Woman in Lars von Trier's Cinema, 1996–2014

R

Ahmed Elbeshlawy

Woman in Lars von Trier's Cinema, 1996–2014

Ahmed Elbeshlawy
School of Professional and Continuing Education
Hong Kong University
Hong Kong

ISBN 978-3-319-82143-6   ISBN 978-3-319-40639-8 (eBook)
DOI 10.1007/978-3-319-40639-8

© The Editor(s) (if applicable) and The Author(s) 2016
Softcover reprint of the hardcover 1st edition 2016
This work is subject to copyright. All rights are solely and exclusively licensed by the Publisher, whether the whole or part of the material is concerned, specifically the rights of translation, reprinting, reuse of illustrations, recitation, broadcasting, reproduction on microfilms or in any other physical way, and transmission or information storage and retrieval, electronic adaptation, computer software, or by similar or dissimilar methodology now known or hereafter developed.
The use of general descriptive names, registered names, trademarks, service marks, etc. in this publication does not imply, even in the absence of a specific statement, that such names are exempt from the relevant protective laws and regulations and therefore free for general use.
The publisher, the authors and the editors are safe to assume that the advice and information in this book are believed to be true and accurate at the date of publication. Neither the publisher nor the authors or the editors give a warranty, express or implied, with respect to the material contained herein or for any errors or omissions that may have been made.

Cover illustration © Jonny Storey Ltd / Getty Images

Printed on acid-free paper

This Palgrave Macmillan imprint is published by Springer Nature
The registered company is Springer International Publishing AG
The registered company address is: Gewerbestrasse 11, 6330 Cham, Switzerland

Acknowledgments

I would like to thank my editor, Lina Aboujieb, for her commitment to this writing project and her reassuring presence all along. I would also like to thank the Palgrave reviewers for the rigorous reading given to the manuscript and the insightful remarks made on it. The professional support of Karina Jakupsdottir and the thorough work of Soundarrajan Sudha cannot be given enough acknowledgment. The book carries its author's signature, but, making it possible carries many other hidden signatures of people whom the writer – most probably – won't have the chance to meet in person.

I cannot possibly describe the debt I owe to those whose mere presence—consciously or unconsciously—spurred my thinking and inspired my writing of this work. My gratitude specially goes to Harleny Hon Siew Kim, Christine Wirth, Wong Kit Man, Diana Jin Yang, Chan Shuk Ngan, Ng Chau Kuk, Zhou Yu and Joyce Cheuk.

Some sections of this book have appeared, in different form, in *Scope*, *fe/male bodies* and *Sexuality and Culture*. I would like to thank the editors of these journals for their interest in my work.

Finally, I would like to thank my dear wife, Rania Kamel, for her unconditional support. And to Malak, Maryem, and Omar: thank you, guys, for the understanding you showed during all those evenings when I had to seclude myself to write.

Contents

1 Introduction: The Lacanian Woman and Lars von Trier's Cinema   1

2 The Danger of the Naive Religious Woman of *Breaking the Waves*   35

3 *Idioterne*: Woman as a Proponent of Real Politics   53

4 *Dancer in the Dark*: Deploying the Siren, Impairing the Sight   69

5 *Dogville*: Woman as an Ideological Cinematic Tool   85

6 *Manderlay*: The Gift, Grace's Desire and the Collapse of Ideology   113

7 The Deployment of the Impossible W~~oman~~ in *Antichrist*   135

8 Besides Melancholia and Beyond Gender: *Melancholia*   155

9 Conclusion, or, Desire as Law: The Loneliness of
   Nymphomaniac between Pornography and Narrative   179

Index   207

CHAPTER 1

Introduction: The Lacanian Woman and Lars von Trier's Cinema

In a book entitled *Everything Is Connected: The Power of Music*, Daniel Barenboim starts with a paradoxical statement that immediately negates itself. He writes: "I firmly believe that it is impossible to speak about music" (5). He doesn't use a more nuanced verb to describe his position like, for example, 'I think', 'I assume', 'I fathom' or 'I feel'. He *believes, firmly*, that it is *impossible* to speak about music. The statement negates itself because, right after it, Barenboim seems to make the impossible possible by writing a sizeable book of more than two hundred pages on precisely nothing but music. The paradox of the (im)possibility of speaking about music is, of course, most appropriate considering the subject matter, which is by its very nature a paradoxical event. Music "says everything and nothing at the same time" (5). It seems to present the world, yet it also presents naught. Defining music, to Barenboim, is even more problematized by the "physical phenomenon that allows us to experience a piece of music, which is sound", since "music expresses itself through sound, but sound in itself is not yet music" (7). It is because of sound that music must be limited in time, yet it puts the listener "in direct contact with timelessness" (10). In music, "joy and sorrow exist simultaneously" and it can "help us forget and understand ourselves simultaneously" (20).

The writer of this book—or more accurately this writing project—feels more or less in the same situation. If I attempt to write about woman, it is precisely because I believe that I cannot write about woman, and not least because I happen to be a man. The project, unwritten as it stands, seems impossible to embark on. Have I any right at all to write about woman?

© The Author(s) 2016
A. Elbeshlawy, *Woman in Lars von Trier's Cinema, 1996–2014*,
DOI 10.1007/978-3-319-40639-8_1

Considering the fact that Barenboim is a celebrated musician, musicologist and philosopher who claims that it is "impossible to speak about music" (5), my task seems to be far more difficult as a man trying to speak about woman. Upon hearing that I wanted to write a book about woman in Lars von Trier's cinema, a feminist intellectual friend of mine seemed to have already taken a critical position towards the unwritten idea, giving me an unforgettably cynical look, as if to say: 'in cinema or outside cinema, how dare you speak about woman in the first place?' Of course, I dare not. That is, I dare not claim that I am going to write something about woman that can be understood in terms of defining what woman is or is not for von Trier, or even for this writer, in cinema or outside. In fact, I cannot even claim that this writing project will constitute anything in the course of a message communicated to its reader. In order to explain this awkward start, which may prove quite discouraging to some readers, I would say that this already declared failure to communicate is precisely the subject matter of this book and what constitutes the secret of its enjoyment on the part of the writer as well as, hopefully, the reader.

In this sense, there is already a resemblance between what constitutes enjoyment in writing this book and what constitutes enjoyment in watching Lars von Trier's distinctive cinematic works, which, even though created to be enjoyed, always seem to question what is enjoyed by the viewer. For what is enjoyed, in this case, simultaneously makes the viewer ill at ease. And, unlike in mainstream cinema, it is neither the violent nor sickening elements that are solely responsible for the viewer's enjoyment of such grotesque scenes of female torture as the ones in which the heroine of *Breaking the Waves* is slashed by two sadistic sailors, or the heroine of *Dogville* is raped in cold blood by all the men of the township, or the heroine of *Nymphomaniac* experiences an orgiastic moment while being violently whipped by a cat o' nine, or the heroine of *Antichrist* mutilates her own clitoris with a pair of scissors. In spite of its notorious legacy of visible misogyny, there is something in Lars von Trier's cinema that goes beyond its perceived gender division and violence against women.

This book, therefore, discusses the corpus of Trier's cinematic production from 1996 to 2014 in order to raise some questions about woman, the deployment of female sexuality, desire, and the idea of subjectivity. It takes into consideration the evolution of film theory and its departure from figures such as André Bazin (*What Is Cinema?*), Christian Metz (*The Imaginary Signifier: Psychoanalysis and the Cinema*) and Laura Mulvey (*Visual and Other Pleasures*), who established certain universalizing assertions about filmmaking and the viewing experience, as well as from the idea of cultural contextualization that deals with the filmic text and its spectator as unique phenomena peculiar to their local circumstances. Instead, it turns to Lacanian psychoanalysis and a number of its contemporary exponents such as Slavoj Žižek, Todd McGowan, Jacques Hassoun, Frances Restuccia and Anna Kornbluh, who offer new Lacanian aspects of ideas of subjectivity, female sexuality, the gaze, melancholy and love, based on which the whole theoretical perspective about the cinematic experience has significantly changed in recent years according to the evolution in Lacanian theory itself and its relation to analyzing cinema.

In light of this, this work adopts the view that the era of looking solely at form or stylistics when analyzing film, based on the popular postmodern notion that a film "should not mean but be" (Abbas 18), is over. The contemporary viewer, whose life is largely spent in front of various screens, now demands more from a cinematic film than visual effects, graphics and digital tricks, which can, after all, be found in other, more interactive, leisure-time activities such as story-based video games on the touch screens of advanced computers and smartphones.

The elements giving value to a cinematic film can be located in either its content or its stylistics, without giving a consistent advantage to one over the other. This, however, should not be understood as the kind of regression into cinematic identification on the part of the viewer that was thoroughly looked at and staunchly attacked by Theodor Adorno in the mid twentieth century. To Adorno, one of the most dangerous characteristics of mass culture was that it took reification beyond its metaphoric sense. It was not just that the products of mass culture illusively reified objects of dreams and fantasies, but that people themselves "resemble[d] products […] they assimilate[d] themselves to what is dead" (*Culture Industry* 95). What was reified came as a result of searching for identity in the wrong place and, in the course of this, acquiring some sort of a pseudo-identity.

That is why Adorno wrote to Walter Benjamin in one of his letters that the "reification of the cinema is all loss" (*Complete Correspondence* 129). While the character on the screen defined the human subject strictly in terms of his/her function in a capitalist society, the spectator assimilated himself/herself to what he/she saw on the screen. That is to say, first, that the human was transformed into dead material. The dead material was then endowed with humanness. Products of mass culture were not exactly seen by Adorno as anti-auratic. The lost aura of high art was compensated for by what he saw as the seriously flawed over-identification with products of low art or mass culture, giving them a "human aura". Human subjects as victims of their own capitalistic drive develop a fetishistic attitude towards the very same conditions that tend to be dehumanizing them. The more they are gradually being transformed into things, the more they invest things with a human aura (*Stars Down to Earth* 100).

Instead, the experience of viewing cinematic films in our contemporary time of visual overproduction, interactive video games, social media, speedy flow of information and instant news should be a search for that which is beyond both interpretation and simple enjoyment; beyond both looking for the constitution of some totality of meaning—either in the film's content or its form—and visual pleasure. McGowan argues that "cinema is first and foremost a site for the revelation of the gaze" (172). The gaze, in Lacanian theory, is defined as the "objet a *in the field of the visible*" (Lacan, *Four Fundamental Concepts* 105); in other words, the ultimately unattainable object-cause of desire, or the real of desire in what is viewed, which, however, "is not a positive entity but a lacuna in the visual field" (McGowan 6), which destabilizes the viewer's position as viewer.

The nothingness of the object-cause of desire traumatizes the viewer as a desiring subject, as the encounter with this uncanny voidness directly puts the subject face to face with its own condition as a mere product of language, an "effect of the signifier" or, as Lacan explains, as that which has nothing to do with ideas of either subjectivity or individuality (*My Teaching* 79). The nullity of the object is itself the nullity of the subject. In other words, the subject at this point is not only threatened by the realization that the object is always already lost but by the prospect of the traumatic loss of desire itself, which is the very condition of the subject's existence. The (non)existence of the objet petit a in the field of the visible is an abyss which instantly corresponds with the destiny of the subject as that which never finds its own tangibility in existence.

In the viewing experience then, the gaze, as McGowan argues, is "not to be located in the spectator" but "in the film itself" (5). The spectator's voyeuristic gaze is disrupted by "the real gaze", which constitutes a "gap within the spectator's seemingly omnipotent look" (6). It is a point at which the viewer feels that he faces something in the visual field that looks back at him, which objectifies him, which marks his death as a subject by virtue of being "subjected to the gaze" (7). The gaze is not something that can be seen on the screen, but makes itself felt through the negative effect of an overpowering unseen seer, or "appears to offer access to the unseen" (6). It does not belong either to the imaginary register or the symbolic order, but to the Real defined as a *fracture in reality* or, as Lacan puts it, "a hole in the symbolic" (*Psychoses* 156).

The gaze is that "inexplicable blank point in the image" that "the Other cannot embody" (McGowan 86–7); therefore, it cannot even be defined as the eye of God in a religious sense. God, in the language of institutionalized religion, is God in language or God *of* language. The gaze, however, neither belongs to language nor can it be fully expressed or defined by it. The Other cannot be entirely foreign since "it is in the Other that the subject is constituted as ideal" or "constitute[s] himself in his imaginary reality" (Lacan, *Four Fundamental Concepts* 144). The Other belongs to the "imaginary reality" of the subject because knowledge as such, to the subject, resides in the Other; it is the Other that "knows", and this Other itself is "posited [...] at the outset" by the subject. Without the Other, "nothing indicates to us that there is a dimension of truth anywhere" (Lacan, *On Feminine Sexuality* 96). This is why Žižek argues that:

> The most radical dimension of Lacanian theory lies not in recognizing [that the subject is barred/crossed-out] but in realizing that the big Other, the symbolic order itself, is also *barré*, crossed-out, by a fundamental impossibility, structured around an impossible/traumatic kernel, around a central lack. (*Sublime Object* 122)

The name of this "traumatic kernel" in the context of the cinematic experience is the gaze. Based on this, in order to continue to be relevant to the highly screen-addicted lives of modern subjects, film viewing should not be marred by taking critical positions or maintaining a sense of resistant reading. On the contrary, one "should not be conscious or critical in a cinematic experience"; one "should submit totally to the logic of the cinematic or dream image" in order to "meet the gaze" (McGowan 13). A film should no longer be viewed and enjoyed as a temporary imaginary escape from the realities of daily life but as a medium carrying possible chances for the viewer to encounter moments in which reality itself is revealed as imaginary. It is only in this sense that a fictional film can be more interesting than a documentary.

For example, Kathryn Bigelow's *The Hurt Locker*'s secret of success is not that it offers a certain dramatization of aspects of the Iraq War but that it contains scenes in which the absence of traditional villains, the absence of face-to-face conflict, the camera's disconnected and queasy motion and the soundless moments before bomb explosions seem to internalize the drama and make the main characters' internal struggles loom larger in their unseen presence than the presence of the images and sounds of the actual war. In turn, the viewer's feeling of sympathy towards the victims of war, on both sides of the conflict, as well as awareness of their own mortality and the nearness of death can be much more genuine in the case of watching Bigelow's film than in the case of watching the surreal images of the actual war in BBC or CNN footage.

By contrast, a recent 'realistic' four-minute *Frontline* documentary entitled *Life in Baghdad: Joy Amid the Chaos of War*—which was made at the time when television and computer screens were flooded with news about the notorious terrorist group ISIL's spread in Iraq and Syria—had an unexpected alienating effect on many of its viewers, though it was clearly made with the intention of showing that, in spite of the news reporting and appalling images of the brutal killings and beheadings conducted by ISIL, there were ordinary people in Baghdad leading ordinary lives just like everyone else. In it, one can see children joyously diving in an irrigation waterway surrounded by heaps of debris, pedestrians and commuters making their way through the shambles of Baghdad, people eating ice cream in a big, carnival-like gathering in the open, et cetera. The first reaction to this short video is to observe the optimism in the faces of Iraqi people laughing and enjoying the simple pleasures of life in spite of the constant fear they are living in.

One scene, however, seems to spoil everything: a decorated limousine carrying a newlywed couple is caught in traffic and surrounded by a group of dancing young men. Somehow this scene does not chime easily with the other scenes of Baghdad. My first reaction was that it was hard to imagine there are still decorated wedding limousine cars on the streets when all one gets nowadays out of Iraq is the sleek, spotless and Hollywood-like images of the carefully directed beheadings of ISIL. This, however, was followed by a moment of deep sorrow for the city, which has transformed over the centuries from being the ultimate cosmopolitan capital of the world in the early middle ages to the contemporary devastated capital of today's Iraq, a land of limousine car weddings and media stunt beheadings.

It is at this moment that one can see the resemblance between the glossy surface of the limousine and the glossy surface of the long knives that ISIL members display in front of the camera before slaughtering their victims. The joyous dance suddenly appears to be more hysterical than joyous; more like a dance of death than of life. The fact that one can hardly see the silhouette of one immobile figure inside the limousine through its closed dark windows seems to question what everyone outside it is celebrating exactly. There is no sign of life inside. The deadly silence of the decorated luxurious limousine amid all the noise seems to betray the sense of constant danger lurking behind the joy and festivities of the Iraqi people, and the car becomes the unintentional dark spot of the short documentary; an object seeming to symbolize all of Iraq's fears and desolation.

If cinema is the usual, most popular, or easiest site for the deployment of ideological mandates, the viewer's ability to subvert those mandates depends on his recognition of the gaze at the moment it shows or the "real point at which [ideology] breaks down" and not on his aptitude for "conscious reflection" upon the ideological structure or message of the film. This requires "allowing oneself to enjoy and to pay attention to the moments of one's enjoyment" (McGowan 15) in the cinematic experience. It is precisely this position of non-critical and non-reflecting enjoyment of the filmic image upon which the current writing project is based. It does not seek to read any of its analyzed filmic texts but to look at certain moments of traumatic enjoyment of certain scenes in those texts in order to show that what is still enjoyed in the cinematic experience is the viewer's occasional loss of his voyeuristic power through recognizing his own presence in what he sees.

As can be understood from the title of the book, its idea is delimited to analyzing the figure of woman in the distinctive cinematic production of the Danish director Lars von Trier, who is one of the most successful, as well as one of the most controversial, directors in the history of cinema. The book's argument goes against both the popular view that von Trier's films are misogynist in nature and the feminist view that they seek to empower women or advocate femininity. Instead, the book argues that woman in the cinema of Lars von Trier stands for the very impossibility of becoming a woman in the Lacanian sense. In other words, woman as portrayed by von Trier's cinema is always an attempt at presenting the viewer with an image of a genderless subject par excellence who is not inhibited by the confines of ideology and culture, and that this attempt itself is always already a failed one. This failure is precisely what constitutes the element of enjoyment in watching the films of Lars von Trier. It is also what gives them their political importance, elevates them above accusations of misogyny, and elevates the director himself above the accusation of being a mere provocateur.

Since this book takes a psychoanalytic approach, certain pitfalls must be illuminated from the start in order to be avoided. The subject of woman is not dealt with here in terms of gender, but in terms of what cannot be encompassed by the idea of gender difference. In her essay 'Freud on Women, Nancy Chodorow writes:

> We are still not able completely to evaluate [Freud's] theory of femininity; indeed, many evaluations find it to be extremely problematic. By contrast, Freud's understandings about male attitudes toward women and femininity do not seem to be shadowy and incomplete at all. They are specific, informative, persuasive, precise, and clear, covering ingeniously a variety of sexual, representational, and neurotic formations. They illuminate for us with passion and empathy, and in full daylight, the mysteries of the male psyche. (246)

Freudian psychoanalysis, therefore, cannot be adequate to discuss woman because Freud, even when his psychoanalytic references to "woman" are in dialogue with an emphatically plural account of a multitude of "women" (224), clearly deals with woman solely as the 'other gender' or that which is the opposite of man. Thus, "theoretical woman in the developmental theory" revolves around the "centrality of penis envy" (226–8), while "clinical woman" serves as Freud's "beginning understanding of the implication of sexual desire […] and sexual trauma […] in the genesis of hysteria" (232), which, in Freud's thought, is a particularly female illness. "Woman as subject-object", which is discussed in terms of the adversarial "mother-daughter relationship", is still strikingly marked by "penis envy" as the daughter "believes either that her mother has chosen never to give one to her and hasn't got one herself, or that, although she doesn't have one, could have arranged things so that her daughter did" (234).

Freud's "defense of the morality and upstanding qualities and capabilities of the women contemporary neurologists and psychiatrists considered degenerate, morally and mentally contaminated, and inferior as a result of their heredity", which Chodorow looks at in her view of "women as they are socially and historically located" in Freud's writings, is framed as a "defense of hysteria" (234–5), defined as something peculiar to the female psyche. While all of the previous accounts seem to alienate as well as subordinate the feminine from a male point of view, they constitute what Chodorow sees as "woman as subject" (226–37) in Freudian thought. Other Freudian accounts, from Chodorow's point of view, constitute "woman as object"; among these, Freud's "manifest, explicit, treatments of women as objects", his depiction of woman as "implicit, latent object in the male psyche" and his account of female "subjectivity and character [as] imagined in the masculine psyche" (237–46).

Freud's position with regard to woman, which is described above by Chodorow, is evident not only in his writings where he deals directly with woman as the other gender, such as 'The Dissolution of the Oedipus Complex' (*On Sexuality* 313–22), 'Some Psychical Consequences of the Anatomical Distinction between the Sexes' (*Standard Edition* 248–60), 'Female Sexuality, with a letter from Freud to Carl Mueller-Braunschweig' (*Freud on Women* 321–41), and 'Femininity' (*New Introductory Lectures* 139–67), but also in his sporadic discussions of the female in *Art and Literature* and *Civilization, Society and Religion*.

For example, Freud believed that "sexual life lays down the pattern for the exercise of other functions" and, in the female sex, the historical sexual suppression of the female and society's stress on the importance of her chastity resulted in women whose "upbringing forbids their concerning themselves intellectually with sexual problems […] and frightens them by condemning such curiosity as unwomanly and a sign of a sinful disposition". Therefore, women are "scared away from *any* form of thinking, and knowledge loses its value for them", resulting in their "undoubted intellectual inferiority" (*Civilization* 50–1). Although Freud clearly stated that the supposed 'intellectual inferiority' of women had unnatural reasons and that Moebius's "physiological feeble-mindedness", which is attributed to women, is "disputable and its interpretation doubtful" (231), he nevertheless seems to structurally read a host of female fictional characters in *Art and Literature* whose beauty or best quality seems to reside in their 'dumbness' or silence in the eyes of their suitors or lovers and, by implication, *readers*—a dumbness that also represents death to Freud. Those fictional characters include Cordelia and Portia from Shakespeare's *King Lear* and *The Merchant of Venice* respectively, Cinderella, Psyche in Apuleius's story, Aphrodite in Offenbach's *La Belle Hélène*, the girl who kills her 12 brothers in Grimms' 'Die zwölf Brüder' ('The Twelve Brothers'), as well as the girl who restores her brothers to life in his 'Die sechs Schwäne' ('The Six Swans') (*Art and Literature* 235–47).

In his analysis of Christoph Haizmann's depiction of the Devil with female breasts, Freud argues that "there is nothing strange about depicting female devils" as anonymous or multitudinous, but it is unusual to feminize "*the* Devil, who is a great individuality, the Lord of Hell and the Adversary of God" in art (405). This cannot be taken as evidence that

Freud himself believed that the Devil, as a "great individuality", cannot be female, or, one can quite justifiably add, that the female cannot be a great individuality, as Freud was merely detecting representations of the Devil in art. However, he does seem to indicate that femininity in itself is a problem or a stigma, since he sees that it must have been the adversarial relationship between the painter and his father as a castrating figure that impelled Haizmann to paint the Devil—a father substitute in Freud's analysis—and project on him the very femininity that the father invokes in the son through the effect of the castration threat. Two things, then, seem to debase/humiliate the father in Freud's reading: the devilish image and the female breasts. In a way, masculinity is associated with "great individuality" while femininity is reduced to an anonymous pair of breasts.

In his analysis of Stefan Zweig's story 'Vierundzwanzig Stunden aus dem Leben einer Frau' ('Twenty Four Hours in a Woman's Life'), which relates the story of a widow (mother of two sons) who tries to save a dedicated young gambler from committing suicide after losing all of his money by casually offering herself to him in bed, Freud considers only male sexual fantasy—in this particular case a "boy's wish that his mother should herself initiate him into sexual life in order to save him from the dreaded injuries caused by masturbation"—as the means by which male imagination "brings the unattainable woman", which is the mother, "within easy reach" by equating her with a prostitute (459). As for female sexuality, Freud dismisses "sudden and mysterious impulses"; therefore, he sees the impulsive behavior of Zweig's heroine—who up to the moment of coming across the young gambler remained faithful to her dead husband—as being caused not by anything related to her own sexuality but by her inability to "escape her quite unconscious transference of love on to her son" (460), embodied by the young gambler.

Generally speaking, the feminine or femininity in Freud's thought does not seem to assume a life of its own and is mostly talked about as a component of the male psyche in terms of the feminine attitude that the boy adopts towards his father as an effect of the castration complex in the course of his psychosexual development.[1] "Being the actual vehicle of the sexual interests of mankind", women, according to Freud, "are only endowed in a small measure with the gift of sublimating their instincts" (*Civilization* 47). Unlike married men, who "very frequently avail themselves of the degree of sexual freedom which is allowed them" (46), women, "when they are subjected to the disillusionments of marriage, fall ill of severe neuroses which permanently darken their lives" (47). The woman as mother becomes the child's "first protection against all the undefined dangers which threaten it in the external world", yet she is "soon replaced by the stronger father, who retains that position for the rest of childhood" (204).

Although Freud criticizes the field of psychology, in which "the contrast between the sexes fades away into one between activity and passivity, in which we far too readily identify activity with maleness and passivity with femaleness, a view which is by no means universally confirmed in the animal kingdom" (295), in his discussion of the early history of the Oedipus complex, he describes the boy's identification with the father as a "typically masculine" attitude rather than a "passive or feminine" (134) one, clearly himself equating passivity with femininity. Yet, it can be argued that Freud's writing does inadvertently point to the problematic position or the ultimate indefinability of woman. For even though Freud tends to place woman on the side of nature and sexuality and man on the side of culture and civilization, his fundamental question, "what does a woman want?", seems to originate from a position that is unsure about locating woman unequivocally on either side.

To Freud, women "come into opposition to civilization" and adopt a "hostile attitude towards it" as a result of being abandoned by man, who has to make "an expedient distribution of his libido" and "withdraws from women and sexual life" for intellectual activities and cultural aims (293). Although this squarely puts woman on the side of nature and sexual life and man on the side of culture and civilization, Freud nevertheless puts a brother on the side of perversion and sexual activity (which is, in this case, healthy, good and positive) and his sister, "being a woman" and thus "possess[ing] a weaker sexual instinct" (43), on the side of neurosis (which is negative and unhealthy).

Thus, the foundation of the family historically depended on man's unwillingness to be "deprived of his sexual object—the women" and woman's unwillingness to be "deprived of the part of herself which had been separated off from her—her child" (290). In this sense, wouldn't it be more appropriate to say that it is man who belongs more to nature due to his elevation of the demands of his sexuality and pathological desires beyond the social bond and with no regard to, or no real concern towards, the family as an institution of civilization, while woman is more committed to the idea of the family, if only by an attachment to that "part of herself"? Putting man on the side of perversion and woman on the side of neurosis seems to destabilize the idea of woman as an enemy of culture and civilization since neurosis is the very mark of culture. It is perhaps more accurate to say that culture is neurotic by definition.

That is why it can be understood from Lacan's analysis of the moral law that the history of religion is marked by a movement from the imaginary to the symbolic; from gods that can be seen to God who cannot be seen but is only manifested in language. The second commandment, "Thou shalt not make unto thee any graven image" (*The Bible*, Exodus 20:4), "excludes not only every cult, but also every image, every representation of what is in heaven, on earth, or in the void"; it eliminates the "function of the imaginary" and establishes a "relation to the symbolic" in the sense of "speech" (*Ethics* 81). Civilization starts with a "primordial law" that "superimposes the reign of culture over the reign of nature" (*Écrits: The First Complete Edition* 229).

To Lacan, the neurotic subject not only identifies himself in language, he loses his own being in the signifying chain; he transforms himself into a signifier and becomes language (*Psychoses* 155). The Neurotic phenomenon thus seems to be inherent in culture since the 'normal' human subject does transform himself or herself into a signifier on a daily basis. Transforming oneself into a signifier maintains the whole system of symbolic exchanges that define one's daily life and regulate all his or her relations with others. By displaying a cultural code, the subject sends a message to the other, which means that he turns himself into a signifier. That makes neurosis the very condition of culture, and it is perhaps most obvious in the case of the religious person who "looks like or behaves like the neurotic" (*My Teaching* 38–9).

The development of psychoanalytic theory by Lacan changes psychoanalysis's relation to the feminine significantly. In accordance with Freudian thought, Lacan asserts that the woman's realization of her own sex is "not accomplished in the Oedipus complex in a way symmetrical to that of the man's, not by identification with the mother, but on the contrary by identification with the paternal object" (*Psychoses* 172). This is precisely what feminizes "virile display" itself in the case of man (*Écrits: A Selection* 322). But he adds that, in the case of the female sex, it is "characterized by an absence, a void, a hole" since there is "an obstacle, a defect, in the way of bringing about the identification that is essential for the [female] subject's sexuality to be realized" due to the lack of "symbolic material" (*Psychoses* 176). Symbolic material in this sense is equivalent to the "paternal object", since it is the lack of it in the case of the female subject that problematizes her relation to it. For there is an established relation between the subject of language and the phallus regardless of the "anatomical difference of the sexes"; and, in the case of woman, "any interpretation of this relation [is] especially difficult" (*Écrits: A Selection* 312).

This absence, however, is precisely *presence beyond the physicality of the object*, the way the absence of the primordial father who is killed by his offspring establishes the powerful symbolic presence of the prohibiting "Name of the Father". Lacan states that "before the name of the father, there was no father" (*Psychoses* 306). On prohibition, he states that "it is as a function of the death of God that the murder of the father which represents it in the most direct way is introduced by Freud as a modern myth", and that

> all the mystery is in [the murder of the father] act. It is designed to hide something, namely, that not only does the murder of the father not open the path to *jouissance* that the presence of the father was supposed to prohibit, but it, in fact, strengthens the prohibition. The whole problem is there; that's where, in fact as well as in theory, the fault lies. Although the obstacle is removed as a result of the murder, *jouissance* is still prohibited; not only that, but the prohibition is reinforced [...] the sole function of the father is to be a myth, to be always only the Name-of-the-Father, or in other words nothing more than the dead father, as Freud explains in *Totem and Taboo*. (*Ethics* 143, 176, 309)

It is crucial to understand that it is *not* prohibition that results in the murder of the father; on the contrary, it is the father's death that establishes the law of prohibition: "the father's death ... this good news, that God is dead, does not seem to me to be of a kind to liberate us, far from it ... the conclusion that forces itself upon us in the text of our experience is that the response to 'God is dead' is 'Nothing is permitted anymore' ... it is certainly not as an attempt to explain what sleeping with the mother means that the murder of the father is introduced into Freudian doctrine. On the contrary it's on the basis of the father's death that the prohibition of this *jouissance* is established in the first place" (*The Other Side* 119–20).

Similarly, it is the "absence of the penis that turns [woman] into the phallus, the object of desire" (*Écrits: A Selection* 356). To be the phallus or the "signifier of the desire of the Other" requires rejecting "an essential part of femininity" or "all her attributes in the masquerade" (321). In other words, the structure of subjectivity in the case of the female, even though she may initially take the same detour as the male subject within a discourse that is predominantly written in the Name of the Father, is nevertheless fundamentally different by virtue of the female's (dis)connection to the phallus. She is somehow outside the system of symbolization but is defined as the very point at which that system collapses. She is not threatened by castration since she is perceived as always already castrated by her anatomical nature, yet this lack itself transforms *her* into a phallus, in other words, into man's real of desire as well as his very sign of castration.

It is in this sense that Žižek equates between woman and the phallus in the economy of desire (*Žižek Reader* 157). "What is foreclosed from the Symbolic returns in the Real of the symptom: woman does not exist […] she returns as a symptom of man" (*Sublime Object* 73). The symptom in psychoanalytic terms, therefore, is not to be understood as a sign to be read or interpreted; it is what leads to the interpretation of signs in the first place. To say that woman is a "symptom of man" from the position of the speaking subject means that woman evokes the sign of castration due to the lack of the phallus, which renders her non-existent in the symbolic order, yet threatening its very collapse as she precisely represents the very hole of the Real, the fracture, the deformity, or the abyss that reminds the speaking subject of its fictitiousness. If women according to common sense exist out there in the imaginary register, woman as a "symptom of man" has a relation to the Real or that which cannot be represented.

Lacan says that "becoming a woman and wondering what a woman is are two essentially different things"; in fact, it is the impossibility of the first state that gives reason to the second since "it's because one doesn't become one that one wonders". The two states of becoming and wondering are even oppositional since "to wonder is the contrary of becoming one" (*Psychoses* 178). In other words, becoming is becoming *in* the discourse while wondering *is* the discourse. How can the subject of language, in the case of woman, be defined as woman if she engages, consciously or unconsciously, in the "wondering"? Put in its simpler yet no less unanswerable form, the question could be: is there a discourse that is feminine? Lacan states that "the metaphysics of the woman's position is the detour imposed on her subjective realization. Her position is essentially problematic, and up to a certain point it's inassimilable (*Psychoses* 178). The inassimilability of the woman's position not only puts her right in the middle of the void upon which subjectivity as such is based, but casts a serious doubt on the existence of the symbolized subject (man) as well. If woman is outside the discourse, this can only be explained by her being its very instigator. In other words, while the presence of man is a symbolic possibility that does not actually explain either man or woman, the absence of woman, in its essence, is an impossibility, because it would be an absence that cancels out the presence of both genders—and the discourse.

It took Lacan nine years, between publishing *Écrit* in 1966 and *Encore* in 1975, to say something on feminine sexuality—hence subjectivity—in a completely different seminar with a completely different mind. Žižek explains how Lacanian thought shifts radically from the notion of the "Other" to the notion of the "One" in *Encore*, from the signifier to the sign, from the symbolic network to the psychosis reflected in Lacan's effort in his last years, which was "directed at breaking through the field of communication-as-meaning" (*Žižek Reader* 29). In short, from discourse to *jouissance*. This Lacanian shift also marks "the two opposed meanings of the word 'existence' in Lacan".

The first means "symbolization, integration into the discursive order [...] in which Lacan maintains that 'Woman does not exist'", and the second is the opposite meaning of "'ex-sistence', the impossible-real nucleus resisting symbolization" (31) to which woman is ultimately committed. Female subjectivity thus is at once reinforced and voided by virtue of the female's connection to the notion of woman. As Lacan puts it: "W̶o̶m̶a̶n̶ cannot be said (*se dire*). Nothing can be said of Woman. Woman has a relation with S($\cancel{A}$), and it is already in that respect that she is doubled, that she is not whole, since she can also have a relation with Φ" (*On Feminine Sexuality* 81). In other words, the subjectivity of the female relates to woman who does not exist in the system of symbolization yet exists at the level of *jouissance* where she, as well as the big Other itself, is crossed out.

Man, as Lacan teaches, is a "creation of discourse", while the same "cannot be said of woman" (*Other Side* 55). If the world that includes the symbolized subject is this façade created out of language, truth, or that which is always already bracketed, or always already sought by philosophical as well as cultural/religious discourses, is what assumes residence outside the façade. That is why Lacan asserts that he "[doesn't] know how to approach the truth no more than woman" since, to man, "they constitute the same conundrum" (*On Feminine Sexuality* 120). The elusive notion of Truth and the elusive notion of Woman share the same commitment to the Real.

Thus, to man, "truth is never [...] more beautiful than at the moment when the light, which he holds aloft as in the proverbial emblem, surprises her naked" (*Écrits: A Selection* 133), since truth, like woman, can only be attributed with adjectives, yet cannot be said to exist. The word 'woman' itself, in Lacanian discourse, leans to the side of being an adjective more than a noun. Hysteria, thus, is not simply seen by Lacan as a disease that befalls woman, and being hysterical is "not her privilege alone", but it is the figure of the hysteric itself that is feminized by discourse; "in saying 'she', we are making the hysteric a woman" (*Other Side* 33).

This is how Lacan explains or expands Freud's ideas on women as historical enemies to culture who "come into opposition to civilization" (Freud, *Civilization* 293). Woman is "called woman (*on la dit-femme*) and defamed (*diffâme*) (Lacan, *On Feminine Sexuality* 85). Yet, in Lacanian psychoanalysis, it is precisely this infamous being, this enemy of culture and religion, who can be said to have a relation to God that is not mediated by language through her mysterious *jouissance* about which she "doesn't breathe a word". The secrecy, however, does not imply any hidden knowledge, since Lacan adds: "perhaps because she doesn't know (*connait*) it" (60). Commenting on his translation of the Lacanian text, Bruce Fink notes that "*connaître* implies something more experiential than *savoir*, and could lead to the following translation here: 'she doesn't experience it'. Lacan is perhaps also playing on the *con*—the French equivalent for the English slang 'cunt'—in *connaître*" (*On Feminine Sexuality* 60). Needless to say, imagining a relation to God that is not mediated by language immediately becomes a horrifying notion for the male subject *created* by discourse.

One of the most interesting literary works to reflect man's fantasy about the ideal woman is Villiers de l'Isle-Adam's *Tomorrow's Eve*, in which the French writer (1838–89) creates the fictional character of a scientist who invents a mechanical woman who represents the dream of the ultimate romantic love. The scientist's genius makes the mechanical woman look, move and talk exactly like a real woman. Moreover, she is eloquent and no less versed in managing a dialogue than a philosopher or a great poet. But what is really significant about her, according to her creator's expressed point of view, is that she is devoid of what men perceive in women as female pettiness and small-mindedness. It is the feminine conscience that the scientist seemingly wants to get rid of by inventing the android—for the usage of man. But this cannot be the whole story. As a female android, the scientist's invention cannot just be devoid of the soul of a woman, but also devoid of the *Eros* of a woman; she is a desexualized creature. Thus, it can be argued that over and above what is seen by the male inventor as female pettiness and small-mindedness, it is female *jouissance* that he really wants to get rid of—that incomprehensible, ultimately mysterious, and perceivably dangerous side of a woman.

In Lacanian psychoanalysis, God, like female *jouissance*, is "radically Other" and cannot be talked about except in terms of complete mystery:

"it is insofar as her jouissance is radically Other that woman has more of a relationship to God than anything that could have been said in speculation in antiquity following the pathway of that which is manifestly articulated only as the good of man." God and female *jouissance*, therefore, belong to the realm of the mystic or what cannot be articulated or talked about. Hence the foreclosure of God in the real, the one, in Lacan's words, who "has not yet made his exit" (*On Feminine Sexuality* 83–4), and the creation of God in language, the God of cultural interpretations. And it is precisely the God of cultural interpretations in whose name all of the historical atrocities of religion have been committed, including those committed against women.

The very foreclosure of this part of the divine—that which is Real and cannot be talked about like female *jouissance*—is what creates the God of the soul, that of love, the spiritual God who resides in language; in other words, that which has nothing to do with the debased body, *of woman*. The dread of woman as an enemy of religion, culture and civilization by virtue of her fundamental connection, in the male imagination, to man's lower body stratum, is in reality an apprehension regarding the hollowness of the subject of religion, culture and civilization, and this makes woman, as Žižek puts it, "the subject par excellence" (*Žižek Reader* 129–35). In other words, "man is woman with phallus" and "subjectivity as such is feminine" (*For they know not* xxi).

The (non)existence of woman to Žižek thus "undermines the reign of the phallus" (*Žižek Reader* 139), casting serious doubt on the existence of the male subject. The masculine/feminine opposition is problematized by nothing but the notion of subjectivity itself, as masculine and feminine become nothing but "two modes of the subject's failure to achieve the full identity of man ... each of them is a 'failed whole'" (*Žižek Reader* 144–5). Yet, what distinguishes woman in this economy is her occasional "*passage à l'acte*" (passage to the act) (Lacan, *Anxiety* 114–30). Lacan differentiates between acting-out and the passage to the act in the sense of being always already caught in the network of socio-symbolic exchange (acting-out), as opposed to achieving an act that breaks away from that network, hence, inevitably, necessitating subjective death (*passage à l'acte*). As Lacan puts it, the *passage à l'acte* is "on the side of the subject inasmuch as he appears effaced by the bar to the greatest extent" (115). In other words, the passage to the act is marked by the subject's emergence at the very moment of its ultimate effacement as subject (a capital S crossed out by a bar).

The passage to the act is thus an act of authentic subjectivity or an act of absolute freedom from the socio-symbolic network, hence, its moment is the "moment of the subject's greatest *embarrassment*" (115); in other words, a moment of abandoning all the obligations regulating the subject's social links to others. Lacan calls this socio-symbolic network "the *stage* of the Other where man as subject has to be constituted" (116), and the *passage à l'acte* is that moment in which the subject "from where he is—namely, the locus of the stage [...], topples off the stage" (115). In other words, the passage to the act creates a fracture in the symbolic order; it unsettles reality as we know it and dents its phallocentric structure because it is neither directed to the Other nor disciplined by its mandates.

Whereas acting-out, as Lacan puts it, "is essentially something in the subject's conduct that is on show" or that is "orient[ed] towards the Other", hence always already "other than what it is" (123), the passage to the act, defined as a rift in reality, is necessarily marked by the trauma of the Real. "*Acting-out is a symptom*", as Lacan asserts, even though the symptom, unlike acting-out, is "not an appeal to the Other" (125), whereas the passage to the act breaks away entirely from this symptomatic structure by being something which highlights subjectivity at the very moment of subjectivity's obliteration. As Žižek puts it, the subject "'undergoes' the act ('passes through' it) rather than 'accomplishes' it: in it, the subject is annihilated and subsequently reborn (or not), that is, the act involves a kind of temporary eclipse, *aphanisis*, of the subject" (*Enjoy Your Symptom* 44). It is an act of "symbolic suicide" (43) which "entails an exit from the symbolic network" (*Žižek Reader* 33) and which is to be "opposed strictly to the suicide '*in* reality'", which "remains caught in the network of symbolic communication" (*Enjoy Your Symptom* 43–4).

The question that essentially arises, then, is why this passage to the act in Lacanian discourse is more accessible to woman than man. The answer to this question has to be addressed through a certain understanding of the structure of desire and its connection to—or rather its independence from—the notion of *jouissance*. Lacan maintains that desire is the desire of the Other (*Écrits: The First Complete Edition* 98, 355, 582, 689, *The Four Fundamental Concepts* 38, 115, 235, *My Teaching* 38). This is not to be simply understood in terms of desiring what the Other desires, but in terms of desire being conditioned by the fantasy the subject creates with regard to the desire of the Other—an Other which the subject poses in the first place.

Lacan's analysis of sacrifice seems to offer his clearest explanation of what he means by the definition of desire as desire of the Other. "Sacrifice," he asserts, "is not at all intended to be an offering, nor a gift, [...] but the capture of the Other in the web of [the subject's] desire." Man's history of heterogeneous sacrifices to a multitude of imagined divinities is a history of inventing the divine Other, furnishing it with a desire that is necessarily similar in its structure to man's desire, then offering it an object that is raised to the level of the *objet petit a* or the assumed object-cause of desire, as if the gods "desired in the same way as we do", even when we know that the offering "might [not] be of any use to them". Sacrifice, then, is nothing but a process by which the subject "tame[s]" the Other in the "snare of desire" (*Anxiety* 277–8).

Hence Žižek's definition of sacrifice as a "'gift of reconciliation' to the Other, destined to appease its desire". However, sacrifice, whose very performance is fundamentally based upon expecting no response whatsoever from the Other, "conceals the abyss of the Other's desire; more precisely, it conceals the Other's lack, inconsistency, 'inexistence'". The subject poses the Other, and sacrifice is a "guarantee that the Other exists: that there is an Other who can be appeased by means of the sacrifice [...] so, even if the act fails in its proclaimed goal, this very failure can be read from within the logic of sacrifice as our failure to appease the Other" (*Enjoy Your Symptom* 56).

Thus, faced with the question "Che vuoi?" (Lacan, *Écrits: A Selection* 345–6), or 'what does the Other want of me?'—a question the subject itself raises—the subject frees itself from its anxiety by devising its own fantasy by which it deceptively answers the question with regard to the desire of the Other. This clearly necessitates the ultimate obscurity of what the Other wants. What the Other wants, in the imagination of its creator, must be unclear. This is due to the fact that what it wants is evoked only by the "Che vuoi?" question and, therefore, exists only as an answer to that question. The answer to the question of 'what does the Other want of me?' can only be articulated in a phantasmal way. The function of this fantasy is to relieve the subject of the anxiety of the "Che vuoi?" It is not accidental that the formula of fantasy ($\$ \lozenge a$), in Lacan's completed graph of desire (*Écrits: A Selection* 348), brings the subject back in the direction of—but not at all in—the imaginary realm.

At the level of a *jouissance* that is beyond the pleasure principle, which occupies the topmost part of Lacan's famous graph of desire, the subject escapes meaning, loses identification, and breaks away from the big

Other's hold; in other words, the subject loses the very foundations of its subjectivity. Freud discusses the pleasure of repetition "beyond the pleasure principle" in terms of the child's fort-da game by which he plays at mastering the experience of displeasure due to the mother's occasional disappearances (*On Metapsychology* 275–349). Lacan explains how a *jouissance* that is beyond the pleasure principle is realized at a certain stage where the subject realizes "that his desire is merely a vain detour with the aim of catching the *jouissance* of the other" (*Four Fundamental Concepts* 184). A *jouissance* that is beyond the pleasure principle thus seems to fall outside the metonymic structure of desire.

By essentially taking place at the level of meaning, acting-out is at its core a political—or a politically correct—act in terms of what one gains or loses through its performative gesture. In other words, it is a political act that remains governed by either the reality principle or the pleasure principle, as it can be argued that it always enjoys—openly or secretly—being bound to the big Other's imagined *jouissance*. It can also masochistically enjoy being the victim of the big Other. The passage to the act, on the other hand, like a *jouissance* that is beyond the pleasure principle, cancels out the existence of the big Other. The only difference is that, in the case of *jouissance*, the big Other gets cancelled out inadvertently or unwittingly on the part of the subject, while in the case of the passage to the act, the subject consciously, determinately, yet also emotionally and with a unique sense of great embarrassment, abandons the façade of the socio-symbolic world, or what Lacan calls the "stage of the Other", and "passes over into the real" (*Anxiety* 113), effectively voiding the existence of the big Other together with its own place of identification in the big Other's discourse—a murderous and suicidal act at once.

The passage to the act is thus more accessible to woman than man by virtue of man's much stronger bond with the desire of the Other as that which guarantees *jouissance* and, simultaneously, by woman's relative remove from the kind of *jouissance* that is symbolized by the phallus. Man's *jouissance* is destined to be always already caught in the economy of desire, as law, as a "commandment". The law that forbids the object of desire (the mother) guarantees at once the imposition of this very desire as law because "in and of herself the mother is not the most desirable object there is" (Lacan, *Anxiety* 106). The mother is the most desirable object because the law guarantees her that place of *the* forbidden object. That is why Lacan maintains that "we have to conceive of jouissance as being profoundly independent of the articulation of desire" (182), and that in general terms "woman turns out to be superior in the domain of jouissance" where she "possesses [...] greater freedom because she doesn't clasp onto this relation to the Other as *essentially*, in such a *wesentlich* manner, as men do, in particular in anything to do with jouissance" (183).

It is in this sense that woman's status is fundamentally interconnected with subjectivity in Lacanian theory. If the subject is a barred subject or a subject that is essentially split by the violent admission into the symbolic order and therefore never consistent with its own signification, then it can be argued that woman is the subject par excellence due to her inadmissibility into that sphere. As Žižek puts it, "it is precisely woman that 'exists', that persists as a residue of enjoyment beyond meaning" (*Žižek Reader* 31). If woman's existence is this intrinsically problematic non-being, man's existence, on the other hand, as Lacan maintains, is a "being of non-being [...] conjugated with the double aporia of a veritable subsistence that is abolished by his knowledge" (*Écrits: The First Complete Edition* 679).

Based on this, Žižek argues that "the fear of woman as a pathological dirty stain, as something that is opposed to spirituality, something that man lowers himself to, or as something that is formulated, connected to and inscribed in man's erogenous zone (phallus) is in its essence a fear of the void that the subject itself is" (*Žižek Reader* 129–35). Her present/absent figure is that of "*woman*" who "does not exist" and who is "*not whole*" (Lacan, *On Feminine Sexuality* 7). This symbolic non-existence in itself is the very negativity on account of which woman is always closer to the negative *passage à l'acte*. "The act as real is 'feminine', in contrast to the 'masculine' performative, that is, the great founding gesture of a new order" (Žižek, *Enjoy Your Symptom* 46).

In Lacanian discourse, W̶o̶m̶a̶n̶ is crossed out not simply because she does not exist in patriarchal discourse—which is, of course, true—but much more importantly because "'woman' is a name for a distortion or inflection of the male discourse" (Žižek, *Metastases* 105). In other words, patriarchal discourse named its own abyss, or that instance of being which perpetually threatens its collapse, 'woman'. This is not to say, however, that Lacanian psychoanalysis either agrees with or tries to resist patriarchal discourse; on one hand, it only reveals the fallacies upon which that discourse bases itself and, on the other, it simultaneously reveals the serious flaws of the feminist discourse that seeks to empower the female through resisting patriarchal discourse and, in the course of this quest, defeminizes her with no less than catastrophic consequences. In short, real female power resides precisely in the figure of the crossed-out ~~Woman~~. To Žižek, it is how this non-existence is understood that distinguishes between Otto Weininger's "woman therefore does not exist" and Lacan's "'la femme n'existe pas'" in the Hegelian sense. Weininger, unlike Lacan, "fails to accomplish [the] Hegelian reflexive reversal of *recognizing in this 'nothing' the very negativity that defines the notion of the subject*" (142–3).

Feminist opposition to patriarchal discourse or "phallocentrism" (151) paradoxically weakens the position of woman, because the strength of that position, unlike the position of man, does not reside in the existence of a feminine discourse in the first place, but in the definition of woman as the *collapse of discourse* as such. As Žižek puts it, the "Limit that defines woman is not epistemological but ontological […] beyond it there is nothing […] Woman *qua* enigma is a spectre generated by the inconsistent surface of multiple masks […] and the Lacanian name for this inconsistency of the surface […] is simply *the subject*" (151–2).

It is astounding how the cinema of Lars von Trier from 1996 to 2014 seems to be largely about deploying certain female figures who particularly evoke—consciously or unconsciously—the enigma of woman as presented in Lacanian psychoanalysis. Whereas Lacan questions "why not interpret one face of the Other, the God face, as based on feminine jouissance?" (*On Feminine Sexuality* 77), von Trier sees that, if there is a positive side to Christianity, it is "just the fact that there's a woman involved [the Virgin Mary]". He simply justifies his view by saying, "so there's not only men [in Christian divinity]" (Lumholdt, *Lars von Trier: Interviews* 194), as if the idea of equality between the genders should be extended to the divine.

However, by expressing this female involvement as mere presence at a minimum level (it is "just a fact"; there is a divine woman there whose presence cannot be denied even if her holy figure is to a certain extent eclipsed by the much more powerful figures of the Father and the Son), von Trier seems to understand that Christianity is still a male religious discourse which literally silences the female figure (the mother herself) in a direct way ("Woman, what have I to do with thee? mine hour is not yet come" [*The Bible*, John 2:4]. In other words, this is between me and my father; a woman should not get involved in this serious affair).

Whereas Lacan sees that the coming into being of the notion of the soul is founded on the very alienation of woman from it (*On Feminine Sexuality* 85), von Trier wonders why the male figure occupies the centre stage of religious discourse: "God has always been a 'he'. Why is 'he' a he?" (Lumholdt, *Lars von Trier: Interviews* 194). In Lacanian psychoanalysis, man usually acts out while woman is more capable of the passage to the act. In Lars von Trier's cinema, as the director himself declares, "whenever there's been a man in the lead role, at a certain point this man finds out that the ideal doesn't hold. And whenever it was a woman, they take the ideal all the way" (148–9).

This, however, is not to be understood in terms of some sort of feminine success or achievement as compared to masculine failure. Just as Žižek maintains that 'masculine' and 'feminine' "are not the two species of the genus Man but, rather, the two modes of the subject's *failure* to achieve the full identity of Man [...] since *each of them is already in itself a failed Whole*" (*Metastases* 159–60), von Trier maintains that what differentiates men from women in his own films is that while "men fail like hell, [...] women fail just as much—only the men don't go the whole nine yards. They abandon ship at the sixth or the eighth" (Lumholdt, *Lars von Trier: Interviews* 197).

The present book, therefore, is based upon a certain Lacanian view, which maintains that woman is a master signifier in language that has some relation to something that is outside language, outside the symbolic order, and threatening its collapse at once. Through looking at the female figures created by Lars von Trier in his films from 1996 to 2014, it attempts neither to explain what woman is in any traditional sense nor to wonder what woman wants in any Freudian sense, but to look at what woman, as a non-existent being, *does* in/to Lars von Trier's cinema and the effect of that on the viewer.

Chapter 2 discusses *Breaking the Waves* as von Trier's early attempt to put the figure of woman at a crossroads with the idea of culture and religion. The film features a woman whose morality is based on her own sense of righteousness, which is determined by an imagined private connection to God. As freeing as it is from the idea of institutionalized religion, the idea of a personal relationship with God cannot be trouble-free since it implies replacing the mediation of culture (in Bess's case the culture of her Calvinist church and highly conservative community) with pure linguistic correspondence with the master signifier 'God'. That such an idea is related to the psychotic phenomenon is an established discourse in Lacanian psychoanalysis. This is not to suggest, however, that Bess is psychotic.

In fact, the main purpose of writing this chapter is to argue for precisely the opposite; that since Bess's form of belief seems to stress that a personal relationship with God can only be established through a human being, and since she does not cancel out the human dimension in religion, she remains a neurotic subject who identifies herself in language and maintains erotic relations with the other. The aim of Chapter 2 is to argue that the naive Bess, who truly loves God, is indeed innocent of all sins but one, and it is *the* ultimate sin a human being can fall in. Bess is nothing but the very representation of that which marks the fall of God himself into sin, which is no less than his very existence in language.

Chapter 3 argues that even though von Trier's *Idioterne*, as the purest example of the Dogma 95 movement, has been discussed by many writers in terms of its politics and its subversion of Hollywood's cinematic techniques, much less attention has been given to the fact that it is as much a film about a woman in mourning and, precisely because of its unprecedented and *unrepeated* abandonment of the normal, fictional or traditional ways of filmmaking, can be considered von Trier's most mournful film. That is to say: *it mourns Dogma 95 as a lost object of love at the very moment of its birth*. The attention given to the unusual pioneering stylistics of the film as a political message communicated through form (Koutsourakis's *Politics as Form in Lars von Trier: A Post-Brechtian Reading* is one of the best examples) seems to have overshadowed the politics of its content, which, literally, seems to mourn the stylistic project of Dogma 95 at the moment it is introduced in cinematic history, since it seems to expect its own failure as a political project with the aim of freeing filmmaking from control and calculation.

Chapter 3, therefore, argues that *Idioterne* is a film that perceives itself fundamentally as a lost cause, and only one thing in it stands in defence of that lost cause: Karen's final act of spassing—an act which marks the end of *her own* work of mourning over her lost child. Her spassing is a final act of identification, a crescendo that precedes the freedom and un-inhibition of her ego as she leaves her family house. It is also an act that stands in defence of the lost cause *Idioterne* presents, as well as the lost cause the film itself *is*.

Chapter 4 looks at *Dancer in the Dark* as a near-perfect conspiracy against the act of film watching itself. The heroine, Selma, is not just a blind sacrificial mother who is suffering passively and rejecting one man's love unrealistically. She is also that impossible female character who is, in many ways, *un-cinematic*. *Dancer in the Dark* can be thought of as von Trier's extreme example of deploying the Lacanian "objet a *in the field of the visible*" (Lacan, *The Four Fundamental Concepts* 105), as the blind heroine herself is the occasional deployment of the gaze. Selma, however, destabilizes the viewer's position, not only with her blind eyes, which are supposed to look and do not see, yet seem to see beyond simple looking, but also with her droning voice, which literally makes von Trier's film hardly anything but a celebration of the idea of the survival of the song—that most primitive art—even in the midst of the most philosophically oriented postmodern politicized cinema of technical prowess mixed with deliberate stylistic playfulness. To enjoy *Dancer in the Dark* is to know how not to watch it as a cinematic work but to *feel it as work* only, or as a process which does not look forward to an end, or as something that never dies except by the very death of the subject; in other words, as something which resembles the subject's libido in its insistent survival as a vital substance, as a force of nature that, *essentially*, has neither eyes to see nor image to be seen.

Chapter 5 looks beyond the idea that *Dogville* is a direct onslaught on America. As one of the most interesting European takes on America, the film seems not to be just a stylistically anti-Hollywood as well as thematically anti-American film, but even an *anti-cinematic* film with its "depthlessness" (Badley 103) and "formal organization" (Koutsourakis, *Politics as Form* 151), which perhaps make it "the ultimate 'staged' film" (Stevenson 104). What is more important, however, from this work's perspective, is that, as a "parody of American ideology" (Schepelern, *Visual Authorship* 164), *Dogville* reflects a vision that tries to render America a feminized as well as desexualized mutant of Europe. Put another way, *Dogville* as a European text seeking to read America is in one way capable of doing so by arguing how America, seen as an inheritor of European civilization, simultaneously feminized and desexualized itself to be different and non-European.

In the course of this, the structural and conscious processes by which *Dogville* invents a desexualized America and relates this desexualization to the idea of murder will be revealed. The two main points to be made, however, are, first, that the violence done to America is a violence that is primarily directed to *cinematic* America—or even to cinema itself as an American invention—through the figure of *woman* as an ideological cinematic tool, and, second, that this anti-American European take on America, in spite of its outspoken aggressivity, seems to mark a certain unconscious erotic affair between the inventing European subject and the invented feminized image of America. This is precisely where the Lacanian intervention occurs.

Chapter 6 looks at von Trier's *Manderlay* as a film that deploys the black body as a cinematic gift and the figure of woman as the collapse of ideology simultaneously. *Manderlay*, as a film dealing primarily with American racism, takes what it perceives as America's democratic ideal—that which is taught to the slaves of Manderlay by Grace—and reveals it as a "social fantasy", which is a notion that Slavoj Žižek designates as a "necessary counterpart to the concept of antagonism" (*Interrogating the Real* 254). What illuminates this social antagonism, however, is Grace's personal experience with Timothy—her sexual fantasy fixing the racist divide in America's social structure. The enjoyment in (watching) *Manderlay* is precisely the enjoyment of the black body as a (cinematic) gift, as an object for the gaze. In this particular point, von Trier's film seems to be more or less in line with several Hollywood productions content-wise, regardless of its minimalist stylistics.

What is different about *Manderlay*, however, is that it takes the black body on a Lacanian detour from sublime to soil, from fantasy to feces; in other words, from the Lacanian objet petit a to the gift. And, as a gift, the same black body loops back and transforms itself again into the objet petit a. It is at this point that *Manderlay* goes beyond its racist discourse. The chapter shows that *Manderlay*, over and above the history of slavery in America and the black/white division, reconsiders the concept of human freedom through disturbing the viewer's common sense of the term in three particular scenes: the scene of Grace's dream, in which we have no access to the dream images except through the narrator's voice; the scene in which Timothy rapes Grace; and the scene in which Grace whips Timothy near the end of the film. In analyzing these three scenes in which the figure of woman plays a major role, three notions will help to radically revise what we take as the common sense of freedom. These three notions are the gift, the object-cause of desire, and fantasy.

Chapter 7 argues that if there is any female character in the history of cinema who comes close to presenting the viewer with the clearest possible image of Lacan's "Woman" who "cannot be said", whom "nothing can be said of [her]" (*On Feminine Sexuality* 81), who is outside the system of symbolization yet threatens its very foundation, it is Charlotte Gainsbourg's character in *Antichrist*. With a shot of hard-core pornography, images of physical and sexual violence, explicit masturbation and genital mutilation, there is no doubt that *Antichrist* is one of the most provocative films ever made. On top of its graphic violence, the film is also commonly seen as the epitome of von Trier's perceived misogyny, even though this is an accusation he flatly denies.

Chapter 7 neither looks for positive traits in *Antichrist* nor dismisses it as an entirely harmful film. To put it quite bluntly, content-wise, there is nothing positive in *Antichrist* and, in terms of stylistics, everything is employed to stress an ultimate fundamental failure to think about the human condition in any optimistic way—which is, of course, nothing new to von Trier's cinema. However, in the imaginary nightmarish world of *Antichrist*, in its ultimate negativity and perceived identification with the idea that women may be evil by their very nature, the film takes an already established historical discourse of female marginalization and identifies with it to the very point of that discourse's self-destruction. Moreover, it is precisely what is seen by some viewers as the film's "clumsy climactic sequence during which Gainsbourg's character takes inspiration from her studies on genocide and comes to embody all the evils done to woman throughout history" (Page) that marks the film's deepest insight into the human condition as such, beyond gender politics. Two stylistic traits in *Antichrist* play major roles in communicating its unsettling message: the employment of voices and sounds, and the employment of the sexual scenes.

Chapter 8 approaches the topic of melancholia through Lars von Trier's cinematic take on it in his film, *Melancholia*, a film seen by many as a sort of deviation from his other works, usually perceived as misogynistic, and even hailed by some as particularly feminist. The argument is that, even though the film deals primarily with melancholia, its focus shifts radically from the category of the melancholic to the category of the hysteric towards its end. By taking a close look at a few certain scenes in von Trier's film, the chapter seeks to show that, in *Melancholia*, there is something else besides melancholia that remains with the viewer long after experiencing the film, which, even though still related to the film's melancholic stasis (both content- and stylistics-wise) and what some of its readers see as its nihilistic drive, is fundamentally situated in the desiring, living, hysterical subject as what constitutes the human condition in general.

To put it in simple language, von Trier's *Melancholia*, regardless of what the director's intentions may have been in terms of what he really wanted to communicate to the viewer, shows that while melancholia may be regarded as an illness afflicting certain people (Lars von Trier himself is known to have experienced severe bouts of depression), being a desiring subject is itself an incurable illness that can be traced back to the subject's very inscription into the symbolic order—an inscription that is melancholic by its very nature since it is based not on a gain but on a certain fundamental loss within the psyche. In the course of this, it will also be shown that nothing hinders coming to grips with a filmic text like *Melancholia* and trying to fully grasp the scope of its radical implications more than feminist readings of it.

Chapter 9 serves as a conclusion to Lars von Trier's cinematic deployment of female figures as *Woman* in the Lacanian sense. Its argument approaches the question of desire through his *Nymphomaniac*—a film which can be quite justifiably seen as the director's most pornographic film. *Nymphomaniac*'s pornography, however, seems to serve as the most effective tool by which the film *departs from* one of the fundamental pornographic rules, namely the play on the metonymic structure of desire, in order to effectively replace the law of desire with the Lacanian idea of *desire as law*, which Lacan discusses in connection with anxiety (*Anxiety* 106–7), as well as in 'Kant with Sade' (*Écrit: The First Complete Edition* 645–68), in which he shows how those two seemingly irreconcilable figures meet at the very limits of moral law where Sade's *Philosophy in the Bedroom* "yields the truth" (646) of Kant's 'Critique of Practical Reason' in spite of the Kantian elevation of the Law above "pleasure ... pain, happiness ... abject poverty ... the love of life—in short, everything pathological" (662). I do not really understand this query. I assume it is about the strikethrough over the word "Woman" in some instances. This is intentional wherever it appears, so, yes, if the word "Woman" is with a strikethrough please keep the strikethrough.

Moreover, *Nymphomaniac* does this in a particularly Sadean fashion; by telling the story of her various sexual exploits, which could have been written by the Marquis de Sade himself, the heroine *becomes* Sade, in the sense that Simone de Beauvoir makes out of the Marquis as mainly a corpus of literature or as one long erotic narrative. And when everything is said, once the heroine becomes able to regard herself as narrative, she, like Sade, becomes "afraid of the reality of the world" (Beauvoir 7). *Nymphomaniac* is not simply about a woman enjoying herself to the point of abuse and bodily damage; it is about a woman whose politically incorrect position with regard to society voids her nymphomania of its supposed worth—*jouissance*.

She learns, even though in an ultimately violent and humiliating way, that it is not by filling up her holes that she will reach a powerful *jouissance* that is beyond the pleasure principle; for the kind of eroticism experienced beyond the pleasure principle has nothing to do with sexual intercourse, requiring as it does communication with the Other on a much higher level (an intellectual level, for example). *Nymphomaniac*, therefore, does not only simply deploy a form of feminine sexuality that is insatiable, non-conformational, and dangerous through the figure of its heroine; it does something far more important, presenting itself to the viewer as an interruption of mainstream cinema, not in the sense of its pornographization but in the sense of mainstreaming pornography itself by presenting it as more problematic and thought-provoking than entertaining.

Finally, I would like to add a certain dimension or adjustment to Abbas's statement that "a film should not mean but be" (18). In its being, a film always means something—either through its content or stylistics or both—even if it does not mean to mean anything. It is the viewer who ultimately makes the film mean or be. In other words, it is the viewer who can either interpret or enjoy, who can either constitute meaning or elevate the cinematic experience beyond meaning. However, even elevating the cinematic experience beyond meaning is not exactly meaningless. Recognizing in a film that which is more than itself may not provide any reading or any critique of it. It provides much more than that; it provides the viewer with a glimpse of the uncanniness of his own real of desire as well as the fictitiousness of his own position as subject, and this, even though traumatic, cannot be meaningless.

NOTE

1. See Freud's recurrent discussion of this in *Art and Literature*, ed. Albert Dickson and trans. from the German under the general editorship of James Strachey (Penguin Books, 1990), pp. 201, 353–4, 405, 448–50.

BIBLIOGRAPHY

Abbas, Ackbar. *Hong Kong: Culture and the Politics of Disappearance*. Minneapolis and London: University of Minnesota Press, 1997.
Adorno, Theodor W. *The Culture Industry*. Edited by J.M. Bernstein. London and New York: Routledge, 2001.
Adorno, Theodor W. *The Stars Down to Earth*. Edited by Stephen Crook. London and New York: Routledge, 2002.
Adorno, Theodor W., and Walter Benjamin. *Theodor W. Adorno and Walter Benjamin: The Complete Correspondence 1928–1940*. Edited by Henri Lonitz and translated by Nicholas Walker. Cambridge, MA: Harvard University Press, 2000.
Badley, Linda. *Lars von Trier*. Urbana, Chicago, Springfield: University of Illinois Press, 2010.
Barenboim, Daniel. *Everything Is Connected: The Power of Music*. Edited by Elena Cheah. London: Weidenfeld and Nicolson, 2008.

Bazin, André, and Hugh Gray. *What Is Cinema?* Berkeley: University of California Press, 1967.
Beauvoir, Simone de. Must We Burn Sade? *The Marquis de Sade: The 120 Days of Sodom and Other Writings*. Compiled and translated by Austryn Wainhouse and Richard Seaver. New York: Grove Press, 1953.
Chodorow, Nancy J. Freud on Women. *The Cambridge Companion to Freud*. Edited by Jerome Neu. Cambridge and New York: Cambridge University Press, 1991.
Freud, Sigmund. *New Introductory Lectures on Psychoanalysis*. Translated and edited by James Strachey. New York: Norton, 1965.
Freud, Sigmund. *On Sexuality.* Vol. 7 of Penguin Freud Library. Edited by Angela Richards and translated by James Strachey. Harmondsworth: Penguin, 1976.
Freud, Sigmund. *Art and Literature*. Edited by Albert Dickson and translated from the German under the general editorship of James Strachey. Penguin Books, 1990a.
Freud, Sigmund. *Freud on Women: A Reader*. Edited by Elisabeth Young-Bruehl. New York: W.W. Norton, 1990b.
Freud, Sigmund. *Civilization, Society and Religion*. Edited by Albert Dickson and translated by James Strachey. London and New York: Penguin Books, 1991a.
Freud, Sigmund. *On Metapsychology: The Theory of Psychoanalysis*. Edited by Angela Richards and translated from the German under the general editorship of James Strachey. Penguin Books, 1991b.
Freud, Sigmund. *The Standard Edition of the Complete Psychological Works of Sigmund Freud*. Vol. XIX (1923–5). Translated from the German under the general editorship of James Strachey, in collaboration with Anna Freud, assisted by Alix Strachey and Alan Tyson. London: Vintage, 2001.
Koutsourakis, Angelos. *Politics as Form in Lars von Trier: A Post-Brechtian Reading*. New York, London, New Delhi and Sydney: Bloomsbury, 2013.
Lacan, Jacques. *Écrits: A Selection*. Translated by Alan Sheridan. London and New York: Routledge, 1989.
Lacan, Jacques. *The Four Fundamental Concepts of Psycho-Analysis*. Edited by Jacques-Alain Miller and translated by Alan Sheridan. Penguin Books, 1994.
Lacan, Jacques. *The Psychoses 1955–1956*. Edited by Jacques-Alain Miller and translated by Russell Grigg. New York and London: W.W. Norton and Company, 1997.
Lacan, Jacques. *On Feminine Sexuality, The Limits of Love and Knowledge: Encore, 1972–1973*. Translated and with notes by Bruce Fink. New York and London: W.W. Norton and Company, 1998.
Lacan, Jacques. *The Ethics of Psychoanalysis 1959–1960*. Edited by Jacques-Alain Miller and translated by Dennis Porter. London: Routledge, 1999.

Lacan, Jacques. *Écrit: The First Complete Edition in English*. Translated by Bruce Fink. New York and London: W.W. Norton and Company, 2006.

Lacan, Jacques. *The Other Side of Psychoanalysis*. Translated and with notes by Russell Grigg. New York and London: W.W. Norton and Company, 2007.

Lacan, Jacques. *My Teaching*. Translated by David Macey. London and New York: Verso, 2008.

Lacan, Jacques. *Anxiety*. Edited by Jacques-Alain Miller and translated by A. Rae Price. Cambridge: Polity Press, 2014.

Lumholdt, Jan. *Lars von Trier: Interviews*. Mississippi, Jackson: University Press of Mississippi, 2003.

McGowan, Todd. *The Real Gaze: Film Theory After Lacan*. Albany: State University of New York Press, 2007.

Metz, Christian. *The Imaginary Signifier: Psychoanalysis and the Cinema*. Bloomington: Indiana University Press, 1981.

Mulvey, Laura. *Visual and Other Pleasures*. Houndmills, Basingstoke, Hampshire [England]: Palgrave Macmillan, 2009.

Page, Nicholas. The Last Temptation of Von Trier: *Antichrist*. *The Big Picture Magazine*. Accessed 10 October 2013. http://thebigpicturemagazine.com/index.php?Option=com_contentandview=articleandid=127: the-last-temptation-of-von-trier-antichristandcatid=34: film-reviewsandItemid=60

Schepelern, Peter. The Making of an Auteur: Notes on the Auteur Theory and Lars von Trier. *Visual Authorship: Creativity and Intentionality in Media*. Edited by Torben Grodal, Bente Larsen, and Iben Thorving Laursen. Copenhagen: Museum Tusculanum Press, University of Copenhagen, 2005.

Stevenson, Jack. *Dogme Uncut: Lars von Trier, Thomas Vinterberg, and the Gang That Took on Hollywood*. California: Santa Monica Press, 2003.

The Bible: Authorized King James Version with Apocrypha. Oxford and New York: Oxford University Press, 1998.

Villiers de l'Isle-Adam, Auguste, comte de. *Tomorrow's Eve*. Translated by Robert Martin Adams. Champaigne, IL: University of Illinois Press, 2001.

Žižek, Slavoj. *The Sublime Object of Ideology*. London and New York: Verso, 1989.

Žižek, Slavoj. *The Metastases of Enjoyment: Six Essays on Woman and Causality*. London and New York: Verso, 1994.

Žižek, Slavoj. *The Žižek Reader*. Edited by Elizabeth Wright and Edmond Wright. Oxford and Malden, MA: Blackwell Publishing, 1999.

Žižek, Slavoj. *Enjoy Your Symptom! Jacques Lacan in Hollywood and Out*. New York and London: Routledge, 2001.

Žižek, Slavoj. *For They Know Not What They Do: Enjoyment as a Political Factor*. London and New York: Verso, 2002.

Žižek, Slavoj. *Interrogating the Real*. Edited by Rex Butler and Scott Stephens. London and New York: Continuum, 2006.

Filmography

Antichrist. Directed and written by Lars von Trier. Irvington, NY: Criterion Collection, 2010.
Breaking the Waves. Directed and written by Lars von Trier. Paris: Pathé, 2003.
Dancer in the Dark. Directed and written by Lars von Trier. Montréal, Québec: Alliance Atlantis, 2007.
Dogma 2: Idioterne (*Dogma 2: The Idiots*). Directed and written by Lars von Trier. Toronto: Alliance Atlantis, 2004.
Dogville. Directed and written by Lars von Trier. Hong Kong: Edko Films Ltd., 2005.
The Hurt Locker. Directed by Kathryn Bigelow. Written by Mark Boal. Santa Monica, CA: Summit Entertainment, 2010.
Life in Baghdad: Joy amid the Chaos of War. Reported by Martin Smith. Produced and edited by Michelle Mizner. Principal Photography Scott Anger. *Frontline*. Accessed 12 November 2015. https://www.youtube.com/watch?v=ftPHG8yGuts
Manderlay. Directed and written by Lars von Trier. Delmar, CA: IFC Films. Distributed by Genius Entertainment, 2005.
Melancholia. Directed and written by Lars von Trier. Hong Kong: Edko Films Ltd., 2011.
Nymphomaniac. Directed and written by Lars von Trier. Hong Kong: Panorama Corporation Limited, 2014.

CHAPTER 2

The Danger of the Naive Religious Woman of *Breaking the Waves*

The question of what a woman is in psychoanalysis does not only bear on gender difference, male and female identities, desire, guilt, ego formation, or even the void upon which the self is based, but on the very existence of discourse as such. This is at the heart of Lacan's discourse about the inexplicability of the notion of woman or the impossibility of becoming one:

> Becoming a woman and wondering what a woman is are two essentially different things […] It's because one doesn't become one that one wonders and, up to a point, to wonder is the contrary of becoming one. The metaphysics of the woman's position is the detour imposed on her subjective realization. Her position is essentially problematic, and up to a certain point it's inassimilable. (*Psychoses* 178)

Becoming is becoming *in* the discourse. Wondering *is* the discourse. It is because of this that the inassimilability of the woman's position not only puts her right in the middle of the void upon which subjectivity as such is based, but casts a serious doubt on the existence of the symbolized subject (man) as well. If woman is outside the discourse, this can only be explained by her being its very instigator. In other words, while the presence of man is a symbolic possibility that does not actually explain either man or woman, the absence of woman, in its essence, is an impossibility, because it would be an absence that cancels out the presence of both genders—and the discourse.

It took Lacan nine years, between publishing *Écrit* in 1966 and *Encore* in 1975, to say something on feminine sexuality—hence subjectivity—in a completely different seminar with a completely different mind. Žižek explains how Lacanian thought shifts radically from the notion of the "Other" to the notion of the "One" in *Encore*, from the signifier to the sign, from the symbolic network to the psychosis reflected in Lacan's effort in his last years, which was "directed at breaking through the field of communication-as-meaning" (*Žižek Reader* 29). In short, from discourse to *jouissance*. This Lacanian shift also marks "the two opposed meanings of the word 'existence' in Lacan". The first means "symbolization, integration into the discursive order [...] in which Lacan maintains that 'Woman does not exist'", and the second is the opposite meaning of "'ex-sistence', the impossible-real nucleus resisting symbolization" (31) to which woman is ultimately committed.

The structure of subjectivity in the case of the female, even though she may initially take the same detour within a discourse that is predominantly written in the Name of the Father, is thus nevertheless fundamentally different by virtue of the female's connection to the notion of woman. In other words, the subjectivity of the female relates to woman who does not exist in the system of symbolization yet exists at the level of *jouissance* where she, as well as the big Other itself, is crossed out. She is outside the system but constitutes its very subversion. She is not threatened by castration, yet it is precisely the lack of the phallus that transforms *her* into man's sign of castration.

Looking at Lars von Trier's *Breaking the Waves* in light of what has been said above seems to add another dimension to an already complicated notion. For here we have a woman who occasionally talks to God, then impersonates Him and talks back to herself as God. Bess, a naive religious girl with a history of psychological problems, marries Jan, a Norwegian oil-rig worker, despite the disapproval of her community's elders who run the village through an authoritative Calvinist church so conservative it does not even allow church bells. Bess immensely enjoys her sexual experience with her husband, and when he eventually returns to his work on the rig, she can hardly bear life without him. Jan makes occasional phone calls to Bess in which they have sexual conversations. Bess's impatience, however, makes her ask God for Jan's rapid return at any cost in one of her prayers where she impersonates God and imaginatively creates dialogues with Him.

In what seems to be God's immediate answer to her prayer, Jan does return, but with a paralyzed lower body that is no longer able to perform sexually. To free her from being tied to him, Jan asks Bess to make love to other men, alleviating her sense of guilt by convincing her that she will do this not for herself but for him; by relating her sexual encounters with other men to him in detail, they can fantasize about being together again and through this she can keep him alive. After her first extramarital sexual experience Jan's condition seems to improve, so Bess dresses up as a prostitute and starts to have sex with strangers. Perceived now as a prostitute by everyone in the village she becomes increasingly estranged and even stone-pelted by the children in the street. It is at this point that "Bess's struggle takes on a load of Christian symbolism" (Badley 83).

In one of the film's most touching scenes, Bess as usual tries to ask God for guidance, but this time she is somehow unable to impersonate Him (God does not reply to her). Horrified by this 'divine silence' she looks up apprehensively with an ashen face and asks "Father, where are you?" just as Jesus cries on the cross "Eli, lama sabachthani? [...] my God, why hast thou forsaken me?" (*The Bible*, Matthew 27:46, 42). Pushed by Dr Richardson (Adrian Rawlins) and Dodo (Katrin Cartlidge), Jan signs a document consigning Bess to a mental hospital. On her way to the hospital she manages to escape. When she is informed that Jan is dying, she takes this as a sign from God that she should sacrifice more than just her body to save his life. In suicidal determination she returns to a ship where she was previously roughed up and cut by two violent sailors. On her way she has a final dialogue (which is in fact a monologue) with God to make sure he is with her. Viciously abused and nearly beaten to death, she is brought to the hospital where she learns that Jan's condition is not improving. Bess dies and the elders of her village decide to give her a sinner's burial condemning her to hell. Right after her death, however, Jan is unaccountably cured. He and his friends steal Bess's body and bury it at sea. Hours later they wake up to the toll of giant bells that seem to be miraculously hanging from the sky.

Breaking the Waves thus shows a woman whose morality is based on her own sense of righteousness, which is determined by an imagined private connection to God. As freeing as it is from institutionalized religion and its – to quote the great James Joyce in what seems to be his description of the Islamic tradition – "search for righteousness" (5), the idea of a personal relationship with God cannot be trouble-free since it implies replacing the mediation of culture (in Bess's case the culture of her Calvinist church and highly conservative community) with pure linguistic correspondence with the master signifier 'God'. That such an idea is related to the psychotic phenomenon is an established discourse in Lacanian psychoanalysis. This is not to suggest, however, that Bess is psychotic.

In fact, the purpose of writing this chapter is to show quite the opposite; that since Bess's form of belief seems to stress that a personal relationship with God can only be established through a human being ("you cannot love words, you cannot be in love with a word, you can love another human being, that's perfection"), and since she does not cancel out the human dimension in religion, she remains a neurotic subject who identifies herself in language and maintains erotic relations with the other. The aim of this chapter is to argue that the naive Bess, who truly loves God, is indeed innocent of all sins but one, and it is *the* ultimate sin a human being can fall into; Bess is nothing but the very representation of that which marks the fall of God himself into sin, which is no less than his very existence in language.

But let us start from the beginning by shedding some light on what neurosis is and how it differs from psychosis in Lacanian psychoanalysis. In 1910, Freud wrote his 'Psycho-Analytic Notes upon an Autobiographical Account of a Case of Paranoia' (*Standard Edition* 12–80) in which he discusses Daniel Paul Schreber's own account of his mental illness, which the latter published in 1903 in the form of a book entitled *Memoirs of My Nervous Illness*. In his discussion of Freud's analysis of the Schreber case, where Schreber's delusional experience is traced back to the fact that he regretted not having had children, Lacan explains the difference between neurosis and psychosis by stating that:

> In neurosis, inasmuch as reality is not fully rearticulated symbolically into the external world, it is in a second phase that a partial flight from reality, an incapacity to confront this secretly preserved part of reality, occurs in the subject. In psychosis, on the contrary, reality itself initially contains a hole that the world of fantasy will subsequently fill. (*Psychoses* 45).

Neuroses thus remain inside the symbolic order, precisely because erotic relations with the other, or that which is a reflection of the self, remain in them. In fact, Lacan says that the neurotic subject not only identifies himself in language, but loses his own being in the signifying chain; he transforms himself into a signifier and becomes language (155). The neurotic phenomenon thus seems to be inherent in culture since the 'normal' human subject does transform himself or herself into a signifier on daily basis. Transforming oneself into a signifier maintains the whole system of symbolic exchanges that defines one's daily life and regulates all his or her relations with the other. By displaying a cultural code, the subject sends a message to the other, which means that he turns himself into a signifier. And since people transform themselves into signifiers every day, it can be argued that human culture is by definition neurotic, or, even more precisely, that neurosis is in fact the very condition of culture.

The return of the repressed, in the case of neurosis, takes place within the signifying chain, totally determined by the symbolic sphere, no matter how concealed that repressed material becomes. It can disguise itself beneath a mask, or beneath various masks, but it always "reappears *in loco* where it was repressed, that is, in the very midst of symbols" (105). The psychotic phenomenon on the other hand is marked by a "hole" in reality, a gap in the subject's symbolic order and, more importantly, it is an unbridgeable gap, a moment of total breakdown which renders the subject's whole signifying chain an inarticulate mess. Delusion thus results from an encounter with the real, or with that which can neither be represented by language nor appear in the register of the imaginary.

The return of the repressed in the case of the psychosis takes place "in altero, in the imaginary, without a mask" (105). The difference between neurosis and the psychotic phenomenon is thus that while neurosis is still based on an erotic relation with the other within a system of symbolic exchange, the psychotic phenomenon is marked by a fundamental impairment to that relation and, in Schreber's case, by conceiving an imagined personal relation with God, the ideological big Other, or the symbolic almightiness of the Name of the Father. In the psychosis, the relation with the imaginary other, with all the aggressivity it carries, and which originates initially in the formation of the ego in the mirror stage, is essentially disrupted. Instead of symbolic exchanges within the symbolic network, the entire signifying *system* is reorganized/disorganized and brought into play in its totality, that is, in its ultimate representation—what Lacan calls the Name of the Father.

Consequently, while the discourse with the other, which is also the self, fades out, the psychotic subject contrives a discourse with the "imaginary father", "the basis of the providential image of God" (*Ethics* 308)—a discourse that, according to Lacan, is defined by a "mobilization of the signifier as speech, ejaculatory speech that is insignificant or too significant" (*Psychoses* 321). One might add here: insignificant, because it does not exactly belong to the world, since it does not constitute a discourse with the other, and, too significant, because it is overloaded with the notion of a correspondence with God. To imagine a correspondence with God, a personal correspondence with God, in which God becomes an active participant, does not simply come about because of an overzealous religiousness.

In Schreber's case, Lacan illustrates a certain detour that starts with the lack of the signifier 'being a father' and ends up at filling the lack by fantasy via the delusional way of "being the female correspondent of God" (77). Being a father is being a father in language since "before the name of the father, there was no father" (306). The natural father is actually nothing but that unfortunate subject who is destined to carry the heavy symbolic load of the Name of the Father, the castrating figure and, at the same time, the basis of the superego. This is why Lacan states that "the sum of these facts—of copulating with a woman, that she then carries something within her womb for a certain period, that this product is finally expelled—will never lead one to constitute the notion of what it is *to be a father*" (293).

In Schreber's case, then, the lack of the signifier 'being a father' is of such complexity as to arouse the Lacanian fundamental question: "Che vuoi?" (Lacan, *Écrit: A Selection* 345–6), signaling an incomprehension on the part of the subject as to the desire of the big Other, with no satisfactory answer. What does it mean to have all the characteristics of virility and yet not become a father? The psychotic in this case bases itself on this encounter of the void behind the desire of the big Other—the unrepresentable and ultimately unexplainable real that violently floods the subject through the fissure in his symbolic world. Delusional discourse follows in which, in Lacan's own words, "the signifiers begin to talk, to sing on their own" (*Psychoses* 294), creating the illusion that there is a discourse between two entities. It is in this discourse that the psychotic subject begins to transform himself into the object of desire of the big Other, in other words, to compensate for the lack of being a father/bearer-of-the-phallus by transforming *himself* into a phallus.

This, however, clearly does not apply to Bess whose relationship to God is intrinsically mixed with her relationship to Jan. Frances Restuccia argues that *Breaking the Waves* "depicts a 'hysterical' W̶o̶m̶a̶n̶ in Love, a 'masochistic,' mystical Woman—that is, a W̶o̶m̶a̶n̶ who doesn't exist—in Lacanian Love, in a sense with God" (187). Although I have certain reservations on using the Lacanian "W̶o̶m̶a̶n̶" here, I am in agreement with

Restuccia that Bess is a woman who is in love with God. When Bess imaginatively relates to the paralyzed Jan a sexual encounter with Dr Richardson (Adrian Rawlins), which never really took place, he immediately realizes she is lying. Bess could have chosen to invent and improvise, relating other imagined sexual encounters with other men whom Jan does not know to feed his imagination.

But Bess, from this work's perspective, is neither trying to show obedience to Jan nor just simply trying to get him miraculously cured. By actually having sexual intercourse with strangers she is trying to *prove* to God that she loves him/Him. Impersonating God in her unusual form of prayers, she commands: "Prove to me that you love him and then I'll let him live." Restuccia argues that Bess "sacrifices her subjectivity for Jan […] In turn, she sacrifices for God as well […] a God Himself beyond the Law […] to Bess, to love a human being, and in turn to love God, beyond language and the Law, is divine 'perfection'" (196). The crucial question that poses itself here, however, is: can God, who is beyond the Law, be talked with/about? And, if Bess's major gesture is sacrifice, in what way does this really escape the Law?

In Christian belief, sacrifice is itself the Law. If Bess sacrifices herself for the love of Jan, or for the love of God, then she is precisely in love *according to* the Law, and not beyond it, since her sacrifice seems to be a kind of small emulation of God's sacrifice; she sacrifices herself to the alleviation of a human being's suffering in imitation of God who sacrifices himself or part of himself to alleviating humanity's suffering. This total identification with the idea of divine sacrifice, which is clearly manifested in the film's portrayal of Bess as a Christ figure, seems to simultaneously glorify and mock God's sacrifice—which seems to lose all meaning the moment we realize that Bess's God *demands* a human sacrifice *in exchange* for saving a human life, as if divine Law can't help falling back helplessly to the rules of symbolic exchange. Indeed, healing, either physical or spiritual, always requires going through some traumatic transformation in the religious imagination: "And certain women, which had been healed of evil spirits and infirmities, Mary called Magdalene, out of whom went seven devils" (*The Bible*, Luke 8:2, 83–4).

In fact, the idea of God manipulating those rules seems to dominate from the start; when Bess asks God to bring Jan back at any cost, she "offers God the first symbolic exchange", which He immediately accepts, setting a ridiculously high cost. Žižek argues that "to save Jan, Bess accepts to betray HERSELF" ('Femininity between Goodness and Act'). This self-betrayal, however, from this work's point of view, is not simply based on "'perfect' Love [or] 'limitless love' [that is] beyond the Law" (Restuccia 196); it is not beyond Bess's religious beliefs, which are marked by total identification with the divine sacrificial gesture and which therefore necessitate emulating God himself in his betrayal of HIMSELF precisely at the moment he lowers himself to the level of symbolic exchange. That is why Lacan sees the story of Christ's sacrifice "not as the enterprise of saving men, but as that of saving God" (*On Feminine Sexuality* 108).

The price Bess pays for this symbolic exchange with God, according to Žižek, is "complete alienation: her *jouissance* is now in words, not in things, not in the bodily sexual activity itself, but in her verbal report on her exploits to the crippled Jan" ('Femininity between Goodness and Act'). What needs to be added here, however, is that this particular price of "complete alienation", which Bess has to pay, seems in turn to designate nothing but the alienation of God himself, whose *jouissance*, as we perceive it, has always already been in words. The history of religion and its relation to the human species, in spite of the heterogeneity of religions, seems to have been the history of repeating the same gesture of foreclosing the idea of God in the Real, as an Other in the most radical sense, in other words, that which cannot be imagined or talked about, through creating God as Father, or as a human being, or indeed through bestowing godly attributes on human beings, but ultimately through creating God in language as what Lacan calls the "Name of the Father" (*Écrit: The First Complete Edition* 480–5). For "within the space of language, we 'regress' to the level of Being" (Žižek, *Interrogating the Real* 182). Once God exists in language, He *is*, but that in itself is necessarily a regression.

Religious discourse in general seems to be nothing but a reflection of man's creation of God in his own (man's) image. Nothing clarifies this more than psychoanalysis. Žižek argues that a "certain 'sacrificial situation' defines the very status of man *qua* 'parlêtre', 'being of language' [...] what is sacrificed in the act of choice is of course the Thing, the incestuous Object that embodies impossible enjoyment—the paradox consisting in the fact that the incestuous Object *comes to be through being lost*, i.e., that it is not given prior to its loss" (*Enjoy Your Symptom* 74–5). This "sacrificial situation" seems to define the very status of God, too, *qua* "being of language" as clearly evidenced by the religious discourse in which human imagination seems unable to escape its assumption that God must have sacrificed something, some impossible *jouissance*, or indeed must have made the same sacrifice as man in order to be of language or to exist in language *qua* the Name of the Father. This sacrifice may not be the sacrifice of the incestuous Object of desire or the maternal Thing. It could rather be "*Father himself*, namely, the obscene Father-*jouissance* prior to his murder and subsequent elevation into the agency of symbolic authority (Name-of-the-Father) (Žižek, Ticklish Subject 314).

There are two answers—one psychoanalytic and the other cultural—to Žižek's skeptical question, "is thus *BW* not the utmost 'male chauvinist' film celebrating and elevating into a sublime act of sacrifice the role which is forcefully imposed on women in patriarchal societies, that of serving as the support of male masturbatory fantasies?" Žižek himself answers the question in Lacanian terms, saying that "not all of a woman is caught up in the phallic *jouissance*: She is always split between [...] attracting the male gaze and [...] a mysterious *jouissance* beyond Phallus about which nothing can be said" ('Femininity between Goodness and Act'). The cultural politics of *Breaking the Waves*, however, are not solely constituted by giving woman this exit from male phallic economy and splitting her being between two worlds, but also by problematizing the concept of God in both worlds. God in the Real, like woman's mysterious *jouissance*, cannot be talked about, cannot be shown or symbolized; while God in language manifests Himself in discourse, in the Word and, in a particularly postmodern cinematic way, in tolling bells hanging from the sky.

That is why, from this work's perspective, the play of 'words' in *Breaking the Waves* in fact goes beyond the assumption that Bess delivers the film's core message when she states "you cannot love words, you cannot be in love with a word, you can love another human being, that's perfection". On the surface of it, Bess's statement seems to be in opposition to what is preached in her church, but, at the same time, it is not precisely clear how it opposes the core of Christian thought, which is based on loving Christ as both God and a human being. Taking a closer look, everything in *Breaking the Waves* shows precisely the opposite: that one cannot love *but* words, that one is always already in love with a word, and that what passes for 'perfection' in love is nothing but our deceptive success in "persuading the other that he has that which may complement us", and which is precisely nothing but self-deception according to Lacan since it is through this persuasion of the other that we "assure ourselves of being able to continue to misunderstand precisely what we lack (*Four Fundamental Concepts* 133).

It does not take much to see with striking clarity that what Bess really lacks—what woman lacks from the film's perspective—is a voice; words of her own. Early in the film, the 'naive' Bess states that "it's stupid that only men can talk in the service", to which her father replies "hold your tongue, woman!" The form of prayers she invents for herself can be seen as her own special religious discourse by which she compensates for her absence in the established religious discourse where only man talks. What is in common between the two discourses, however, is that God must be a He—something Bess *wouldn't want* to change for a particular reason that will be discussed here shortly. Caroline Bainbridge reiterates after Björkman that throughout von Trier's films, "religion and the organization of religion are frequently attacked, but the idea of God is not", and that is why "Bess refutes advocation of belief in the Word and the Law by saying 'you can't love the Word. You can only love a person'" (Bainbridge 14–15).

But isn't the "idea of God" *preconditioned* by nothing but words? It can be argued that it is precisely the idea of God that is attacked because God always already manifested himself in the Word/Law. Beneath the surface of the staged opposition between Bess's idea of God and the elders' idea of God there is no real opposition because Bess herself loves the words, and the viewer cannot miss the very existence of God throughout *Breaking the Waves* as nothing but words that run on Bess's lips, with the exception of the last scene in which von Trier replaces the words with the bells. The question that Bainbridge poses with regard to the "narrative parallels" of Bess's sexual conversations with Jan on the telephone and her conversations with God, "Is 'love' to be understood in religious terms or is it rather premised on carnal desire?" (106), seems to be somewhat misleading because in the conversations both with Jan and with God, love depends on words, sexual or otherwise.

In fact, it can be argued that the film's major theme is love in the form of words, and Jan's accident and subsequent immobility should not only be seen as the cause of Bess's "complete alienation" (Žižek, 'Femininity between Goodness and Act') but also as the cause of her complete transfer to and disappearance in the realm she always already loved and preferred; a world of "make-believe", as Dodo tells her, or a world of words. This is why it is quite futile and beside the point to try to determine Jan's true intention when he tells Bess, "I want you to find a man to make love to and then come back here and tell me about it." From the present work's point of view, the moral question is not even posed in the first place, because the film's sole concern is to show the sheer power of the word. Her relationship to Jan, like her relationship to God, becomes pure discourse.

When Bess drinks and dances in an attempt to sexually arouse Dr Richardson and make him sleep with her, he keeps asking her to "stop dancing and talk to me!" Again, looking for the moral here would be pointless because the point, in accordance with the film's core idea, is to show through him that it is only through the *word* that the other's body can be truly accessed and, through her, that *talking* is the one thing she won't offer; only her body. When, in a later scene, Dr Richardson utters the magical sentence "I love you", she can't even tolerate his presence any more, while in the scene that immediately follows she is utterly traumatized by God's silence (her inability to impersonate God and talk on his behalf).

In all this, it is the idea of the word that reigns supreme in *Breaking the Waves*. And, in light of it, the scene in which Bess bravely opposes the idea of loving words inside the church becomes much more ambiguous and problematic than commonly assumed. It is as if Bess is opposed to the very idea that entirely shapes her life and her love. The priest angrily declares that "no woman speaks here", but he cannot prevent her from having a final dialogue with God before her suicidal act. The play of the Word still goes on even after Bess's death; Dr Richardson expresses a wish in front of the judge to change his medical report about Bess and, instead of neurosis, he suggests that the deceased suffered from being "good". The elders decide to bury her with no proper funeral and the priest tells her relatives that he "must say about Bess what must be said". It becomes urgent and a "must" for the religious institution to have the final *word* on her life and her destiny in the afterlife.

But, naturally, it is not up to any of the characters to have the final word in a von Trier film; it is von Trier himself who decides to side with Bess's form of belief and announce God's presence—that is to say, Bess's version of God—in the final scene by the giant bells in the sky. Perhaps what Peter Schepelern sees in von Trier's early films as the director's success in creating a universe "where everything was under the absolute control of the *auteur* artist who functioned as God or a puppeteer" (*Purity and Provocation* 64) can be applied here. But ultimately, the final scene, as Žižek suggests, seems to serve as a "postmodernist appendix", which shows that "miracles effectively do occur, as an aesthetic spectacle, without 'really believing it', but also without any ironic or cynical distance" ('Femininity between Goodness and Act').

It can be argued thus that the film's final gesture of affirming the presence of God is paradoxically a sign of *disbelief* in God's existence. True believers, like Bess, must die in doubt, not in entire belief, because belief loses its very meaning if its ultimate dimension is revealed. To Lacan, belief by its very definition must "presuppose in its basis that the ultimate dimension that it has to reveal is strictly correlative with the moment when its meaning is about to fade away" (*Four Fundamental Concepts* 238). In this sense, the giant bells in the sky are *not* exactly an affirmation of God's presence, precisely because they are meant to remove the audience's *doubt*—and with it belief itself.

The typical feminist critique of religious discourse, which suggests that it is man who invented God in his own male image or, more interestingly, that "patriarchy attacked and finally managed to overthrow the ancient established religions of the Mother Goddess, who preceded male gods in every mythology in the world" (Walker 268), seems to repress the fact that this is a fight over nothing but a master signifier in language. Lars von Trier himself, who is commonly perceived by many viewers as a misogynist, in what seems to be a feminist moment, asks "God has always been a 'he'. Why is 'he' a he?" (194).

The answer, over and above both the religious discourse and the feminist critique of it, is that perhaps male and female cooperated and in a way even conspired to make God male; man wanted to make him male in his own image to establish some sort of symbolic authority over woman, and woman, with a more complicated and ambitious intention, wanted to make God male in order to complete the circuit and render God, as his male inventor, a creation of language and no more. Put another way, man invented an ideology and woman subverted it by what Žižek refers to in a number of his essays as the literal identification with ideology. According to Žižek, "*the stepping out of (what we experience as) ideology is the very form of our enslavement to it*" (*Žižek Reader* 60).[1] The same ideological power applies to the religious discourse in general. While what can produce a kind of disheartenment of an ideological discourse is the "playful identification"[2] with it, subverting ideology, in Žižekan thought, can be achieved by nothing but a total and literal identification with its mandates or "the procedure of the ultra-orthodox subversion of the law through the very overidentification with it".[3]

While man historically abstracted himself as God, as can be evidenced in the discourse of religion, woman abstracted the abstraction itself. She did not really try to revise or critique the religious discourse and its male God; she took man's ideological invention as it is and pushed it even further to the very limits of the completely unbelievable. It is an affirmation and a fundamental destabilization of religious discourse at once. Thus, while a feminist critique of the religious discourse works against the grain, revealing its male-oriented foundations, it does not seem to the present writer to be an effective way to destabilize that discourse or the persistence of its framing of the feminine as subaltern in texts that are extremely judicious and soggy with masculine stresses.

The feminist reading of *Breaking the Waves*, and of religion itself, seems to be neither the best of readings, nor does it seem to constitute any real resistance to the supposed male-oriented mandates of religion. A Lacanian reading seems to be certainly more effective; it does not resist the religious discourse – on the contrary, it pushes it violently to its very limits and, in doing so, it completely subverts it. Bess, according to this Lacanian reading, is not in opposition to the religion of the elders and their God; on the contrary, she is in complete identification with their discourse. The difference between a symptomatic anti-religious feminist reading of *Breaking the Waves* and a Lacanian reading is thus itself the difference between resisting power ineffectively by creating that academically assured yet practically already aborted stance of resistance to power and ideology, and a Baudrillardian "challenge to power to be power, power of the sort that is total, irreversible, without scruple, and with no limit to its violence". Baudrillard states that "it is in facing this unanswerable challenge that power starts to break up" (60–1).

The power of the religious discourse breaks up precisely at the point of its exhaustion, where the Word is everything and where woman does not exist in it. Yet, Lacan states that "it is insofar as her jouissance is radically Other that woman has more of a relationship to God than anything that could have been said in speculation in antiquity following the pathway of that which is manifestly articulated only as the good of man" (*On Feminine Sexuality* 83). In Lacanian discourse, God and female *jouissance* belong to the realm of the mystic or what cannot be articulated or talked about. God, in the Real, has none of the attributes given to him in the language of religion(s). He, like female *jouissance*, is "radically Other" and cannot be talked about except in terms of complete mystery. Hence the foreclosure of God in the Real, the one, in Lacan's words, who "has not yet made his exit" (84), and the creation of God in language, the masculine God.

Žižek argues that:

> While the explicit Law is sustained by the dead father qua symbolic authority (the 'Name of the Father'), the unwritten code is sustained by the spectral supplement of the Name of the Father, the obscene specter of the Freudian 'primordial father' [...] the obscene father-enjoyment subordinated to no

symbolic Law, the total Master who dares to confront face to face the Real of terrifying *jouissance*. ('Move the Underground')

Bess in *Breaking the Waves* does not simply show us that God's nature is different from what is preached in church; she rather shows us that total and unconditional naive identification with the church's discourse directly leads to the inevitable fall of God Himself from "symbolic authority" to the "obscene father-enjoyment subordinated to no symbolic Law". God's enjoyment in *Breaking the Waves* demands nothing less than the sadistic torture of the body of the true believer to the point of death. It is there that woman destroys the image of God in the language of religion(s), while maintaining at the same time, through her own *jouissance*, a relationship with a mystic God who resides beyond man's universe.

Notes

1. This idea is also elaborated by Žižek in 'Fantasy as a Political Category', *The Žižek Reader*, eds Elizabeth Wright and Edmond Wright (Oxford and Malden, MA: Blackwell Publishing, 1999), p. 97; 'How Did Marx Invent the Symptom?', *The Sublime Object of Ideology* (London and New York: Verso, 1989), p. 30; and 'Are Cultural Studies Really Totalitarian?', *Did Somebody Say Totalitarianism? Five Interventions in the (Mis)use of a Notion* (London and New York: Verso, 2001), p. 226.
2. Žižek's example on this is how the Bosnian rock group Top lista nadrealista consolidated Bosnian solidarity during the war in Bosnia against Serbian racism through playful identification with the racist obscenities themselves. 'Passions of the Real, Passions of Semblance', *Welcome to the Desert of the Real! Five Essays on September 11 and Related Dates* (London and New York: Verso, 2002), p. 18.
3. Žižek gives the example of Heinrich von Kleist's hero in the novella *Michael Kohlhaas: From an Old Chronicle*, in which the hero identifies himself completely with law and justice to the very limits of overthrowing both in the process. 'The Myth and Its Vicissitudes', *Did Somebody Say Totalitarianism? Five Interventions in the (Mis)use of a Notion* (London and New York: Verso, 2001), pp. 32–4.

Bibliography

Badley, Linda. *Lars von Trier*. Urbana, Chicago, Springfield: University of Illinois Press, 2010.

Bainbridge, Caroline. *The Cinema of Lars von Trier: Authenticity and Artifice*. London and New York: Wallflower Press, 2007.

Baudrillard, Jean. *Forget Foucault*. Translated by Nicole Dufrense. Los Angeles, CA: Semiotext(e), 2007.

Freud, Sigmund. *The Standard Edition of the Complete Psychological Works of Sigmund Freud*. Vol. XIX (1923–5). Translated from the German under the general editorship of James Strachey, in collaboration with Anna Freud, assisted by Alix Strachey and Alan Tyson. London: Vintage, 2001.

Joyce, James. *Finnegans Wake*. Great Britain: Penguin Books, 2000.

Lacan, Jacques. *Écrits: A Selection*. Translated by Alan Sheridan. London and New York: Routledge, 1989.

Lacan, Jacques. *The Four Fundamental Concepts of Psycho-Analysis*. Edited by Jacques-Alain Miller and translated by Alan Sheridan. Penguin Books, 1994.

Lacan, Jacques. *The Psychoses 1955–1956*. Edited by Jacques-Alain Miller and translated by Russell Grigg. New York and London: W.W. Norton and Company, 1997.

Lacan, Jacques. *On Feminine Sexuality, The Limits of Love and Knowledge: Encore, 1972–1973*. Translated and with notes by Bruce Fink. New York and London: W.W. Norton and Company, 1998.

Lacan, Jacques. *The Ethics of Psychoanalysis 1959–1960*. Edited by Jacques-Alain Miller and translated by Dennis Porter. London: Routledge, 1999.

Lacan, Jacques. *Écrit: The First Complete Edition in English*. Translated by Bruce Fink. New York and London: W.W. Norton and Company, 2006.

Restuccia, Frances L. 'Impossible Love in Breaking the Waves: Mystifying Hysteria'. *Lacan and Contemporary Film*. Edited by Todd McGowan and Sheila Kunkle. New York: Other Press, 2004.

Schepelern, Peter. '"Kill Your Darlings": Lars von Trier and the Origin of Dogma 95'. *Purity and Provocation: Dogma 95*. Edited by Mette Hjort and Scott Mackenzie. London: British Film Institute, 2003.

Schreber, Daniel Paul. *Memoirs of My Nervous Illness*. Translated and edited with introduction, notes and discussion by Ida Macalpine and Richard A. Hunter. London: W. Dawson, 1955.

The Bible: Authorized King James Version with Apocrypha. Oxford and New York: Oxford University Press, 1998.

Trier, Lars von. '9 A.M., Thursday, September 7, 2000: Interview by Kjeld Koplev'. *Lars von Trier: Interviews*. Edited by Jan Lumholdt. Jackson, Mississippi: University Press of Mississippi, 2003.

Walker, Barbara G. *Man Made God: A Collection of Essays*. Seattle, WA: Stellar House Publishing, LLC, 2010.
Žižek, Slavoj. *The Sublime Object of Ideology*. London and New York: Verso, 1989.
Žižek, Slavoj. *The Žižek Reader*. Edited by Elizabeth Wright and Edmond Wright. Oxford and Malden, MA: Blackwell Publishing, 1999.
Žižek, Slavoj. *The Ticklish Subject: The Absent Centre of Political Ontology*. New York and London: Verso, 2000.
Žižek, Slavoj. *Enjoy Your Symptom! Jacques Lacan in Hollywood and Out*. New York and London: Routledge, 2001.
Žižek, Slavoj. *Did Somebody Say Totalitarianism? Five Interventions in the (Mis)use of a Notion*. London and New York: Verso, 2002.
Žižek, Slavoj. *Welcome to the Desert of the Real! Five Essays on September 11 and Related Dates*. London and New York: Verso, 2002.
Žižek, Slavoj. *Interrogating the Real*. Edited by Rex Butler and Scott Stephens. London and New York: Continuum, 2006.
Žižek, Slavoj. 'Femininity between Goodness and Act'. *The Sinthome 14*. Accessed 31 July 2014. http://www.lacan.com/symptom14/?p=43
Žižek, Slavoj. 'Move the Underground! What's Wrong with Fundamentalism?—Part II'. Accessed 20 August 2014. http://www.lacan.com/zizunder.htm

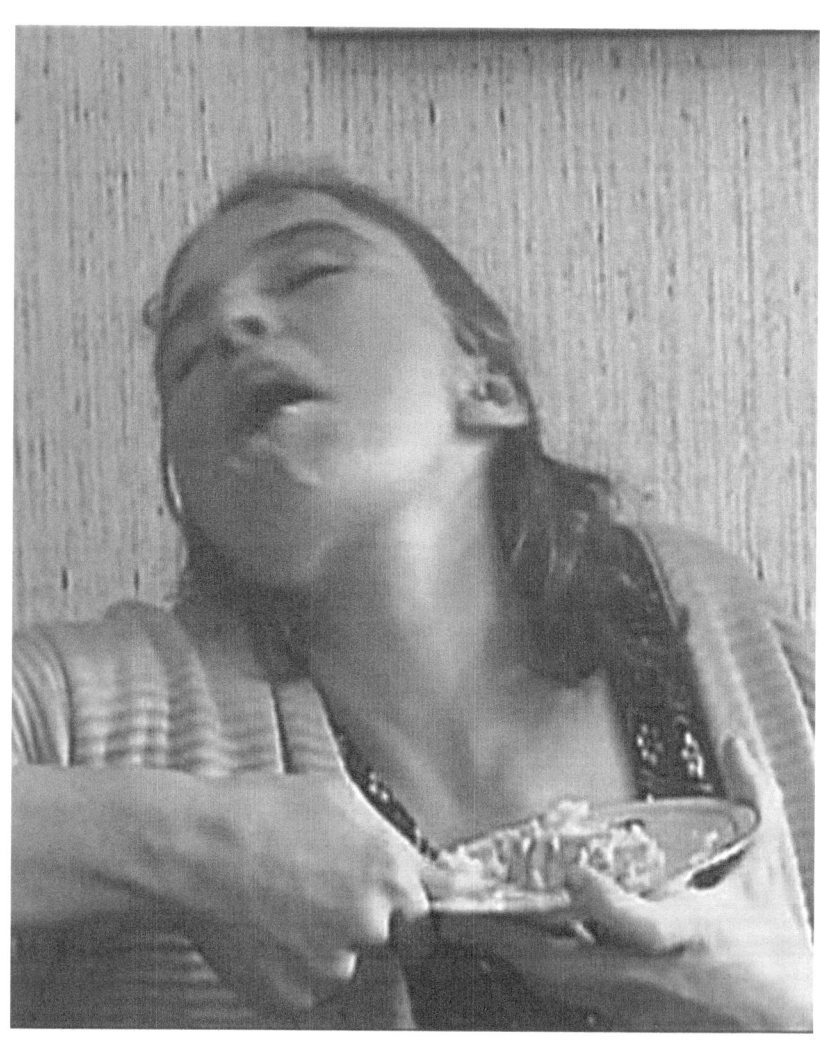

CHAPTER 3

Idioterne: Woman as a Proponent of Real Politics

Lars von Trier's *Idioterne*, as the purest example of the Dogma 95 movement, has been discussed by many writers in terms of its politics and its subversion of Hollywood's cinematic techniques. *Idioterne* is deservedly perceived by several writers as the Dogma 95 work par excellence. Peter Schepelern writes that it is "the ultimate Dogma work, because it not only uses but is *about* the Dogma rules" (*Purity and Provocation* 65). Berys Gaut writes that the film is "in part about the conditions of its own making, a kind of documentary of its own genesis" (95). Much less attention is given to the fact that *Idioterne* is as much a film about a woman in mourning and, precisely because of its unprecedented and *unrepeated* abandonment of the normal, fictional or traditional ways of filmmaking, it can be considered von Trier's most mournful film. That is to say: *it mourns Dogma 95 as a lost object of love at the very moment of its birth.*

One common feature that connects mourning to melancholia is that, in Freud's words, they both involve "grave departures from the normal attitude to life". At the same time, mourning is different from melancholia because "it never occurs to us to regard it as a pathological condition and to refer it to medical treatment. We rely on its being overcome after a certain lapse of time, and we look upon any interference with it as useless or even harmful" (*On Metapsychology* 252). Similarly, the Dogma 95 movement as a whole can be seen as a temporary cinematic condition in Europe whose symptoms started to fade away significantly right after their appearance, until the movement broke up in 2005. Von Trier's *Idioterne*

© The Author(s) 2016
A. Elbeshlawy, *Woman in Lars von Trier's Cinema, 1996–2014*,
DOI 10.1007/978-3-319-40639-8_3

is one of Dogma's earliest, purest examples, both abiding by and breaking the rules. It is Dogma's most symptomatic as well as most diagnostic film.

Although Freud clearly makes a distinction between mourning and melancholia by putting the former on the level of consciousness and referring to the latter as "an object-loss which is withdrawn from consciousness" (254), he seems nevertheless to point to what can be considered a certain pretense inherent in the melancholic position, no matter whether one thinks about it as conscious or unconscious; in other words, no matter whether one thinks that the subject does not know what he represses in accordance with psychoanalysis, or thinks the subject always knows what he represses in accordance with deconstructive thought. Freud says that those afflicted with melancholy "are not ashamed and do not hide themselves, since everything derogatory that they say about themselves is at bottom said about someone else" (257). Melancholy as an ailment or as a pathological identification with a lost object is something, but what the melancholic transfers to himself of what he sees as negative traits in the other is something else and may not be unconscious.

Even though the whole text of 'Mourning and Melancholia' is based on the idea of the loss of a beloved or of "some abstraction which has taken the place of one, such as one's country, liberty, an ideal, and so on" (252) as the primary cause of either mourning or melancholia, the single real-life example that Freud mentions in this canonical text seems to cast real doubt on the notion of melancholia as an unconscious position free from all pretense. Freud writes: "The woman who loudly pities her husband for being tied to such an incapable wife as herself is really accusing her *husband* of being incapable, in whatever sense she may mean this" (257).

Because this negative mirroring does not seem to be entirely free from a subjective conscious position, other thinkers clearly see that melancholy may not be easily identifiable as a result of an entirely unconscious identification. When it comes to abstractions like the motherland or national roots, Žižek, for example, argues that melancholy is "an exquisitely *postmodern* stance, the stance that allows us to survive in a global society by maintaining the appearance of fidelity to our lost 'roots'" (*Did Somebody Say* 142). Mourning, on the other hand, is arguably free from this kind of pretense since it takes place on the level of consciousness. It can, of course, be fake mourning, but it cannot be something the subject represses; in other words, it cannot be a lie that the subject pretends to be unaware of.

Idioterne, therefore, seems to be a work of mourning over Dogma 95 since it anticipates its own failure as a political project with the aim of freeing filmmaking from control and calculation. It is a film that perceives itself fundamentally as a lost cause, and only one thing in it stands in defense of that lost cause: Karen's final act of spassing—an act which, to put it in Freudian language, marks the end of *her* work of mourning over her lost child. Freud writes: "when the work of mourning is complete the ego becomes free and uninhibited again" (*On Metapsychology* 253). Karen's spassing, which is perceived by Linda Badley as a reversion "into the child she has lost" (66), is a final act of identification, a crescendo that precedes the freedom and un-inhibition of her ego as she leaves her family house. It is also an act that stands in defense of the lost cause that *Idioterne* presents, as well as the lost cause the film itself *is*.

Karen's act of spassing in the final scene of *Idioterne* is no less than what Žižek describes as a "Leap of Faith, faith in lost Causes, causes that, from within the space of skeptical wisdom, cannot but appear as crazy" (*In Defense* 2). The film itself seems to share the dialectical tension that Žižek observes as a common ground between Marxism and psychoanalysis; in both theories, "theory is not just the conceptual grounding of practice, it simultaneously accounts for why practice is ultimately doomed to failure" (3). Similarly, *Idioterne* not only illustrates and practices the Dogma rules, but simultaneously shows that the practice of Dogma has to fail. Žižek argues that while the phenomena of political totalitarianisms (like Stalinism and fascism) are obviously monstrous and historical failures, one should perceive that "*this is not the whole truth*: there was in each of them a redemptive moment which gets lost in the liberal-democratic rejection—and it is crucial to isolate this moment" (7). If one is allowed the nonchalance of equating *Idioterne*, as the ultimate Dogma film, with those historical political monstrosities, one can argue that it is obviously a failure in von Trier's history of filmmaking as the experiment was never repeated and was not exactly true to its rules in the first place; but this is not the whole truth: there was a redemptive moment—the moment in which woman is shown to be *the* political subject par excellence.

The corpus of critical literature that has been written about *Idioterne* asserts that the film sticks to as well as destroys the Dogma rules simultaneously. As Gaut suggests, the film's stylistics clearly show that von Trier's directing of it is itself an act of spassing (94–5), or an act of losing control with the aim of opposing the individual vision to making a film. Yet, he also perceives that "Dogma's implicit oppositions of individual vision to truth, and of art to truth, are simply too crude. And the manifesto's apparent equation of truth with an anti-bourgeois vision is also too simple, even by the light of Dogma's own film practice" (99). Through his arguably unrivaled attempt to lose control, von Trier ends up being too much in control of what he is doing, shooting several scenes himself with his handheld camcorder.

Gaut notes that "80 to 90 per cent of the footage was shot by von Trier himself [...] he even inserts himself into his film, conducting interviews with his cast from behind the camera" (97). Schepelern states that "even when von Trier relinquishes control, he is still totally in command. He still makes the rules" (*Purity and Provocation* 66). Badley argues that:

> Trier has it both ways: Dogme's documentary 'elements' may enhance the 'realism' of fictional films, but Trier's audible presence in *The Idiots* has the opposite effect of calling attention to the illusion in which the film appears factual and unscripted. Revealing that the film is his fiction or game (as Dogme is a Trier-authored game), his intrusions turn pseudodocumentary into metafiction. (63)

Thus, considering the fact that the film abides by as well as destroys the Dogma rules at the same time, it can be argued that its political significance rests solely on Karen's act in the final scene. In fact, there are writers who even question von Trier's "commitment to Dogme as anything more than just a temporary fling" since "his pre and post-*Idiots* films flagrantly violate all the Dogme rules, and he's never expressed any desire to make another Dogme film" (Stevenson 45). Stevenson thus argues that *Idioterne* "was not a 'necessary' film for [von Trier] to make, not a natural film for him to make or a film he *had* to make. It was a film he made as an act of solidarity, as a commitment to his Dogme brothers" (45–6).

In light of this, he sees *Idioterne* and the Dogme movement itself as "all about fiction filmmaking, not documentary" and thus seems to consider Mogens Rukov's theoretical debate about whether the film is "true to the moment or not", in which he criticizes von Trier's use of porno actors in the group sex scene as manipulative and dishonest (215). It is precisely this pointless debate of "being true to the moment" or not—which is, of course, something that cannot be determined in favor of one view or the other with regard to the making of *Idioterne*—that highlights the fact that it is Karen's act that is the only thing about the film that can be described as "true to the moment", that is to say, the only true ethical or political lesson.

Linda Badley writes that *Idioterne* is "about the carnivalesque performance of disability and excess as access to the sublime" (54). Many evidences, content-wise as well as form-wise, seem to connect the film's portrayal of the collective political act to the Bakhtinian idea of carnival and its subsequent uses in the field of cultural politics. It can be argued that the film's portrayal of the group of idiots' carnivalesque behavior as well as von Trier's carnivalesque stylistics take the carnivalesque itself, as Peter Stallybrass and Allon White theoretically do, beyond being the historic ritual of European culture as well as beyond Bakhtin's folkloric system, and approach it as "an instance of a wider phenomenon of transgression" (Stallybrass and White 26). *Idioterne* is clearly a film that attempts to be transgressive in every possible sense. Its content, its form, its relation to mainstream filmmaking, and even its relation to the other von Trier films – all seem to carry the notion of carnival, as Michael Gardiner sees it through "Bakhtin's own bacteriological metaphor", as "an antibody living within a pathological social body, always threatening to rupture it from within" (Gardiner 37).

Von Trier's "spassing" filmic form, which Gaut sees in his wobbly images, a camera not keeping up with the speaking characters, a crossed axis of action, intentionally bad editing and out of focus shots that are "clumsily framed and sometimes mismatched" (Gaut 94), produces no relief in the viewing experience, which, in order to keep up with the film's irretrievable heterogeneity, is forced to adopt thoroughly transmogrifying and restless perspectives. The film presents the carnivalesque as a ceaselessly dynamic, confrontational, dicey, unpredictable and self-mocking mode of existence. Stoffer's idea about capitalist societies in which "everybody is getting richer but nobody is feeling happier" suggests a stable apolitical condition which the group of spassers seeks to disrupt by creating their own carnivalesque "antibody" within society.

However, the group's carnivalesque spassing does not suggest any kind of social struggle other than releasing their "inner idiot". As Stoffer admits to Karen, being an idiot or pretending to be an idiot "is a luxury, but it is also a step forward. Idiots are the people of the future". His idea seems to carry a Bakhtinian open-ended futurity. The staged idiocy seems to psycho-dynamically oppose any rationalistic desire to draw conclusive outlines for systems of social organization, and thus questions the triumph of any ideology. It's a position which seems to correspond with Bakhtin's stress on the inconclusiveness of the carnival sense of the world which "knows no period", is "hostile to any sort of *conclusive conclusion*", and sees that "everything is still in the future and will always be in the future" (*Problems* 165–6).

The intentionally anarchic way in which von Trier made *Idioterne* is meant to suggest that the film does not contain any projected, ideologized or performance-bound plans, but on the contrary is *contained by* a carnivalesque sense that emanates from its director and everyone participating in it. In accordance with Bakhtin's carnival, it is a film that tries to show the viewer that it is "not contemplated and, strictly speaking, not even performed; its participants *live* in it, they live by its laws as long as those laws are in effect; that is, they live a *carnivalistic life*"(122).

Because of the film's staged inability to stabilize, its viewing experience is nothing but a series of the viewer's impulses to preserve some sort of subjective position as a viewer. As Badley suggests, *Idioterne* destabilizes "the audience's understanding of what is 'real,' it prevents passive looking; it requires that we engage with it in order to recover meaning" (63). One is even tempted to suggest that, excluding its final scene, the film does not seek to mean anything; it only tries to preserve itself as something to be looked at, its perpetual rebirth is its drive to be, which cannot take place except in a particular way of living the experience of no-longer-being-there. It seems to follow Ackbar Abbas's postmodern logic that "a film should not mean but be" (19). Its negation of itself as a meaningful text, however, is by no means absolute or self-destructive, and this is precisely where its transgressions acquire the sense of the carnivalesque. It seeks to problematize the idea of identity whether for its director, its actors, the characters in it, or the viewer who is bound to be caught in its presentation of identity as no more than a fake crown on the head of a fake king in carnivalistic festivities.

One scene—hardly talked about by the film's many commentators—seems to symbolize this fake crowning: the scene in which the group of spassers cheer Jeppe as Stoffer and Miguel carry him on their shoulders with a crown made of plants attached to his headband after his clumsy ski down the steep wooden slope. Bakhtin describes carnivalistic fake crowning as the main ritual that symbolizes the core idea of carnival: *the demolition of identity*. That demolition is played out by what Bakhtin calls the "crowning/decrowning dualistic ritual":

> The primary carnivalistic act is the *mock crowning and subsequent decrowning of the carnival king* [...] crowning already contains the idea of immanent decrowning [...] from the very beginning, a decrowning glimmers through the crowning [...] the ritual of decrowning completes, as it were, the coronation and is inseparable from it. (*Problems* 124–5).

Jeppe and his carriers soon fall to the ground, the others mockingly cover him with small tree branches and Miguel playfully strangles him. Many writers justifiably see the character of Stoffer as symbolic of the director.[1] However, Jeppe, in his crowning/decrowning scene, seems to much more powerfully symbolize the celebrated director who did his best to undermine his own position, lose control over his material and change the dominant rules of filmmaking, no matter how unsuccessful his attempts at this seem. In fact, the simultaneous crowning and decrowning of Jeppe seems to correspond with the simultaneous crowning and decrowning of the viewer's subjective position as viewer. Caroline Bainbridge writes that *Idioterne* invites the viewer to "empathize with Stoffer (Jens Albinus) and his friends as if their masquerade of mental retardation is real", thus the viewer "mirror[s] Karen's (Bodil Jorgensen) immediate response to the group" only to be shocked later on, like Karen, when "the 'spassers' reveal the joke once they have climbed inside the taxi" (91).

Murray Smith expresses the same idea: "A little way into the cab ride and, quite abruptly, the rug is pulled from under our feet [...] *we* have been taken for a ride by the film" (112). It is a moment in which we as viewers realize that "the joke is on us as much as Karen" (Badley 63). This "decrowning" of the spectator is what marks the film's political significance and its disruption of the pleasure of viewing. As Badley suggests, "the film's unresolved dialectic between performing and 'being', acting and therapy, documentary and fiction ultimately forces the audience, like the Idiots, to reflect on the ethical implications and responsibilities of spectatorship" (68). Bainbridge expresses the same view when she writes that the film "forces us to consider our relation to the image, to speak an ethical or political perspective on our cinematic experience" (97). As for von Trier, he seems to summarize it all in the brief taxi scene where the word "POLITIKEN" is written on the back of the headrest of Susanne's front seat and where Karen—and the viewer—realize that they have been duped by the spassers who start giggling mischievously.

But von Trier's film also shows, beyond any doubt, that a true political act is actually neither carnivalesque nor collective in nature; it does not have a loud voice. On the contrary, a true political act is particularly individual, distinctively silent, stemming from nothing but some pathological identification; a desire that goes "beyond the pleasure principle" (Freud, *On Metapsychology* 275–338). A true political act is not in any sense performative but rather suicidal in a very personal way. Therefore, Badley notes that:

> The group disperses and their experiment fails. Their failure seems to expose the limitations of performance which, like Carnival, is primarily an escape valve for elements and impulses repressed by the dominant culture. Exposing the film's (and Dogme's) *lack* of authenticity, *The Idiots* seems able only to force a negative version of the 'truth' from its characters—until the devastating final scene that allows the 'idiot technique' and the film to succeed. (66)

Spassing, premeditated and perceived by Stoffer's group as a collective action, seems to always already cancel out its political significance from the start as some sort of resistance to the capitalist apparatus or rejection of bourgeois culture. Performed collectively, it cannot escape the performance as its essential aspect; for the collective is inevitably performative even if it involves symbolic, even real, suicide. In war, for example, collective suicide may not necessarily mean courage. The idea of 'kill yourself and cause maximum damage', which Japanese pilots adopted and applied so casually in their historic attack on Pearl Harbor, loses the dimension of bravery significantly once it is perceived and framed as a collective action. It might indeed be far more difficult and socially suicidal for a soldier in war, among his fellow soldiers, not to go ahead with a suicidal attack than to do it with the others. In such circumstances, making the individual decision not to do it with the others would probably be far more courageous and consequential.

The failure of Stoffer's group of spassers to perform spassing in front of their family members or acquaintances does not only reveal the falsity of their individual commitment to their project (which can also be symbolic of the individual commitment of the Dogma directors to the Dogma rules), but the falsity of collective spassing as a political stance in the first place. The group sex scene is perhaps the film's best illustrative instance of false cultural politics. On the importance of the scene and the penetration shots involved, von Trier comments that "it is dangerous. There are people there pretending to be retarded while really fucking. This provides exactly the kind of transgression of limits that this scene and the film as a whole need" (quoted in M. Hjort, *Purity and Provocation* 150).

Yet, the scene is also designated as the one major point in *Idioterne* where von Trier's Dogma rules appear to be least "true to the moment" (Stevenson 215), as Stevenson observes based on Mogens Rukov's assertions. In accordance with these assertions, Hjort argues that the viewer "somehow senses the rote or mechanical nature of the copulation, which, although real, paradoxically comes to stand in stark contrast with the authenticity of a certain kind of pretence or performance" (*Purity and Provocation* 150). Over and above the fact that the stylistics at this point betray Dogma's claims of authenticity, however, is the fact that the transgressive content itself, contrary to what von Trier thinks, appears *less* transgressive precisely because of the collective performance involved in it. The actors had to stay on set and perform while actual penetration was taking place, which gives the scene a distinctive carnivalesque feel whose highest point is nothing but the brief shot of penetration itself (performed by porno stand-ins).

As in Bakhtin's idea of the carnivalistic "grotesque body", the emphasis at this point is on the "apertures or convexities, or on various ramifications and offshoots: the open mouth, the genital organs, the breasts, the phallus, the potbelly, the nose" (Bakhtin, *Rabelais* 26). While this appears transgressive, it is hard to see how the scene escapes being just another one of the hundreds of thousands of porn scenes targeting male eroticism in which women are always objectified as catalysts for male sexual arousal. Does Nana's enthusiastic readiness to have a "spasser fuck" offer anything to the viewer but a fantasy world in which all anxiety about rejection disappears? Is Susanne's initial rejection and later agreement to participate in group sex anything but part of that fantasy world? Pornography, as Susan Bordo argues, is not just about objectifying women, it is a "context in which the repressed penis [...] can come out of hiding and exhibit itself without shame or fear of rejection" (41).

The carnivalesque orgy in the film does not appear to address the viewer in any other way. On this reading, in accordance with Bordo's analysis of pornography, "it *is* the penis which has the stake here, *not* the phallus; for despite 'the pervasive presence of erections' in pornography, these are erections that are exposed precisely in order to be validated" (41). The brief shot of Stoffer's erect penis in the showers seems to belong to this category of erections. Murray Smith suggests that the film poses the question: "Does Stoffer want to know what ('liberated', 'innocent', 'uninhibited') retarded sex feels like—or does he just want to fuck his friends, literally and thus metaphorically?" (115). The question is indeed an important one; however, if it shifts its focus to the viewer, it gains even more importance: does the viewer experience the scene as "dangerous" and "transgressive", as the director claims it to be—or does *he* just use it to serve his onanistic fantasies like any other porn scene?

The aforesaid seems to leave us only with Karen. Badley argues that "it is impossible to pick out a protagonist until the last fifteen minutes, when

Karen (Bodil Jorgensen), a soft-spoken, middle-aged housewife, emerges to create the moment that is the film's raison d'être" (58). *Idioterne* is one of those films that have to be viewed twice in order to be fully grasped and enjoyed. On the first viewing, the viewer is not likely to give any weight to the opening scene in which Karen visits a playground then takes a ride in the streets of Copenhagen in a horse-drawn carriage. Plainly dressed, looking pale and sort of lackluster, her hands hanging in front of her chest as if she doesn't know exactly what she should do with them, her smile curious and bleak at the same time as she looks at her surroundings with childish interest, Karen seems to carry some sort of authentic idiocy in her before knowing anything about Stoffer and his group of spassers. This authentic idiocy, unlike Stoffer's staged one, has nothing to do with engagement with any ideological mandates based on a political position, a belief, or a revolutionary spirit.

Whereas Stoffer believes that "idiots are the people of the future", Karen's authentic idiocy does not look forward to any future. It is an idiocy marked by pathological identification with a lost object of love (her dead child), and therefore, it corresponds directly with the idea of standing firmly in defense of a lost cause such as Stoffer's idea of spassing or, indeed, Lars von Trier's idea of Dogma 95. Neither Stoffer nor von Trier were able to hold on to their projects for too long. The former comes to a conclusion that "it was all a lie"; the latter never repeated the experience of directing a film strictly according to the Dogma 95 rules. It is no coincidence that, in his films, von Trier projects the idea that, while both men and women fail just alike, "men don't go the whole nine yards. They abandon ship at the sixth or the eighth" (197). While men at some point realize that the "ideal doesn't hold", women "take the ideal all the way" (148–9).

Even though it is the presence of Karen in the opening and final scenes that gives any sense or value to what happens in the film in between those two scenes of "emotional directness" (Smith 111), her presence in most parts of the film is marginal. She neither participates in collective spassing nor likes "poking fun" at other people. More importantly, she stays away from the mass of naked bodies participating in the action in the group sex scene, which is considered to be von Trier's most inauthentic scene in the film. Compared to the other women in the film, Karen *appears* to be weaker in character, less confident and less confrontational. In fact, compared to the other von Trier heroines, Karen seems to be particularly unremarkable. She does not look lively and innocent like Bess of *Breaking the Waves* or strong and stoic like the talented blind Selma of *Dancer in the Dark*. She does not display the powerful figure of the femme fatale like Grace does in *Dogville*; she is neither a horrifying intellectual like "She" of *Antichrist* nor a melancholic beautiful bride like Justine of *Melancholia*.

Karen is just a regular housewife with no career, no intellect, no talent and no power. She does not even display the fetishistic or voyeuristic cinematic image of the female that Laura Mulvey saw back in the seventies as "styled" according to the "determining male gaze [which] projects its phantasy onto the female figure" (*Literary Theory* 589). Instead, Karen seems to be an exemplary case of the zero existence of a woman; a woman *tout court* whose only qualification is just being a woman. Precisely because she seems to be deprived of individual winning features that distinguish her, the listlessness of Karen stands for 'woman' as such. She is *the* particular non-subject which at once substantiates subjectivity. Her position in one way seems to be equivalent to the position of the "Muslim" with regard to humanity that Žižek designates as the "'inhuman' indifference" that is *"inherent to 'humanity'"*. In his analysis of the Muslim as a human category, Žižek argues that "as deprived of almost all specific positive human features, [the Muslims] stand for humanity 'as such'". Karen's relation to the other von Trier heroines seems to resemble the Muslim's relation to humanity in which he exists as a "man *tout court*, without any further qualifications" or as a "'living dead'" (*Did Somebody Say* 76–7).

Karen as an exemplary non-subject, however, is von Trier's almost perfect cinematic tool by which he puts in focus an act of authentic subjectivity. Badley argues that:

> Karen's initiation, education, and final performance thus provide the centerpiece in a kind of workshop in how to achieve a 'Real' act (as Slavoj Žižek calls it) of absolute freedom that produces a rift in the symbolic order, disrupting the phallic economy and the psychic apparatus of (masculine) reality. (69)

In Lacanian language, the Real act is called *"passage à l'acte"* (passage to the act). As Lacan puts it, "the moment of the *passage à l'acte* is the moment of the subject's greatest *embarrassment*, with the behavioral addition of *emotion* as a disorder of movement" (*Anxiety* 115). Furthermore, because she does not attract the viewer in any other way, Karen literally becomes the act. Even though the final scene in *Idioterne* is dominated by Karen, she nonetheless seems to virtually disappear as she starts to spass while eating cakes with her family under the expectant eyes of Susanne.

The viewer's attention at this point is drawn to the munched food which starts to spill out of her mouth, on her relatives' reaction to that, their surprised and embarrassed looks, the seemingly uncontrolled movement of her seemingly mentally retarded head and, of course, on the sudden violent reaction of her husband as he slaps her face. Karen's act, in accordance with Žižek's analysis of the Lacanian "*passage à l'acte*" (*Žižek Reader* 33), highlights Karen's subjectivity as well as obliterates that subjectivity at once. As Žižek puts it, the subject "'undergoes' the act ('passes through' it) rather than 'accomplishes' it: in it, the subject is annihilated and subsequently reborn (or not), i.e., the act involves a kind of temporary eclipse, *aphanisis*, of the subject" (*Enjoy Your Symptom* 44). It is an act of "symbolic suicide" (43) which "entails an exit from the symbolic network" (*Žižek Reader* 33) and is to be "opposed strictly to the suicide '*in* reality'" which "remains caught in the network of symbolic communication" (*Enjoy Your Symptom* 43–4).

The dread of woman as an enemy of religion, culture and civilization by virtue of her fundamental connection, in male imagination, to man's lower body stratum, is in its reality an apprehension towards the hollowness of the subject of religion, culture and civilization. The present/absent figure of Karen thus corresponds directly with "*woman*" who "does not exist" and who is "*not whole*" *(pas toute)* (Lacan, *On Feminine Sexuality* 7). Žižek explains how this symbolic non-existence in itself is the very negativity on account of which woman is the subject par excellence (*Žižek Reader* 129–35). While she 'passes to the act', man as a barred subject only acts out, performs. "The act as real is 'feminine', in contrast to the 'masculine' performative, i.e., the great founding gesture of a new order" (*Enjoy Your Symptom* 46).

While Karen's act is feminine in this particular sense of symbolic suicide that seeks no less than a radical change of the world, it can be argued that the scene which shows Stoffer running naked down the street in pursuit of the car of the man from the council and shouting "Søllerød Fascists!" stages a "'masculine' performative". It is a scene which presents Stoffer's ultimate act of spassing as 'acting-out' or lashing out at capitalist society in mostly a symbolic way (not unlike the Marxist academic, for example, who makes his living out of thrashing capitalism inside the classroom—a vociferous Marxism devoid of any Marxist praxis—which is in a way like 'spassing out' from time to time while being nothing but one of the functionaries of the capitalist system).

In other words, it is a political act which remains within the pleasure principle as it can be argued that, secretly, it masochistically enjoys being the victim of the social big Other. It is in this sense that woman's status is fundamentally interconnected with subjectivity in Lacanian theory. If the subject is a barred subject or a subject that is essentially split by the violent admission into the symbolic order and therefore never consistent with its own signification, then it can be argued that woman is the subject par excellence due to her inadmissibility into that sphere. As Žižek puts it, "it is precisely woman that 'exists', that persists as a residue of enjoyment beyond meaning" (*Žižek Reader* 31). If woman's existence is this intrinsically problematic non-being, man's existence on the other hand, as Lacan puts it, is a "being of non-being [...] conjugated with the double aporia of a veritable subsistence that is abolished by his knowledge" (*Écrit: The First Complete Edition* 679).

Karen's final act of spassing, where she 'acts' being an idiot yet lives her most authentic moment as a political subject, can be read as a moment of total identification with her lost object of love: the dead child. Previously, she was particularly disgusted and disgruntled over expensive food (caviar) dripping out of the laughing mouths of the group of spassers, or she was reproachful like a mother teaching her child not to waste food or let it drop out of one's mouth. In her spassing act at the end, she manages to direct her disgust at her uptight family as well as show them in a way that may be difficult for catalogue conservatives like them to understand that she is the only true mourner, even though she did not attend her child's funeral. She is the only one who is ready to identify with the child in terms of producing what in Lacanian language is called "an untimely release"[2] and take the consequences bravely. Even her disappearance from the funeral can now be seen in a different light as part of this mournful identification within a child's game; as if saying to her child 'you abandon me, I abandon you'.

Commenting on the final scene of *Idioterne*, Badley writes: "When Karen exits, the spectator is left with her, in a blank space outside boundaries hitherto established, with no safe entry back in" (68). Real politics puts the subject face to face with the real, and as the viewer assesses the magnitude of Karen's act of social suicide, he is bound to feel the full weight of assuming subjectivity through undergoing a transmogrifying act that reveals the abyss that lies beneath social identity and the facade that the subject itself is. *This* is the ultimate "decrowning" of the viewer.

NOTES

1. Linda Badley and Berys Gaut among them.
2. Lacan talks about the infant's "untimely release of his intestinal content" as an occasion of a "*passage à l'acte*" in his analysis of the function of oblativity, which, I think, is similar to the untimely and inappropriate release of munched food from the mouth in the presence of others in the case of Karen. *Anxiety*, ed. Jacques-Alain Miller, A. Rae Price (Cambridge: Polity Press, 2014), p. 261.

BIBLIOGRAPHY

Abbas, Ackbar. *Hong Kong: Culture and the Politics of Disappearance*. Minneapolis and London: University of Minnesota Press, 1997.
Badley, Linda. *Lars von Trier*. Urbana, Chicago, Springfield: University of Illinois Press, 2010.
Bainbridge, Caroline. *The Cinema of Lars von Trier: Authenticity and Artifice*. London and New York: Wallflower Press, 2007.
Bakhtin, Mikhail M. *Problems of Dostoevsky's Poetics*. Edited and translated by Caryl Emerson. Minneapolis: University of Minnesota Press, 1984.
Bakhtin, Mikhail M. *Rabelais and His World*. Translated by Helene Iswolsky. Bloomington: Indiana University Press, 1984.
Bordo, Susan. 'Reading the Male Body'. *Building Bodies*. Edited by Pamela L. Moore. New Brunswick, NJ: Rutgers University Press, 1997.
Freud, Sigmund. *On Metapsychology: The Theory of Psychoanalysis*. Edited by Angela Richards and translated from the German under the general editorship of James Strachey. Penguin Books, 1991.
Gardiner, Michael. 'Bakhtin's Carnival: Utopia as Critique'. *Critical Studies. Vol. 3 No. 2—Vol. 4 No. 1/2*. Edited by Myriam Diaz-Diocaretz. Amsterdam and Atlanta, GA: Rodopi, 1993.
Gaut, Berys. 'Naked Film: Dogma and its Limits'. *Purity and Provocation: Dogma 95*. Edited by Mette Hjort and Scott Mackenzie. London: British Film Institute, 2003.
Hjort, Mette. 'The Globalisation of Dogma: The Dynamics of Metaculture and Counter-Publicity'. *Purity and Provocation: Dogma 95*. Edited by Mette Hjort and Scott Mackenzie. London: British Film Institute, 2003.
Lacan, Jacques. *On Feminine Sexuality, The Limits of Love and Knowledge: Encore, 1972–1973*. Translated and with notes by Bruce Fink. New York and London: W.W. Norton and Company, 1998.
Lacan, Jacques. *Écrit: The First Complete Edition in English*. Translated by Bruce Fink. New York and London: W.W. Norton and Company, 2006.
Lacan, Jacques. *Anxiety*. Edited by Jacques-Alain Miller and translated by A. Rae Price. Cambridge: Polity Press, 2014.

Mulvey, Laura. 'Visual Pleasure and Narrative Cinema'. *Literary Theory: An Anthology*. Edited by Julie Rivkin and Michael Ryan. Massachusetts and Oxford: Blackwell Publishers, 2001.
Schepelern, Peter. '"Kill Your Darlings": Lars von Trier and the Origin of Dogma 95'. *Purity and Provocation: Dogma 95*. Edited by Mette Hjort and Scott Mackenzie. London: British Film Institute, 2003.
Smith, Murray. 'Lars von Trier: Sentimental Surrealist'. *Purity and Provocation: Dogma 95*. Edited by Mette Hjort and Scott Mackenzie. London: British Film Institute, 2003.
Stallybrass, Peter, and Allon White. *The Politics and Poetics of Transgression*. Ithaca, NY: Cornell University Press, 1986.
Stevenson, Jack. *Dogme Uncut: Lars von Trier, Thomas Vinterberg, and the Gang That Took on Hollywood*. California: Santa Monica Press, 2003.
Trier, Lars von. '9 A.M., Thursday, September 7, 2000: Interview by Kjeld Koplev'. *Lars von Trier: Interviews*. Edited by Jan Lumholdt. Jackson, Mississippi: University Press of Mississippi, 2003.
Žižek, Slavoj. *The Žižek Reader*. Edited by Elizabeth Wright and Edmond Wright. Oxford and Malden, MA: Blackwell Publishing, 1999.
Žižek, Slavoj. *Enjoy Your Symptom! Jacques Lacan in Hollywood and Out*. New York and London: Routledge, 2001.
Žižek, Slavoj. *Did Somebody Say Totalitarianism? Five Interventions in the (Mis)use of a Notion*. London and New York: Verso, 2002.
Žižek, Slavoj. *In Defense of Lost Causes*. London and New York: Verso, 2009.

Filmography

Antichrist. Directed and written by Lars von Trier. Irvington, NY: Criterion Collection, 2010.
Breaking the Waves. Directed and written by Lars von Trier. Paris: Pathé, 2003.
Dancer in the Dark. Directed and written by Lars von Trier. Montréal, Québec: Alliance Atlantis, 2007.
Dogma 2: Idioterne (*Dogma 2: The Idiots*). Directed and written by Lars von Trier. Toronto: Alliance Atlantis, 2004.
Dogville. Directed and written by Lars von Trier. Hong Kong: Edko Films Ltd., 2005.
Melancholia. Directed and written by Lars von Trier. Hong Kong: Edko Films Ltd., 2011.

CHAPTER 4

Dancer in the Dark: Deploying the Siren, Impairing the Sight

In her most influential essay, 'Visual Pleasure and Narrative Cinema', Laura Mulvey accurately shows how cinema reflects two different tactics by which male imagination avoids the castration anxiety represented by the female. Although she does not refer to Lacan's *On Feminine Sexuality* directly, in which he says that woman "is doubled, that she is not-whole, since she can also have a relation with Φ" (81),[1] Mulvey clearly based her critique of narrative cinema on the Lacanian idea of woman as outside the system of symbolization and as the threat of that system's subversion. Woman is not threatened by castration since she is castrated by nature, yet this lack of the phallus transforms *her* into a phallus; that is to say into man's real of desire, but also—more importantly to Mulvey—into man's very sign of castration.

Thus, in the realm of the cinematic, Mulvey argues that "the male unconscious has two avenues of escape from this castration anxiety". One of the avenues is voyeurism, which Mulvey describes as a "preoccupation with the re-enactment of the original trauma (investigating the woman, demystifying her mystery) counterbalanced by the devaluation punishment or saving of the guilty object". The other avenue is "fetishistic scopophilia", which is defined by Mulvey as a "complete disavowal of castration by the substitution of a fetish object or turning the represented figure itself into a fetish so that it becomes reassuring rather than dangerous" (*Literary Theory* 591).

One of the most important aspects that make Lars von Trier's *Dancer in the Dark* an anti-mainstream film is that it seems to destroy both avenues in the most radical sense of deploying the gaze precisely where the viewer expects to see a woman. Selma is not just a blind sacrificial mother who is suffering passively and rejecting one man's love unrealistically. She is also that impossible female character who is, in many ways, *un-cinematic*. *Dancer in the Dark* can be thought of as von Trier's extreme example of deploying the Lacanian "objet a *in the field of the visible*" (Lacan, *Four Fundamental Concepts* 105), as the blind heroine herself is the occasional deployment of the gaze. Selma, however, destabilizes the viewer's position not only by her blind eyes that are supposed to look and do not see, yet seem to see beyond simple looking, but also by her droning voice, which literally makes von Trier's film hardly anything but a celebration of the idea of the survival of the song—that most primitive art—even in the midst of the most philosophically oriented, postmodern, politicized cinema of technical prowess mixed with deliberate stylistic playfulness.

Dancer in the Dark is set in a small town in Washington State. Selma, a partially blind Czech migrant who works in a stainless-steel factory, lives with her ten-year-old son in a backyard trailer rented to her by a local policeman and his wife. Selma's rapidly fading eyesight is due to a hereditary illness that will also affect her son unless she can save enough money to pay for an operation. So, she works extra time in the factory and pins hairpins to cardboard at home, saving every penny she earns for her son's operation, while pretending all the time in front of everyone that she can see. Apart from work, she enjoys rehearsing the role of Maria in an amateur theatrical production of *The Sound of Music*. What she enjoys most, however, is indulging every now and then in her own particular fantasy in which she imagines singing and dancing to her heart's content as the cornerstone performer in musical numbers created in her imagination out of the grim surroundings of her daily life.

As the film's plot progresses, Selma's songs erupt out of the monotonous sound of machinery in the factory, engines of a passing train, spinning of a phonograph disc, sketching pencils clattering on sketching boards, a distant church choir finding its way to her ears through a ventilation shaft, marching steps of prison guards, and her own heartbeats. As she goes almost completely blind, she loses both her job and her Maria role. Her landlord steals her savings after being bankrupted. Attempting to regain her money from him, Selma accidentally shoots him with his own gun. He refuses to let go of the money purse and asks her to kill him. After shooting him several times, he still breathes and she still can't pull the purse out of his hands, so she picks up his metal safe deposit box and hits his head repeatedly with it before regaining her money.

Selma runs away. Jeff, a man who loves her unrequitedly, meets her and drives her to the hospital for the blind where she pays for her son's operation with all the money she has. Eventually, she is arrested and tried. She does not defend herself much in court and does not say that she is blind, believing that this might ruin what she did in order to secure the operation to save her son's eyesight. She is sentenced to death by hanging. She sings in her prison cell and imagines singing in another musical during the march to the gallows. With the hanging rope around her neck, she sings her "next to last song" (her last in the film) before she gets abruptly silenced by long-drop hanging.

In spite of the fact that among *Dancer in the Dark*'s viewers and commentators there are true lovers of Selma as well as dedicated haters, both parties seem to agree that Björk created an onscreen woman character quite alien to the category of the cinematic. Even though the film, as Linda Badley suggests, "deploys the most hackneyed of 'woman's picture' tropes, the mother consumed by sacrificial maternal zeal [...] embellished with the maudlin theme of the woman going blind" (88), this overdone picture is seriously destabilized by what Kent Williams describes as Björk's "emoting for the camera" in a performance which "hasn't been thought out, either by her or by her director" (*Isthmus*). As a character, Selma (or Björk) is this "ugly duckling with the weird voice" (Grodal 163) who is, quite understandably, "indigestible as a character" (Rosenbaum) with a "stupid grin with which she greets virtually every misfortune"—a kind of a "dumb animal" (Rosenbaum). But, perhaps this indigestibility of the character of Selma, notably frowned upon by mainly male viewers, has to do with her being "stubbornly self-sufficient, insisting she has no use for a man" (Badley 87).

Perhaps Selma is von Trier's response to "cultural assumptions and dominant perceptions of what is to be understood as femininity" (Bainbridge 138). Indeed, she has no use for a man, but, much more importantly, she has no use for a male viewer in the Mulvey sense. When watching *Dancer in the Dark*, it doesn't take long before even the viewer with the least self-awareness as a viewer discovers that s(he) is not supposed to look at a blind woman more than s(he) is supposed to look at the ways s(he) is made to *literally* look at his/her own blindness. The claustrophobic close-ups and the danger of being blind and too close to machines, sharp metal, a speeding truck or a moving train reflect not only the uneasiness the viewer may feel through identification with Selma, but also the uneasiness of being destabilized as a voyeuristic or fetishistic viewer.

Criticizing the film's almost unmusical musical numbers and von Trier's use of multiple cameras in them, as opposed to his usual Dogma-style handheld shaky camera in the non-musical parts of the film, D'Angelo asserts that "nothing is gained by seeing Selma board the train from five different angles in rapid succession; it's a technique that calls attention to itself" (*Scenic Routes*). Indeed it is. In fact, this ungainly viewing experience applies to the whole film. If there is neither acting nor filmmaking in the usual sense, there is supposed to be no watching/seeing in the usual sense. And, unlike previous and subsequent films by von Trier, the idea is not only a Brechtian alienatory way of creating art that addresses the viewer's intellect rather than his emotions – that is, maximizing the distance between the viewer and the work, or, in other words, minimizing the distance between those who consciously make the work of art and those who consciously consume it.

The idea of *Dancer in the Dark* from this work's perspective is to make a film that feels like a near-perfect conspiracy against the act of film-watching itself. The viewer is not supposed to watch *Dancer in the Dark* in the first place; s(he) is rather supposed to resist the impulse to watch and, like Björk's "emoting for the camera" (Williams)—and oddly enough, contrary to Brechtian non-identification with the work of art—emote according to what s(he) sees on the screen, and that is to freely and unabashedly weep—there is virtually nothing to laugh at or be amused by in the film. To enjoy *Dancer in the Dark* is to know how not to watch it as a cinematic work but to *feel it as work* only or as a process that does not look forward to an end, or as something that never dies except by the very death of the subject; in other words, as something resembling the subject's libido in its insistent survival as a vital substance, as a force of nature that, *essentially*, has neither eyes to see nor image to be seen.

Selma is the very embodiment of that life-substance; a blind being displaying nothing of the cinematic feminine "*to-be-looked-at-ness*" (Mulvey, *Literary Theory* 589), nothing for either scopophilic or voyeuristic fantasy. It is at this level of viewing awareness—if we can still describe this kind of experience as one of viewing—that eroticism strongly manifests itself in a seemingly un-erotic film. In addition to that, the unworldly oversentimentality of the story mixed with Björk's acutely non-cinematic acting makes it hard to identify with Selma simply as a stoic blind mother. Rosenbaum does have a point. The only thing that remains is her voice and her survival as pure song up to the last moment of her life. It is difficult to see Selma or to identify with her character because she is *not* a woman; she is pure and primitive song always going against all the odds and, like the libido itself, surviving beyond man's enlightenment-driven comprehension.

This is why those who expect to watch *Dancer in the Dark* as an interpretable film cannot possibly enjoy it. It is not for nothing that Björk called von Trier "an emotional pornographer" (Graham) or that von Trier described their working relationship as "almost like a sexual thing" (Roman 95). These statements seem incompatible with a film that is virtually devoid of any sexual scenes, and the relationship between von Trier and Björk during the making of it was reportedly devoid of any real intimacy (in fact it was quite adversarial). To use one of Susan Sontag's most perceptive thoughts about creating and consuming art "against interpretation", *Dancer in the Dark* falls under the category of works of art that, "in place of a hermeneutics", call for an "erotics of art" (14). It does not offer the viewer the representation of anything erotic but rather directly engages him/her in the erotics of representation itself. D.H. Lawrence once wrote about what he called "blood knowledge" or the "vast vital flux of knowing that goes on in the dark, antecedent to the mind", which Adam and Eve, according to Lawrence, must have experienced before the introduction of the "beastly apple" that started the "other sort of knowledge". Lawrence writes:

> When Adam went and took Eve, *after* the apple, he didn't do any more than he had done many a time before, in act. But in consciousness he did something very different. So did Eve. Each of them kept an eye on what they were doing, they watched what was happening to them. They wanted to KNOW. And that was the birth of sin. Not *doing* it, but KNOWING about it. Before the apple, they had shut their eyes and their minds had gone dark. Now, they peeped and pried and imagined [...] and they felt uncomfortable after. They felt self-conscious [...] the sin was self-watching, self-consciousness. (90-1)

To Lawrence, thus, the devil lies in representation, in presenting something for the eyes to watch. Perhaps this is why he does not mention anything about 'tasting' the apple. The danger of that apple, or the sin related to it, like the sin related to the sexual organs, is that it was primarily something to watch. "Blood knowledge" cannot be achieved except by the 'shutting of the eyes'. Blindness is its essential precondition. "Mind-knowledge", on the other hand, depends on watching. The way *Dancer in the Dark* is made seems to suggest that the act of representation is a sin, and therefore eliminates presenting the heroine for the voyeuristic or fetishistic gaze of the viewer, substituting for it an alternative mode of eroticizing the work and engaging the viewer in it on its own terms or idea of what eroticism is.

In this sense, *Dancer in the Dark* can perhaps be described as von Trier's most ambitious work. It does not only confuse the viewer by mixing reality and fantasy like some of the earlier von Trier films (*Idioterne*, *Element of Crime* and *Epidemic* are examples). In fact, it draws clear stylistic lines between reality and fantasy, alternating between "two extreme states—that of the pure fantasy of the musical numbers and the documentary realism of the narrative" (Graham). Nor does it only destabilize the subjectivity of the viewer (*Antichrist* and *Melancholia* are manifest examples). It calls for a viewer who can themselves be blind, like Selma; a viewer who, instead of watching the heroine, can literally engage with her in an erotic relation that does not depend on seeing the female form but on being infatuated by the category of the feminine as such, defined as "blood knowledge", which precedes any representation for the eyes.

The song, or Selma as pure song, is nothing but femininity in its most primitive form of the mythical singing sirens in Homer's *Odyssey*, the temptresses who represent irresistible pleasure by their sheer singing voices. It can be argued that Hollywood's famous musicals come precisely from what Horkheimer and Adorno call the "happily hapless meeting of Odysseus with the Sirens" after which "all songs have ailed; the whole of Western music suffers from the absurdity of song in civilization" (47). It is this incompatibility between song and civilization—an ailment that the American musical in particular seems always to try to cure or eliminate with bright lights, lavish costumes, calculated dancing movements and heavily orchestrated songs—that *Dancer in the Dark* stresses by creating a musical that does not bear any resemblance to similar cinematic productions from the past. "No Hollywood musical has ever looked anything even remotely like this" (D'Angelo), even though von Trier himself claims that he acts "from admiration for the way musicals are" (Graham)—a claim many people find it hard to believe since von Trier's musical numbers in the film seem to draw attention only to his unusual technique of making a musical and not really to the musical itself at all.

Yet, there is something crudely natural in all of Selma's songs that does not sit well with the highly mechanized and noisily artificial music created by different machines, and that is her singular voice, which seems somehow dissociated from the music. Unlike Hollywood musicals in which singing voices are always in calculated unity with the music as well as the visual, Selma's singing voice seems to emanate out of defiance to the artificiality of the musical despite the character's staged love for musicals. Torben Grodal argues that Björk's "strongly subjective and expressive voice is the absolute opposite of the integration of the individual in a social system of fine singing in the classical musical" (162). If 'Cvalda' (the song Selma sings in the factory to the industrious sound of machinery) is a celebration of the mechanical or a celebration of labor, the film as a whole can be seen as a celebration of the survival of the mythical power of the song as the "motive force of all art-music" (Horkheimer and Adorno 47).

In terms of the musical and its cinematic history, Selma/Björk is an anti-Odysseus figure; she is a siren droning away unabashedly against all we think constitutes the beauty of musicals, completely unconcerned about the havoc she creates in the genre. This is one thing Lars von Trier couldn't, and wouldn't want to, completely control. Commenting on the way musicals are made in *Dancer in the Dark*'s press kit, von Trier states that he is "not trying to subvert or destroy anything" (quoted in R. Graham). Understandably, many readers of the film do not believe in the sincerity of this statement—especially when the stylistics seem to promote the very style of making the musical numbers rather than their content—yet it does seem that the numbers of *Dancer in the Dark* contain an uncontrollable element, which is Björk herself and her gripping natural voice.

The artificial mastery cinematic productions always maintained over musicals and the tone of singing voices in them, including von Trier's own mastery over his material, seems to resemble the image Horkheimer and Adorno draw of human civilization (Odysseus's ship) striding forward on the way of enlightenment, detaching itself from "myth" or the sirens and their infatuating song.[2] Aware that it is "impossible to hear the Sirens and not succumb to them", Odysseus, who is "technically enlightened", "acknowledges the archaic supremacy of the song" by having himself "bound to the mast" of the ship under his command. "The bound listener is drawn to the Sirens like any other. But he has taken the precaution not to succumb to them even while he succumbs" (Horkheimer and Adorno 46).

Von Trier, a cinematic Odysseus in his own way, senses the supremacy of Selma as pure song, as mythical siren, devoid of, as well as above, all the powerful elements of audiovisual control that surround her and accompany her voice. It is no coincidence that Björk's voice attains its deepest impact upon the viewer in two particular scenes where she sings with no accompanying music. At her lowest moment, when she cannot sing in her solitary cell because she hears no music, distant church hymns come to her ears through the ventilation shaft in the wall, urging her to sing again, at first reluctantly, then buoyantly and impulsively as usual. The mystical invoking the mythical. In the hanging scene, her last "next to last song" comes entirely music-less out of nothing but her own body, emanating from her heartbeats. The siren at her peak, the song at its most powerful sway over its listeners, the listeners—in the film and out—in complete submission to the mythical "motive force" (47) that predates all music.

Earlier in the film, Selma says she likes to leave the theatre right after the next to last song in a musical so that she avoids having to see the end of it all. She does avoid an end to the song in a way because she dies singing. "When the song and her life are truncated, the film simultaneously contradicts and supports her assertion. It is indeed her last song but she has escaped before its end" (Badley 98). The blind mother sacrifices her life to save her son's eyesight, but Selma as pure song survives precisely as that to the very last moment of her life. *Dancer in the Dark* may be "an ugly and cold parody or caricature of the classical American musicals" (Grodal 160), as some American critics see it, or it can be simply an "anti-American narrative" (Graham) offering a "horrific view of the American justice system" (Rosenbaum). Its characters and scenes may be "drawn with a cartoon-like simple salience, for instance in the sense that Selma is the blind girl-tragedy to outperform the most tear-jerking, blind girl-films ever made, as well as the most unselfish mother ever to breathe" (Grodal 160).

It may be a highly politicized work of art; Angelos Koutsourakis, for example, sees it as "a musical that narrates a story and at the same time criticizes the very generic elements that it manipulates. Selma draws our attention to this when she says that she likes musicals because "in a musical nothing dreadful ever happens" (*Politics as Form* 35). Koutsourakis argues that the film's form and content "thematize cinema as a commodity, only to bring this principle under discussion and to question the social reality that produces escapist forms of entertainment". So, "Selma insists that her son has his eyesight healed" so that he will be able to "'see' and not be fooled like her, whose passion for musicals made her imagine the United States like a depoliticized utopia" (36). To Koutsourakis, the film's stylistics carry its political message; in the hanging scene, "the camera's frantic movement combines distanced coldness with emotional excess", provoking the viewer's sense that "Selma's death is not tragic" and that it is "meant to provoke anger rather than pity and fear, forcing the audience to think beyond the limits of tragic unavoidability, implying that different social conditions could have prevented this violent finale" (40).

Yet, the film's strongest political message from the present work's point of view seems to be the survival of the song to the very moment of death as a triumph of the mythical crude droning of the sirens over the calculated cinematic musical, whether it comes from Hollywood or out of Lars von Trier's eccentricities. Selma is not only an anti-American figure or an anti-Hollywood figure. She is an anti-cinematic figure; the very representation of the "absurdity of song in civilization" (Horkheimer and Adorno 47). The survival of her as pure song to the moment of death is nothing short of the survival of the libido itself to the moment of death. As song, she is indestructible.

For her, the urgency to sing resembles the urgency by which Sade writes his sexual stories in Philip Kaufman's *Quills* in whatever way possible. Being stripped gradually of anything that might enable him to communicate his stories to others, he still communicates them somehow to the moment of his own death. When his quills and ink are confiscated, he writes with wine or with his own blood on bed sheets and clothes. Deprived of all kinds of sheets and clothes, he relates a new story mouth to ear through several fellow patients in the asylum to be dictated to his laundress. When his tongue is cut out, he decorates his dungeon with another story using his own feces as ink. It is precisely this libido-like indestructability of the desire to sing and the desire to write that constitutes the major political element in von Trier's *Dancer in the Dark* and Kaufman's *Quills*.

Dancer in the Dark, as Badley and Grodal note, does deploy one of the most oversentimental as well as overrepresented blind woman images in the history of cinema, but it does so only to invoke a blind *viewer* who neither watches the film in the Mulvey sense nor even thinks about it in a Brechtian sense, but "feels" it in the way Lévinas explicates Bergsonian intuition as a "feeling without support in representation", which is "no longer interpreted as a reverberation of a knowing about an affectivity enclosed in itself, but as contact with being, more direct than sensation". There is no doubt that in this kind of feeling, in this realm which escapes representation, "what passed for the blindest and deafest in us goes the *farthest*" (*Entre Nous* 37).

Thus, the blind siren upon which *Dancer in the Dark* stakes everything seems to call for a viewer who *senses* her in the way Lévinas defines sensing as "neither a lame *thinking* nor a shortcut" but as a "way of subjecting oneself to a force" (41). Selma, from this work's point of view, addresses neither the thinking Brechtian viewer seeking to dissect art without identification with it nor the common viewer who takes the "shortcut" of dealing with his castration anxiety through either voyeurism or fetishism, but a viewer who simply enjoys regressing to what Lawrence calls "blood knowledge" (90–1), which is the same thing Horkheimer and Adorno call "myth", or that which enlightened man has to shun and run away from.

The singing siren belongs to a lost or forgotten feminine universe or a realm that woman dominates and which precedes the masculine one. Glimpses of that mythical—and mystical—feminine realm do occur occasionally, even in the midst of literary productions that are soggy with masculine stresses. Lizzy Welby, for example, finds a rare presence of a "'feminine' form" in Rudyard Kipling's verse, which is known primarily for its celebration of masculine bravado and British imperial view of the world. She notices that *The Deep-Sea Cables* is "imbued with a tenderness for and fear of a 'lost' maternal realm", it "sings of a time before a masculine order and calls for an embracing of the feminine within" (17). Kipling's poem speaks of the depths of the sea as the "womb of the world" where "words, and the words of men, flicker and flutter and beat" wakening "timeless things" and killing "father Time". This is also a world of *darkness*, and *blindness*, where "blind white sea-snakes are" (94).

Dancer in the Dark thus calls for a viewer who neither looks for the political message behind what he sees nor takes the unconscious "shortcut" of scopophilic or voyeuristic fantasy, but submits to the mythical force of the singing siren in an experience that does not only deform the musical, as many critics suggest, but quite effectively deforms the cinematic visual as well. For this kind of engagement with the film would be at the heart of what Derrida calls the "abocular hypothesis" or the "epoch of sight" (*Memoirs* 127) in which tears define the function of the eyes away from sight. Tears veil or blind sight as well as fragment or deform what is seen, but at the same time they mark a moment of *seeing* beyond what is presented to vision, a moment of incommensurable "blood knowledge" (Lawrence 90-1) in which sight does not matter and is not the primary function of the eyes. Derrida writes:

> If tears *come to the eyes*, if they *well up in them*, and if they can also veil sight, perhaps they reveal […] an essence of the eye. […] Deep down, deep down inside, the eye would be destined not to see but to weep […] to have imploration rather than vision in sight, to address prayer, love, joy, or sadness rather than a look or gaze. (*Memoirs* 126)

In opposition to viewers who tend to detest the film for what they see as its excessive and unwarranted sentimentality, as well as viewers who admire it just for that, a viewer who really enjoys *Dancer in the Dark* is not one who weeps out of sympathy with the sacrificial blind mother. This is precisely where von Trier's film radically differs from films that deploy the sentimental presentation of the "most hackneyed of 'woman's picture' tropes" (Badley 88) or the "tear-jerking, blind girl-films" (Grodal 160). A viewer who truly enjoys this film is one who weeps out of identification with that which feels uncanny, alien or mythical, within the context of cinematic viewing as an integral part of a highly refined and technologized human civilization, yet at the same time feels inexplicably close to and part of a human nature embedded in a pre-subjective world—a world in which woman rules and sirens drone with no musical instruments, while man, in the wider sense of humanity, unlike the cunning and enlightened Odysseus, *unequivocally* "throw(s) himself into the arms of the seductresses" (Horkheimer and Adorno 46).

Blinding the viewer of *Dancer in the Dark*, then, does not only involve neutralizing the voyeuristic or fetishistic gaze as explained above but, much more importantly, making the viewer see more through intuitive insight than what can be seen through sight; in other words, to reveal the fact of blindness itself as a condition of civilized man or to make the viewer come face to face with his/her own blindness. It is precisely this encounter with the *self*—and not the encounter with the blind woman on the screen—that brings tears to the viewer's eyes; tears that *cloud as well as sharpen vision at once*. This kind of blindness, to put it in a Derridean way, "opens the eye"; it is a "gaze veiled by tears" or a "revelatory or apocalyptic blindness" that "reveals the very truth of the eyes". This tearful gaze "neither sees nor does not see" because it is "indifferent to its blurred vision". Its main concern is neither to look at the external physical sight distorted by tears nor to bother about sight itself as the perceived function of the eyes, but to wonder and to strive, however unsuccessfully, to "know from where these tears stream down and from whose eyes they come to well up" (Derrida, *Memoirs* 127).

In the context of viewing *Dancer in the Dark*, the civilized subject weeps neither in response to Selma's brutal hanging, made almost unbearable by close-ups and panicky camera movement creating an "uncomfortable intimacy" (Graham)—which von Trier characteristically pushes to unbelievably sentimental limits—nor in response to Selma allowing her "psychological pain hitherto expressed in musical sequences carried out in her imagination to spill over into reality" (Bainbridge 112), but in response to her siren-like voice singing with no music; in other words, not in response to the suffering of the other, but in response to *looking upon the remove at which he is made to look upon his own pre-subjective nature, which he has radically alienated from his civilized self.*

Being at play with blindness in this particular way, the accusation of misogyny itself that is often directed at the director of *Dancer in the Dark* gains a whole new paradoxical dimension. The blind, according to Derrida, are "subject to being mistaken" as well as "*the subject of mistake*" (*Memoirs* 94) and, "subject to being *mistaken*", they are also the "*subject of punishment*" (102). Selma is indeed all of that within the context of the film, as well as to the disappointed habitual Mulvey viewer. Within the film, she is mistaken for a criminal and is vilified by the prosecutor for being a thieving, murderous and typically anti-American migrant; a "romantic, certainly communistic woman who worships Fred Astaire but not his country". To the conventional cinema consumer, she is initially mistaken for being a woman, an object of the gaze, a figure that should be "simultaneously looked at and displayed", with an appearance "coded for strong visual and erotic impact" (Mulvey, *Literary Theory* 589).

Von Trier makes sure she gets punished for both; for being a murderer according to the American justice system, as well as for being a non-woman to the viewer. She must be tortured and killed not only for being a murderer but also for not satisfying the male gaze, for not giving it what it wants. Needless to say, trying to pinpoint whether this belongs to the director's commonly perceived misogynistic tendencies or to his equally argued feminist crux is futile. Equally futile is trying to find out whether *Dancer in the Dark* is a European director's celebration of the American musical or a display of what a European director sees as American phoniness contextualized in an idea of America as a "land of Technicolor dreams and almost no social security" (Badley 93).

Commenting on David Kleinberg-Levin's analysis of the human capacity for weeping and its relation to vision, in which he describes weeping as "speech of our nature" (Kleinberg-Levin 397–465), Chloé Taylor writes that "the comparison of tears to speech" enables us to

> Think of the eyes (and eyes in tears) as ears, and also as mouths, as speaking to the other in 'words' that oral language may not contain or allow [...] because tears can be words, words spoken, words responding to, and also, like writing, words/seen/. (15)

This is the kind of response *Dancer in the Dark* seeks to get from the viewer—a viewer who does not use the eyes to see (the film largely succeeds at presenting nothing much to see) but to respond to, in weeping, or engage directly in a dialogue based on a form of speech that has less to do with the rational or civilized speaking subject endowed with 'vision' or 'knowledge' than with an intentionally regressive subject who does not resist the powerful pullback of the voice of the sirens; an anti-Odysseus who, instead of blocking his ears and opening his eyes, shuts his eyes or blinds them with tears, and opens his ears to the infatuating song of the sirens.

Notes

1. Φ refers to the phallus. Lacan, however, explains that he designates Φ as the phallus "insofar as [...] it is the signifier that has no signified, the one that is based, in the case of man, on phallic jouissance". On Feminine Sexuality, The Limits of Love and Knowledge: Encore, 1972–1973, trans. with notes by Bruce Fink (New York and London: W.W. Norton and Company, 1998), p. 81.
2. This is the main theme of the chapter entitled 'Excursus I: Odysseus or Myth and Enlightenment', in Horkheimer and Adorno's *Dialectic of Enlightenment: Philosophical Fragments*, ed. Gunzelin Schmid Noerr and trans. Edmund Jephcott (Palo Alto, CA: Stanford University Press, 2002), pp. 35–62.

Bibliography

Badley, Linda. *Lars von Trier*. Urbana, Chicago, Springfield: University of Illinois Press, 2010.

Bainbridge, Caroline. *The Cinema of Lars von Trier: Authenticity and Artifice*. London and New York: Wallflower Press, 2007.

D'Angelo, Mike. 'The Big Numbers Are the Lowlight of *Dancer in the Dark*'. *Scenic Routes*. Accessed 3 September 2014. http://www.avclub.com/article/the-big-numbers-are-the-lowlight-of-idancer-in-the-96765

Derrida, Jacques. *Memoirs of the Blind: The Self-Portrait and Other Ruins*. Translated by Pascale-Anne Brault and Michael Naas. Chicago and London: University of Chicago Press, 1993.

Graham, Rhys. 'Dancer in the Dark'. *Senses of Cinema*. (December 2000, Issue 11). Accessed 15 November 2014. http://sensesofcinema.com/2000/current-releases-11/dancer

Grodal, Torben Kragh. 'Frozen Flows in von Trier's *Oeuvre*'. *Visual Authorship: Creativity and Intentionality in Media*. Edited by Torben Kragh Grodal, Bente Larsen and Iben Thorving Laursen. Copenhagen: Museum Tusculanum Press, University of Copenhagen, 2005.

Homer. *The Iliad and Odyssey of Homer*. Translated into English blank verse by William Cowper. London: Printed for J. Johnson, 1791.

Horkheimer, Max, and Theodor W. Adorno. *Dialectic of Enlightenment: Philosophical Fragments*. Edited by Gunzelin Schmid Noerr and translated by Edmund Jephcott. Palo Alto, CA: Stanford University Press, 2002.

Kipling, Rudyard. *Selected Verse of Rudyard Kipling*. London: Collector's Library, CRW Publishing, 2012.

Kleinberg-Levin, David Michael. 'Keeping Foucault and Derrida in Sight: Panopticism and the Politics of Subversion'. *Sites of Vision: The Discursive Construction of Sight in the History of Philosophy*. Edited by David Michael Kleinberg-Levin. Cambridge, MA: MIT Press, 1997.

Koutsourakis, Angelos. *Politics as Form in Lars von Trier: A Post-Brechtian Reading*. New York, London, New Delhi and Sydney: Bloomsbury, 2013.

Lacan, Jacques. *The Four Fundamental Concepts of Psycho-Analysis*. Edited by Jacques-Alain Miller and translated by Alan Sheridan. Penguin Books, 1994.

Lacan, Jacques. *On Feminine Sexuality, The Limits of Love and Knowledge: Encore, 1972–1973*. Translated and with notes by Bruce Fink. New York and London: W.W. Norton and Company, 1998.

Lawrence, D.H. *Studies in Classic American Literature*. Harmondsworth: Penguin Books, 1977.

Lévinas, Emmanuel. *Entre Nous: Thinking-of-the-Other*. Translated by Michael B. Smith and Barbara Harshav. London and New York: Continuum, 2006.

Mulvey, Laura. 'Visual Pleasure and Narrative Cinema'. *Literary Theory: An Anthology*. Edited by Julie Rivkin and Michael Ryan. Massachusetts and Oxford: Blackwell Publishers, 2001.

Roman, Shari. *Digital Babylon: Hollywood, Indiewood and Dogme 95*. California: IFILM and Lone Eagle Publishing, 2001.

Rosenbaum, Jonathan. 'Doing the Hustle [Dancer in the Dark]'. *Chicago Reader* (October 27, 2000). Accessed 27 October 2014. http://www.jonathanrosenbaum.net/2000/10/doing-the-hustle

Sontag, Susan. *Against Interpretation*. London: Vintage Books, 2001.

Taylor, Chloé. 'Hard, Dry Eyes and Eyes That Weep: Vision and Ethics in Lévinas and Derrida'. *Postmodern Culture*, 16, no. 2, January 2006. Accessed 10 December2013.http://www.pomoculture.org/2013/09/10/hard-dry-eyes-and-eyes-that-weep-vision-and-ethics-in-levinas-and-derrida

Welby, Lizzy. 'Introduction to Selected Verse of Rudyard Kipling'. *Selected Verse of Rudyard Kipling*. London: Collector's Library, CRW Publishing, 2012.

Williams, Kent. 'Dancer in the Dark'. *Isthmus*. Accessed 19 September 2014. http://isthmus.com/archive/reviews/dancer-in-the-dark/

Filmography

Antichrist. Directed and written by Lars von Trier. Irvington, NY: Criterion Collection, 2010.

Dancer in the Dark. Directed and written by Lars von Trier. Montréal, Québec: Alliance Atlantis, 2007.

Dogma 2: Idioterne (*Dogma 2: The Idiots*). Directed and written by Lars von Trier. Toronto: Alliance Atlantis, 2004.

Element of Crime. Directed by Lars von Trier. Written by Lars von Trier and Niels Vørsel. NY: Criterion Collection, 2000.

Epidemic. Directed by Lars von Trier. Written by Lars von Trier and Niels Vørsel. USA: Home Vision Entertainment, 2004.

Melancholia. Directed and written by Lars von Trier. Hong Kong: Edko Films Ltd., 2011.

Quills. Directed by Philip Kaufman. Written by Doug Wright. Los Angeles, CA: Fox Searchlight Pictures, 2000.

The Sound of Music. Directed by Robert Wise. Written by Ernest Lehman. Beverly Hills, CA: 20th Century Fox Home Entertainment, 2000.

CHAPTER 5

Dogville: Woman as an Ideological Cinematic Tool

There seems to be little doubt that Lars von Trier's *Dogville* is a direct onslaught on America. When the director was asked back in 2001 why he chose, once again after *Dancer in the Dark*, to set his new film in America, he simply assumed a reactionary position:

> I was very provoked by lots of American journalists in Cannes. They were angry because I'd made a film about the U.S.A. although I hadn't been there [...] I didn't think it was such a great sin. Besides that is just what American filmmakers have always done [...] they never went to Casablanca. (Lumholdt, *Lars von Trier: Interviews* 208)

Yet, *Dogville*, as one of the most interesting European takes on America, seems to be not just a stylistically anti-Hollywood, as well as thematically anti-American, film, but even an *anti-cinematic* film. The film's "formal organization", which "valorizes the role of the audience in the construction of meaning", and its "separation of elements", which seems to "negate the singularity of meaning", constitute a "challenge" to the "cinematic institution and the understanding of the medium as a consumable reflection of reality" (Koutsourakis, *Politics as Form* 151). *Dogville* is "the ultimate 'staged' film", staged not only in a mechanical sense, but also in the physical and verbal communication between the actors, whose "exchanges" have a "measured, deliberate, theatrical feel" and are "devoid of any spontaneity" (Stevenson 104). *Dogville* is thus largely a film about the film industry itself, in which the key word "illustration"—being so frequently mentioned by the narrator and the film's central male character, Thomas Edison Junior—plays a major part in communicating that idea to the viewer.

Cinematic America is indeed *Dogville*'s major 'illustration'. Though the film might be understood as a critique of human nature in a universal sense rather than an anti-American onslaught, the director, unequivocally, cuts short the possibility of such interpretation by ending the film with a series of shocking photographs, presumably pointing to America's social injustices. The film's "depthlessness", according to Linda Badley, reflects a "uniquely American shallowness, the composite result of its pragmatism, parochialism, and historical amnesia". The "mise-en-scène designated not the United States so much as a replica of the American imaginary constructed by the mass media" (Badley 103). What is more important, however, is what the film does to the cinematic experience itself. The "lack of cinematic verisimilitude makes active viewing, or reading, necessary, turning cinema into a 'literary' experience" (104).

Dogville even challenges the Dogma 95 manifesto itself, which was mainly created as a challenge to institutional standardized filmmaking and the tradition of Hollywood. In fact, it is considered to be the very "antithesis of Dogme", in spite of its minimalist approach. It presents "von Trier's world, his story"; therefore, thoroughly unlike *Idioterne*, its actors do not "supply their own characters since the characters […] act out the story [von Trier] had written or, in the case of the secondary actors, decorate the story. Like mannequins made of flesh and blood" (Stevenson 103). *Dogville*, thus, is "its own manifesto" (Badley 103). In terms of stylistics, "while employing very few props and no special effects in the Hollywood understanding of the term, those few props […] and the extensive use of sound and lighting effects, assume […] a central importance in bringing the fictional setting and characters to life" (Stevenson 103). In terms of content, *Dogville* is a "nihilistic mockery of Marxist as well as American values". On the one hand, "the working class [is made up of people who] will exploit if they find someone to exploit and enslave", and on the other, the film is a "parody of American ideology as promoted by hundreds of American B movies, the clichés and the idealism that is really only veiled egotism" (Schepelern, *Visual Authorship* 164).

The argument that follows will show that what *Dogville*, as a cynical as well as a Brechtian cinematic work, says about America reflects a vision that tries to render America as a feminized as well as desexualized mutant of Europe. Put another way, *Dogville* as a European text seeking to read

America is in one way capable of doing so by arguing how America, seen as an inheritor of European civilization, simultaneously feminized and desexualized itself to be different and non-European. In the course of this, the structural and conscious processes by which *Dogville* invents a desexualized America and relates this desexualization to the idea of murder will be revealed. The two main points to be made, however, are, first, that the violence done to America is a violence primarily directed to *cinematic* America—or even to cinema itself as an American invention—through the figure of woman as an ideological cinematic tool, and, second, that this anti-American European take on America, in spite of its outspoken aggressivity, seems to mark a certain unconscious erotic affair between the inventing European subject and the invented feminized image of America. This is precisely where the Lacanian intervention occurs.

In his essay 'America First', Michael Wood writes: "Home is what we know we ought to want but can't really take. America is not so much a home for anyone as a universal dream of home, a wish whose attraction depends upon its remaining at the level of a wish" (40–2). It is exactly this that *Dogville* seems to aim at demolishing. For the America invented in it is in fact a home, but obviously only for a certain type of people. It is the "universal dream of home" that is targeted by indicting America's ideas of home, community, hospitality and, above all, the altruistic democratic ideology represented by the writer character, Thomas Edison Junior, who plays the enlightened philosopher, the possible instigator of social change and the one who is looked upon as a savior, *and*, at the same time, the one who turns out to be the weakest and most treacherous of all of Dogville's inhabitants. All of this makes von Trier's film unapologetically cynical. But what kind of cynicism does one find in it? To what extent does this cynicism constitute a political position taken via artistic transgression? Or is it mere cynicism? Is there anything more to it than being a sign of paranoiac repression?

A cynical work of art always causes such controversy around its message and its usefulness in the field of cultural politics. Cynicism is always caught between being politically active through transgressive satirical laughter, unbound sensuality and body politics, and being that "enlightened false consciousness" Peter Sloterdijk describes in his *Critique of Cynical Reason* as the "modernized, unhappy consciousness, on which enlightenment has labored both successfully and in vain" (5). In its first instance, cynicism would take roots in the Bakhtinian realm of carnival, and the cynical work of art would belong to that special political "antibody" which Michael Gardiner, as one of the Bakhtinian circle of thinkers, perceives through "Bakhtin's own bacteriological metaphor" as "living within a pathological social body, always threatening to rupture it from within" (37). In its second, however, it falls back into Sloterdijk's "enlightened false consciousness" and its dilemmatic postmodern condition of being "well-off and miserable at the same time"—a consciousness which "no longer feels affected by any critique of ideology" because "its falseness is already reflexively buffered" (5).

But somehow *Dogville* seems to be devoid of the carnivalesque sense. There seems to be an elaborate kind of satire as well as a sharp cynicism in John Hurt's tone and deliciously tortuous style of narration, but certainly no satirical laughter. It 'hurts', but from above, from what seems, or rather *sounds*, to be an aristocratic tower, and not from below, not from a carnivalistic sense of a social public sphere. From the very opening scene, Hurt's voice introduces the viewer to an obvious miniature representation of small-town America in a particular time that defined the future of modern America, the time of Thomas Edison. With an unfailing British tongue that seems to reflect how America was seen by the aristocratic and socially hierarchical nineteenth-century Europe as simple, sentimental, honest and urbanely primitive, Hurt starts his narration with:

> This is the sad tale of the township of Dogville. Dogville was in the Rocky Mountains in the U.S. of A., up here where the road came to its definitive end, near the entrance to the old abandoned silver mine. The residents of Dogville were good, honest folks, and they liked their township. And while a sentimental soul from the east coast had once dubbed their main street Elm Street, though no elm had ever cast its shadow in Dogville, they saw no reason to change anything. Most of the buildings were pretty wretched. More like shacks frankly. The house in which Tom lived was the best though and, in good times, might almost have passed for presentable.

It can be argued thus that the all-seeing-eye view of the town of Dogville the film opens with, and which persists all along, penetrating physical barriers that had to be made invisible, reflects the degree of contempt with which Lars von Trier looks down upon his material. But it also communicates an unmistakable Brechtian message that advocates the alienatory way of creating art while being hostile to the illusionary method that targets the viewer's emotions rather than his or her intellect. It is relevant to the present discussion to draw attention to some of the many subtle references to Brecht's works before discussing what America meant to Brecht himself as the most appropriate introduction to Lars von Trier's 'Dogvillian' America.

While the film's staging and style persistently detach the viewer and impede identification with the characters, the ghastly content evokes Brecht's *Die Dreigroschenoper* (*The Threepenny Opera*). The name of the town itself, Dogville, seems to play on the allegorical character of "Dogsborough" in *Aufhaltsame Aufstieg des Arturo Ui* (*The Resistible Rise of Arturo Ui*). While the film obviously intends the vicious image it invents to be representative of a collective American psyche, which, it seems to claim, underlies the ostensible kindness and deceptive simplicity of small-town America, "Dogsborough", in Brecht's *Arturo Ui*, is an American citizen who is "reputed to be honest" but whose "morals go overboard in times of crisis", "a hard-boiled broker, who takes a lawyer with him to his lawyer's" and, above all, someone who should be "educated" (12–14) by others who are more experienced in matters of life and human nature—in Brecht's symbolism: Europeans. Dogville's society, like that of *Der Gute Mensch Von Setzuan* (*The Good Person of Szechwan*), is portrayed as a society that rhapsodizes over virtue and generosity while its practice contradicts both. In the interlude following scene nine of that particular play, one of the three gods comments on such a society in a way that could as well describe Dogville's:

> What a world we have found here: nothing but poverty, debasement and dilapidation! Even the landscape crumbles away before our eyes. Beautiful trees are lopped off by cables, and over the mountains we see great clouds of smoke and hear the thunder of guns, and nowhere a good person who survives it! (*Good Person* 98)

Shen Teh, taking her mask off in scene ten, retorts to the three gods' shocked reaction to her gesture with: "Your original order to be good while yet surviving split me like lightning into two people. I cannot tell what occurred: goodness to others and to myself could not both be achieved" (105). Shen Teh's disguise in most of the play and the taking off of her mask close to its end corresponds with Grace's hidden identity, which is not revealed to the people of Dogville until the last scene of the film, where she transforms from the town's victim to its judge and prosecutor. Brecht's symbolism of the three gods disappearing in a mechanical pink cloud that descends from the ceiling of the theatre in scene ten after giving up the prospect of finding a single good person on Earth is evoked in *Dogville* by the alternative dramatic appearance of a god-father in one of the "Cadillac series 355 C" in order to punish Dogville for not having a single good person living in it. Even using real-life photographs as a background for the end credits evokes Brecht's ending of *Mutter Courage und ihre Kinder* (*Mother Courage and Her Children*), with documentary images of Lenin, Stalin and Mao backgrounding the action on the stage.

What America meant to Brecht himself cannot but have a powerful influence on his followers and admirers, and Lars von Trier is no exception in this regard. In his essay 'America Before and After', one of the authorities on Brecht, James K. Lyon, writes:

> Much like a social scientist, Brecht tended to see the world in terms of 'models'—in this case models constructed out of Marxist ideological views and out of his poetic imagination. His sociological model for America when he arrived was based on the assumption that it represented the most advanced form of capitalism and consequently the most uncivilized, inhumane form of human existence. (341)

As a socialist and anti-fascist, Brecht's experience in America after fleeing Nazi Europe was not seen by him as devoid of harassment due to his ideological commitment to communism and to his famous confrontations with the film industry, which he perceived as capitalistically exploiting. His entanglement with Hollywood's film industry clearly marked an unhappy phase in his life, as Martin Walsh argues in his essay 'The Complex Seer: Brecht and the Film', where he writes:

> It is clear that Brecht regarded his work in the cinema as simply a means to earn his living. Hollywood was always eager to secure <<name>> writers, and Brecht churned out scripts, which were so chewed over in the studio factories that his ideas were invariably modified beyond recognition. (10)

Arguably, nothing could have made a writer like Brecht more bitter and resentful than altering his ideas so as to produce right-wing, conformist works that he undoubtedly detested. Thus, his sad lines about selling his talent in the form of lies to earn a living in a poem entitled *Hollywood*, which is cited by Walsh in the same essay (11)—an instance of the economy of desire being sacrificed for the economic.

Brecht's experience of exile in America is epitomized by his being investigated as a witness in 1947 by the House Committee on Un-American Activities, one of 19 personalities deemed unfriendly to American values and ideology. James K. Lyon cites his statement before that committee in which he said: "I am not a film writer, and I am not aware of any influence I have had on the film industry, either politically or artistically", a statement Lyon sees as summarizing "not so much his view of himself as a writer, but the realities of his life in the film world" (71). Needless to say, contrary to Brecht's own words, he had an everlasting artistic imprint on the film industry, especially in Europe. *Dogville* is one of the most obvious effects of that. America seems to have been such a hostile place to Brecht—and he in turn such an intimidating figure to it—that even American Marxists themselves were not on particularly good terms with their European comrade. In 'The Ideological Brecht', Lyon gives an account of the mood that defined Brecht's controversial relationship with members of the Marxist American left wing:

> Joseph R. Starobin, an active member of the American communist party at the time, recalls an experience that captures the atmosphere that often prevailed. In the company of other Communists, he met Brecht and Gerhart Eisler at a soiree in New York City in 1943 or 1944. It was, Starobin says, 'a painful evening, with Brecht lying astride a bed, contemptuous of everybody.' The exile, he claims, shared the 'general European self-centeredness and arrogance' that American Communists sensed in their European counterparts. (288)

Even the destruction of the town of Dogville in the film's last scene could be argued to symbolize the "destruction of America" that Brecht seems to have carelessly announced out of his political overenthusiasm at some point during his life of exile in the United States. Lyon writes:

> In 1947 he strongly espoused the cause of Henry A. Wallace, who was emerging as a third party candidate for president. Bentley recalls hearing Brecht say that, if Wallace were not elected, the alternative for America would be World War III. There was no middle ground. And when the House Un-American Activities Committee launched its investigation of Hollywood in 1947, Brecht announced to friends the imminent destruction of America. (303)

Dogville, as a film that, style-wise, belongs to Brechtian cinema, as well as one that obviously pays such a high homage to Brecht, his works, his ideology and his life, is thus obviously a work that tries to *mutilate* the image of America. And because an image is never just an image, or, to put it in a Žižekan way, "an appearance is never 'merely an appearance', it profoundly affects the actual sociosymbolic position of those concerned" (*Plague of Fantasies* 26); the invented image, like fantasy, not only covers up gaps in the sociosymbolic network of its inventor, an instance of which in the present context would be the destabilization of his or her very constructed subjectivity, but it can actually infuse or confuse reality with the phantasmal—either for its producer or its consumer.

A pertinent starting point would be the character of the philosopher/writer, "Thomas Edison". It is obvious enough where Tom got his name from. Thomas Alva Edison (1847–1931) is the celebrated American engineer whose great inventions substantially defined the modern age. Two of his most important contrivances were film projectors and motion pictures. The fact that this historical piece of information is almost forgotten seems to obliterate the notion that it is not just because of Hollywood's hegemony over the international film industry that people tend to think of the world of movies as an American one. Cinema *is* an American invention, and the history of film is largely an American history. It is true that the French Lumière Brothers developed the first commercially successful film projection system. Yet, their work was mainly inspired by Edison's earlier motion picture devices like the kinetoscope and kinetograph where the idea of creating the illusion of movement out of successive pictures was first introduced.

One exceptionally revealing European text dealing with the character of Edison is Villiers de l'Isle-Adam's *Tomorrow's Eve*, in which the French writer (1838–89), who was actually a contemporary of Thomas Alva Edison, creates the fictional character of a scientist whose name is *Thomas Alva Edison*, "the man who made a prisoner of the echo" (7). Not so different from the Thomas Edison of *Dogville*, Villiers' fictional scientist is a man whose "favorite foible is to think himself ignorant, by a kind of legitimate naïveté. Hence that simplicity of welcome and the mask of rough frankness—sometimes even the show of familiarity—with which he veils the icy realities of his thought" (8).

Perhaps there is no better example in the present context of how the fictional problematizes the sense of reality in the case of anything related to America than the advice the writer of *Tomorrow's Eve* gives to his reader as a preface to the main text. In 'Advice to the Reader', Villiers makes an exceptionally meticulous effort to show the reader that his fictional character of Thomas Edison refers to the "legend" that "has sprung up in the popular mind regarding this great citizen of the United States" and not to the real American engineer. And since the legend is completely separate from the real man, the writer seems to suggest, it belongs to the world of literature.

So, with a Catholic impulse to eradicate all confusion, he starts his advice with: "It seems proper to forestall a possible confusion regarding the principal hero of this book." Yet, his repeated emphasis on the need to eradicate such confusion somehow seems to reflect how much he is himself confused. Later he writes: "The Edison of the present work, his character, his dwelling, his language, and his theories, are and ought to be at least somewhat distinct from anything existing in reality." The affirmative "are" is not only diluted by "at least somewhat distinct" but immediately undermined by the following skeptical "ought to be". It is as if Villiers is at odds, trying to convince *himself* that the legend, in his mind, is truly something separate from reality. Even after making his point thrice, somehow his feeling that it is not established firmly enough persists. So, at the end of his advice he adds:

> Let it be understood, then, that I interpret a modern legend to the best advantage of the work of Art-metaphysics that I have conceived, and that, in a word, the hero of this book is above all 'The Sorcerer of Menlo Park', and so forth—and not the engineer, Mr. Edison, our contemporary. ('Advice to the Reader')

This is his final statement, by which he tries to convince the reader and himself that the judgment that the legend belongs to literature while the real belongs to the real world has been established. Yet, as a conclusion arrived at after this most apologetic preface, Villiers' statement seems to be very shaky indeed, as if trying laboriously to suppress a fundamental suspicion: that the fictional might in fact still be more established than the real. If *Dogville* can be considered a film of any significance in the field of cultural politics, the questions it would be posing in such a case would be of this kind: is reality actually distinguishable from what has been created as a legend? Is America distinguishable from what has been created by Hollywood as cinematic America? Or, to take the issue further, how much of the reality of America has been created by cinematic America? None of these questions can have a clear-cut answer.

In *Tomorrow's Eve*, Thomas Edison creates a mechanical woman, *Hadaly*, who represents the dream of the ultimate romantic love. Edison's genius makes Hadaly look, move and talk exactly like a real woman. Moreover, she is so eloquent and no less versed in managing a dialogue than a philosopher or a great poet. But what is really significant about Hadaly, according to her creator's expressed point of view, is that she is devoid of what men perceive in women as female pettiness and small-mindedness. The feminine conscience is what Edison was able to get rid of by inventing the android—for the usage of man.

As a female android, Hadaly seems to have everything except the soul and Eros of a woman. She is a desexualized creature who may be thought of as the male subject's ultimate object of pornographic imagination; a sexually attractive woman who is devoid of what he perceives as the threatening, inexplicable, "enigmatic" or "mystical"[1] female *jouissance*. Besides that, Hadaly's cinematic movements and gestures in the scenes in which she plays the heroine of a romantic love story are numerous and unmistakable. At the end of Villiers' eccentric novel, the mechanical woman is destroyed by an accidental fire onboard a transatlantic liner on her way to Europe. It seems that, by giving the celebrated American name "Thomas Alva Edison" to his scientist character, Villiers de l'Isle-Adam's text implies that his fictional scientist, who wanted to invent a mechanical woman, ended up, *in reality*, inventing only cinema instead. The displacement seems to suggest that cinema, as an American invention, is desexualized at birth, the implication of which brings to the surface a whole discourse that seems to be lying deep in a certain European subject's unconscious: that America, at its highest symbolic representation, is portrayed as a desexualized woman.

With more or less the same Thomas Edison as a central character among the inhabitants of Dogville, the strange atmosphere of anti-eroticism in the film shrewdly presents the sexual either in its most violent/sadistic form or as being entirely dominated by the economic. On the one hand, raping Grace is made to be the only way to have sex with her; on the other, all the town's inhabitants seem to be asexual creatures, each of them in his or her own way. The first rape scene could be considered one of the most disturbing rape scenes in the history of motion pictures. Lars von Trier was actually able to put in it his whole perspective of the power discourse and its relation to sexual exploitation. The victimizer's suggestive short statements of vicious entrapping are contrasted with the victim's bewildered yet apprehensive questions:

—I wouldn't try to run away
—Why would I want to run away Chuck?
—I wouldn't try to holler either
—Why would I want to do that?

The persuasion takes its philosophical turn when Chuck tells Grace, "I need your respect, Grace," to which she replies, "You have my respect, Chuck." He follows up by repeating: "I want your respect." The demand for respect somehow verbally replaces sexual desire, as if the metonymic structure of desire[2] assumes no disguise at all, in a clear message that defines the relationship conventionally assumed between the powerful and the powerless, the male and the female, the ruling and the ruled, the colonizer and the colonized, the master and the slave, or, in Marxist terms, the bourgeoisie and the proletariat.

"In omitting walls," Badley writes, "Trier has stripped away the institutional and domestic facades that conceal the violence of the underlying political economy while evoking an image of Foucauldian surveillance, inverting the image of small-town hospitality into a vision of regulation and repression in which sexuality is converted into increasingly sadomasochistic forms" (Badley 108). When the direct talk of force starts to take place with Chuck's statement "I can force the flowers to bloom early in the Spring, I can force you", the camera, in one of the most cynical moments of the film, which hardly ever fails to draw a suppressed titter, if not an outright guffaw, moves to a contemplating Tom taking a stroll 'outside' Chuck's house.

This is where the satirical factor in the film reaches its highest point. The lack of physical barriers seems to point to the classic role of the philosopher in human civilization—to contemplate while power has its way right in front of his eyes. And while Chuck's grim 'practicality' unabashedly declares that friendship cannot exist between two people when one of them has the opportunity and power to exploit the other, Tom's assumed position of the enlightened model of man, in spite of the fact that his own sexual desire matches Chuck's, makes him recoil from acting in the same manner. His pathetic position is revealed by his brief awkward questions to Chuck and the latter's unruffled tone and suggestive invitation right after the rape scene:

—Have you seen Grace?
—She is at my place.
—She is busy?
—Not anymore, go right in.

Yet he opts to walk away after standing reluctantly at the invisible door of the house, a gesture attesting to his complete awareness of what Grace has been through. Hurt's voice cuts in right after that, only to add to the viewer's discomfort with his cynical "yet again, Grace had made a miraculous escape from her pursuers with the aid of the people of Dogville". For the truck driver, Ben, the sexual is attained only through the economic. He visits prostitutes when he has enough money to have sex, and when he rapes Grace in his truck he makes a point of assuring her beforehand that this is "not personal", philosophizing the whole situation according to the rules of the "freight industry". Grace, in fact, becomes a receptacle for the town's psychic troubles, an unpaid prostitute who not only suffers humiliation silently but who often masochistically defends her tormentors as well. As for Tom, the sexual, though sought after all along, counts for nothing compared to his desire to maintain a sense of 'author-ity' over Grace and everybody else in the town, including his own self; the authority of being the 'author' of everybody and everything around him.

Tom's leadership of the people of Dogville as their 'enlightened' teacher again evokes Odysseus and his marines pulling their ship away from the sirens and their infatuating song. The movie seems to represent a static moment, however, where the ship stops, takes aboard one of the beautiful sirens, and risks listening to the song for two weeks—needless to say with disastrous results. Tom, whom the film projects as some kind of small-time Odysseus, "complies with the contract of his bondage, and, bound to the mast, struggles to throw himself into the arms of the seductresses" (Horkheimer and Adorno 43) for whom Grace stands. His character is where the humanist, the artist, the savior and the philosopher intersect, and it is exactly this character that carries the ultimate sacrifice and the ultimate guilt within. He seems to represent what Adorno and Horkheimer call "the introversion of sacrifice" (46) as what the history of human civilization always meant. Tom's life's project is to acquire an identity as an author, and for that he always proves capable of sacrificing anything. It is fitting, in the film's discursive narrative, that this particular character becomes the ultimate victim in the last scene of vigilante justice that Grace brings to the town.

Perceived as a cinematic critique of America and the American people, *Dogville*'s main point seems to be to make the anonymous viewer ill-at-ease. For the "universal dream of home" (Wood 42), of liberty and democracy, the idea that epitomizes the human experience and its achievements to be at stake ought to be a gloomy idea. There seems to be little doubt that *Dogville* does not view America as just another civilization in the course of human history. As Hurt states in the opening scene, Dogville is "up here where the road came to its definitive end"; in other words, where the human experience seems to be coming to a close. Yet it is the portrayal of the society of Dogville itself that is meant to make the viewer ponder the question: is this really where the road comes to an end? The satirical message of *Dogville* subtly suggests that it is certainly ironic that the road should come to its definitive end in such a place, where hospitability, overcoming human selfishness, the ability to forgive and, above all, friendship are all impossible.

Dogville's inhabitants are portrayed as gregarious but not friendly. A gregarious person tends to associate with people of his/her type, which does give some sense of belonging to a group or a certain society or a family. But one of the main messages that *Dogville* seems to be communicating is that friendship demands more. Friendship demands acceptance of, and erotic rivalry with, the other as such. This could be one of the reasons why the inhabitants of Dogville, in spite of their common human differences, are portrayed in such a way, so as to strike the viewer as outlandishly alike. A stark similarity can be observed between them and a group of people that Dickens's hero "Martin Chuzzlewit" meets in a hotel bar in America. Criticizing Dickens's work in his essay 'Institutional America', Peter Conrad writes:

> The Americans Martin encounters are without exception listless, hollow-cheeked, tedious, and portentously verbose. The company in the hotel bar endlessly replicates the set of five or six types he has already met. When you've seen a thousand Americans, you've seen one. Their common worship of individualism has ended by effacing their individuality. They all value personality as a commodity, but because it is the same ideal personality which everyone wishes to acquire, the result is homogeneity. (57)

Dogville, not unlike Dickens's story—which may be thought to be less popular than his other masterpieces in English literature—is an artistic work that invents an image of America that is meant to reflect a superficial and pretentious innocence, mixed with a religious hypocrisy that suppresses the erotic. Therefore, representing the sexual as always twisted, unnatural and dominated by the economic seems to be targeting what is perceived by the inventor of *Dogville* as the innocent and religious nature of small-town America. In other words, one of the reasons why the sexual is suppressed, or, why America is desexualized, could be a particular view that sees the idea of sexuality as incompatible with what is commonly perceived as America's puritanism, pragmatism and religious nature.

In spite of the fact that one of America's postures is that of being the home of commercialized sex, the religious spirit and the idea of innocence were always taken to be markers distinguishing America from Europe. America has always been thought to differentiate itself from Europe by a number of things, chief among them religiosity and references to God in national emblems. In *Democracy in America*, Tocqueville writes:

> America is still the place where the Christian religion has kept the greatest real power over men's souls; and nothing better demonstrates how useful and natural it is to man, since the country where it now has widest sway is both the most enlightened and the freest. (291)

Tocqueville's observation, even if debatable, does point to the uniqueness of America's character as a country whose quest for enlightenment, power, democracy and modernization is paradoxically mixed with an avowedly religious spirit. Religious eschatology is therefore used by the creator of *Dogville* to subtly suggest that such eschatology must be firmly established in America's beliefs and ought to be at its strongest in the American mind.

The film seems to make use of religious eschatology as well as mock it. Its epitome, reached in Grace's transformation from historical victim or the sacrificed son of God to the revengeful Christ of the Day of Judgment, can be interpreted in terms of the Freudian "return of the repressed" (*The Origins of Religion* 372–6), but what establishes its satirical message is that it is made to look like a typical American stunt with guns blazing all around. The film seems to communicate to the viewer that the idea of the ultimate sacrifice, which is the core of Christianity and constitutes its Aufhebung, or its (anti)thetical departure from Judaic thought, seems to be alien to itself due to its incompatibility with the eschatology. The final dialogue in the film between Grace and her father sums up the whole idea. He tells Grace: "Rapists and murderers may be the victims according to you, but I call them dogs, and if they are lapping up their own vomit the only way to stop them is with the lash." The last scene of *Dogville* thus seems to symbolize the philosophical triumph of the Old Testament God, the father, over the New Testament merciful God, Grace, evoking "an aura of genocidal wrath and biblical inevitability" (Badley 110).

The father's discourse suggests that God sacrificing himself, or part of himself, purposefully to alleviate the sin of humanity – that is, to make humanity sinless or innocent – seems to be a sacrifice of himself for himself. "Arrogance" is the key word by which this position is described, and through which the idea is communicated to the viewer in one of the most engaging dialogues in the history of filmmaking:

Grace: So I am arrogant, I am arrogant because I forgive people.
Father: My God, can't you see how condescending you are when you say that. You have this preconceived notion that nobody can possibly attain the same hig h ethical standards as you [...] I cannot think of anything more arrogant than that. You forgive others with excuses that you would never in the world permit for yourself.
Grace: Why shouldn't I be merciful?
Father: You should be merciful when there is time to be merciful but, you must maintain your own standards, you owe them that. The penalty you deserve for your transgression they deserve for their transgressions.
Grace: They are human beings.
Father: And does every human being need to be accountable for their own actions? Of course they do. You don't even give them that chance, and that is extremely arrogant.

At the same time, the eschatological idea of God returning to punish humanity for its sins completely destroys the core idea of sacrifice. Eschatology thus cannot but be human imagination inevitably reflecting human psychic turbulences; a limited imagination that seems to be unable to take off any farther than asserting—consciously or unconsciously—that the repressed has to return somehow, someday, in some form or another. What is supposed to be a divine scheme about where humanity originates from and where it is going seems to always fall back helplessly in what Lacan describes as "the realm of what is considered acceptable or, in other words, the realm of prejudices" (*Ethics of Psychoanalysis* 251). *Dogville* is a text that is aware of what it ridicules, though what is ridiculed in it is itself what is being used to communicate its final message of retribution.

The film's final message is certainly a violent one, not to mention that the idea of murder casts its shadow on it from its start to the very end. The figure of Grace, in spite of her victimization, seems to carry the air of the femme fatale. Jan Simons argues that Grace is nothing but a "game puppet" over which the father and Tom are competing for control, and "whoever wins gets to imbue the dummy, Grace, with any attributes he wants (his own values, ideals and views)" (119–20). Yet Grace's aura and charm captivate, if not Dogville, then certainly the viewer. The idea that she ends up being the ultimate murderess, if carefully contemplated, actually carries no surprises. The conversion of the ultimate martyr to the ultimate murderer is in fact one of the most likely conversions. Grace seems to carry the germ of Sophocles' heroine Antigone. There is no tyranny in her, and this means, precisely, no human weakness.

In his analysis of the tragedy of *Antigone*, Lacan writes about Creon: "We will see later what he is, that is, like all executioners and tyrants at bottom, a human character. Only the martyrs know neither pity nor fear" (*Ethics of Psychoanalysis* 267). He differentiates between Creon's and Antigone's antagonistic positions by pointing out that Creon's tyranny belongs to the 'normal', barred subject; in other words, it belongs to the 'sane' human being who is constituted by his symbolic network, while Antigone's martyrdom marks her total identification with her desire for death. At such level of identification with one's own desire, there can be no difference between killing the self and killing the other. So, when Grace finally decides to kill everybody in the town, she also *literally* kills her own old, forgiving self, without which she cannot be 'Grace' anymore.

Her symbolic suicide—which clearly marks an elemental shift from forgiveness to revenge, from divine-like mercy to divine-like wrath, indeed from arrogant non-action to extreme reaction—is represented by von Trier through a slight stylistic alteration of lighting accompanied by Grace's/Kidman's changing facial expression. With her neck still marked red by the abusing collar neck ring which Dogville's people had devised to keep her enslaved, the side look and the turn of the head foretell her transfiguration and the bloodbath she is about to order. But it is the style of the execution that evokes a countless number of similar scenes in Hollywood movies when guns start going off systematically and party-like. If the people of Dogville are made to represent the society of small-town America, Grace herself is the ultimate representation of the familiar cinematic Hollywood image of the lonely American cowboy, the vigilante killer, who saves the day by executing justice in his own way with his own gun—American ideology at its purest.

Cinematic America is thus represented in *Dogville* simultaneously and divergently as desexualized as well as murderous. The affinity between desexing and murder seems to have a certain implicit—sometimes explicit—legacy in literature and film. As for Hollywood productions, the examples range from classic cowboy films with the lonely American hero who lives mainly in continuous transition between cities and townships, often away from what defines and confirms his sexuality, woman, up to the *Terminator* series. The difference between *A Fistful of Dollars* and *Terminator* is that, in Sergio Leone's film, the hero is a man whose slow movements, slow speech and the unbelievable, mechanistic and superhuman speed with which he uses the gun resemble that of a machine, while in James Cameron's film, the hero is a machine that looks like a man. Both the desexualized machine-like man and the desexualized man-like machine, however, have the same cinematic cowboy ethics. As for literature, it can be argued that the establishment of such a theme of murderous desexualization goes back in the history of literary production at least to Shakespearean drama.

One of Shakespeare's most vivid images of the desexualized murderer is the Roman general Caius Martius, the male protagonist in *Coriolanus*, who is portrayed in most of the play as a desexualized war-machine. In act II, scene I, after capturing the city of Corioles and securing victory over the Volsces, Martius is given, as his mother Volumnia points out, "the whole name of the war", "Coriolanus". He gets his new identity out of what he destroys. From then on, Shakespeare's verses seem to give him a kind of mechanistic, inhuman quality. Thus, Volumnia's words: "Death, that dark spirit, in's nervy arm doth lie, which, being advanced, declines, and then men die" (533). But the most telling words come from Cominius in scene II, where he describes Martius's unrivalled systematic slaughter of the enemy in the battle of Corioles: "His sword, death's stamp, where it did mark, it took from face to foot. He was a thing of blood, whose every motion was timed with dying cries" (544). The resemblance between him and the cinematic terminator is striking.

Yet it seems Shakespeare's most illuminating contribution to this discourse marking the affinity between desexualization and murder is a female character. In her famous soliloquy in act I, scene V of *Macbeth*, Lady Macbeth prepares herself for murder by saying: "Come, you spirits that tend on mortal thoughts, unsex me here, and fill me from the crown to the toe, top-full of direst cruelty" (112–13). The somewhat scholastic notion of referring Lady Macbeth's actions to her love for her husband as a devoted wife has been rectified by the view that this is the very thing she wants to disown: womanhood. But why "unsex"? And why "here"? Or more precisely, *where* is "here"?

We are not helped by the fact that some of Shakespeare's many editors inserted a stage direction that says "touching her heart".[3] The use of the verb "unsex" followed by an unidentified "here" puts this now very popular editorial stage direction in doubt. The prayer undoubtedly indicates a desire for a removal of something, but is it really just feminine qualities as compared to male ones that are meant to be removed? In other words, does Shakespeare really want to say that in order to become a killer you have to be masculine? And what does it mean to unsex oneself if the unsexing does not actually guarantee or secure gender inversion? Strictly speaking, rejecting womanhood still does not seem to either fulfill the wish of Lady Macbeth or get us very far through the intricacies of Shakespeare's mind.

While John O'Connor interprets "unsex me here" typically as "remove all my feminine qualities" (26), Horace Howard Furness Jr states that "the very point here emphasized is that she abjured womanhood". He then includes the typical stage direction: "*me here* [Touching her Heart]" (78). Other possibly more skeptical editors, perhaps out of a sense of facing something that defies direct interpretation, chose not to comment on Lady Macbeth's line at all. Kenneth Muir, in the 1991 Arden Shakespeare edition of *Macbeth*, simply skips it – quite unexpectedly, one needs to add, since that edition in fact gives extensive comments on "Come you spirits that tend on mortal thoughts". The elaborate interpretation of evoking the spirits of death and destruction is followed by an unexplained complete silence about the purpose of such evoking.

In her *Shakespeare's Division of Experience*, Marilyn French points to what she sees as an "ambiguity about gender roles in Macbeth" that makes Lady Macbeth in her soliloquy resolve "to align herself with the male principle" in a play in which imagery "is divided into masculine and feminine categories" and in which priority is given to the masculine "courage, prowess, the ability to kill" over the feminine "compassion, nurturance, and mercy" (241–51). French thus seeks to locate the Shakespearean tragedy in a violent masculine realm marked by an acute gender division, which is quite uncharacteristic of Shakespeare, who often plays with genders in his plays.

In the Oxford Shakespeare edition of *Macbeth*, Nicholas Brooke seems to take an opposite view. He first gives priority to the interpretation of "mortal thoughts" as "human thoughts" over "deadly thoughts". He then comments on "unsex me here" in the following manner:

> 'Sex' governs all the range of human experience ('mortal thoughts') that follows: kindness, remorse, pity, fertility; it is, in short, her humanity and not simply her femininity that Lady Macbeth wishes away—the thoughts are very close to those which disturb Macbeth in I.7. (113)

Brooke's editorial comments break away from the gender differentiation discourse. It is significant that he mentions "fertility". Fertility relates directly to the body and to sexuality. His primary comment that "sex governs all the range of human experience" removes barriers between humanity and sexuality. But why would Lady Macbeth wish away her fertility? It is Freud who has the answer to this question, even though he seems to mix the cause with the effect. With regard to Lady Macbeth's character analysis, nevertheless, he reaches to the core of the issue—quite characteristically of him—with one word. "Barrenness" is the key word by which Freud unlocks the character of Lady Macbeth. In his essay 'The Character of Lady Macbeth', Freud writes:

> It would be a perfect example of poetic justice [...] if the childlessness of Macbeth and the barrenness of his Lady were the punishment for their crimes against the sanctity of generation—if Macbeth could not become a father because he had robbed children of their father and a father of his children, and if Lady Macbeth suffered the unsexing she had demanded of the spirits of murder. I believe Lady Macbeth's illness, the transformation of her callousness into penitence, could be explained directly as a reaction to her childlessness, by which she is convinced of her impotence against the decrees of nature, and at the same time reminded that it is through her own fault if her crime has been robbed of the better part of its fruits. (42)

Yet, it is not clearly justified that Lady Macbeth's barrenness, as Freud seems to allude, comes as a result of her unusual prayer to the spirits, in a Shakespearean attempt at poetical justice. If she is a barren lady, there is no reason to discard the possibility that she would be in a position to know this long before the tragedy takes place. Her barrenness could in effect be the instigator of the murder and not the effect of it. The point in such a case would be: 'unsex me here, as I am already barren and useless, as I will not be able to found a dynasty of kings, and not even of noblemen; as I have nothing to lose, why not have a shot at the throne.' In such a case, it would not be Lady Macbeth's intention to be a killer punished by barrenness, as Freud seems to suggest. It would be her barrenness that made her a killer by wishing to give up the only thing she still possesses: her sexuality, since she is already, de facto, not a woman. In her case, abjuring womanhood is meaningless.

In a memorable performance of the play, performed by an English cast on the stage of the Egyptian Opera House in Cairo in 1989, this writer witnessed a Lady Macbeth who violently, unequivocally, and with a loud sound that gave the audience a pain in the stomach rather than a hard-on, slapped her female organ instead of touching her heart. Although this came as a surprise that caught the audience off guard, somehow it didn't seem or sound vulgar. It didn't seem out of context either. Her unusually deepened voice, her direct look into the eyes of the audience in the rows closest to the stage—and not, for instance, up in the air as she is supposed to be talking to the spirits—and her violent gesture seemed desperate to communicate a very articulate message, a message that was obviously meant to be corrective of a long-standing tradition of interpretation. A message that says: it could just as well be desperation, and not ambition, that dictates Lady Macbeth's actions in the first third of the drama.

Therefore, in view of such a message, Lady Macbeth's words would point to a radical desire for castration so as to constitute a certain lack. But the lack is supposed to be already there in the female. The lack in this case is not of an organ, whether it is the heart or the genitals. It is a lack that does not differentiate between genders. It is a lack of sexuality itself that she desires, or, the removal of that which makes her aware of her human body. And sexuality, though exceeding by far the representation of single or particular human organs, has been orthodoxly associated with the genitals more than any other parts of the body.

It doesn't seem just a coincidence that the greatest dramatist of all time makes his hero in *Coriolanus* address his wife in a direct manner only twice, in two moments which stand out in astounding contrast to each other. At the height of his victory and his newly war-acquired identity and self-confidence in act II, scene 1, Caius Martius addresses Virgilia as "my gracious silence" (535), while in act V, scene 3, at his lowest moments, with no identity, and knowing that he will not be able to keep the promise he made to the Volsces and will probably be killed by them, he calls her "best of my flesh" (633). Yet, it is at this latter moment, when he refers to the materialist and the body instead of the ideological, that he is truly at his best, when he could abandon the idea of taking revenge on his own people.

It seems that what Shakespeare really wanted to say in *Macbeth* as well as in *Coriolanus* was that conscience, or, that which works against the killing instinct, comes out of an awareness of the body, while the death of conscience is, *always*, a marker of cutting off the life of the body. What makes Martius an exceptional tragic hero, however, is Shakespeare's ambiguous presentation of him—a presentation that seems to make *Coriolanus* as a play at one and the same time a tragedy and a satire, with a hero who seems to inspire both sympathy and laughter. His epic figure as the awesome Roman general is mixed with a sort of a boyish attitude that makes him his mother's boy. His unrivalled accomplishments as a highly experienced warrior are only matched by a kind of immaturity and innocence that make him a social and political failure.

It is thus not strange that *Dogville* seems to subtly associate these ideas of desexualization and murder with its main attack target: what it perceives as American innocence. American innocence is, in fact, a theme that has been handled by many writers in various ways. Michael Wood, for example, argues that America talks itself into being innocent via cinema with a discourse that suggests that:

> The innocence of victims stems from the principle that says that victims must be innocent, that unless you are innocent, you are not a victim. If you are guilty, even only slightly, the whole question changes, since merely getting more than your just deserves is plainly a matter of moral accounting rather than a miscarriage of justice.

He then argues that "at the back of all this lurks the American weakness for the idea of purity, for the notion of an entirely unflecked innocence" (140). While Wood investigates the effect of Hollywood's representations of American innocence on American society, Edward Said examines America's political motives behind that image of innocence that, for him, is already established in the collective American psyche. In an essay entitled 'The Other America', Said questions the American "collective we", which he perceives as:

> A national identity represented without apparent demurral by our president, our secretary of state at the UN, our armed forces in the desert, and our interests, which are routinely seen as self-defensive, without ulterior motive, and in an overall way, innocent in the way that a traditional woman is supposed to be innocent, pure, free of sin. (*Al-Ahram Weekly*)

Though this seems to be a human image of America as woman, it is not so far away from Hadaly who, as a machine that stands for cinema, cannot be but innocent, pure and free of sin. Ihab Hassan, for another example, creates one of the most sublime versions of American innocence in which it is seen as a form of positive neurosis that constitutes a "regressive force that prevents the self from participating fully in the world [...] As a result, the greatest values affirmed by the American conscience have often been affirmed against the ruling spirit of the land" (*Radical Innocence* 40).

What can be drawn from all of these accounts of American innocence is that America is always expected to go beyond just the country and its national interests. Everybody overloads the symbol with their own romantic images. Some (mis)recognize in it an un-worldly spiritual detachment, an epic quality and an unrivalled conscience. Some question its isolationism. Some read violence underneath its image of innocence. And some mutilate it, as will be argued in what follows, out of love—a love, however, not for America, but for something that does not exist—yet. With regard to *Dogville*, the conclusion that is to be drawn here is that, in spite of its totally negative image of cinematic America—or precisely because of that—the film seems to belong to those works that mutilate America out of disappointed love. As one of numerous phantasmal representations of America, it overloads its invented image of it with its own romantic, or traumatic, fantasies.

Like Villiers de l'Isle-Adam's *Tomorrow's Eve*, *Dogville* presents us with one of the principal heroes of the modern age, the Odysseus of enlightenment, who lives in an America that is made to sacrifice the sexual for a mixture of the scientific, the economic, the religious and, in *Dogville*, the killing instinct. No human civilization has been more mythologized or dehumanized in the history of man. The myth seems to have gone even beyond Hollywood's wildest dreams. The fundamental difference between *Tomorrow's Eve* and *Dogville*, however, as texts created by European subjects, is that the European subject himself is represented in Villiers' novel by the second major character in it, Lord Ewald, while in *Dogville* the European subject seems to shut himself outside the story, looking upon America without looking upon the self—a kind of repression that does not fail to point to the fact that this subject, just as Lord Ewald loves Hadaly, the mechanical android that represents the perfect romantic love, is himself in love with what ideological cinematic America represents.

Love, in Lacanian thought, is a coin that always carries aggressivity on its other side. Because love is of a "fundamentally narcissistic structure" (*Four Fundamental Concepts* 186), the object of love is both a confirmation of the lover's ego and a destabilization of that ego simultaneously. Because the lover always (mis)recognizes what he loves in the object of love, he tends to overload it with more than it can afford. Lacan sums this up in the following words: "I love you, but, because inexplicably I love in you something more than you—the *objet petit a*—I mutilate you" (268). Similarly, what the critique of America by the European subject seems to unconsciously say is: 'I love you, but, because inexplicably I love in you something more than you—the myth, the dream, the universal home, the unattainable, that which goes beyond the country, or, that which never reified/will never reify—I mutilate you.'

In other words, love is a letter which "always arrives at its destination"[4] because the addressee, as Žižek puts it, is "from the very beginning the sender himself" (*Enjoy Your Symptom* 13), and the content of the message is his own being. It emanates from the subject and is reflected back on the subject, precisely because it is the field where the ego most practices its favorite ritual, self-alienation, or, that first erotic relation with the self which establishes itself in the mirror stage. Lacan states that:

> There is a sort of structural crossroads here to which we must accommodate our thinking if we are to understand the nature of aggressivity in man and its relation with the formalism of his ego and his objects. It is in this erotic relation, in which the human individual fixes upon himself an image that alienates him from himself, that are to be found the energy and the form on which this organization of the passions that he will call his ego is based. (*Écrits: A Selection* 21)

It comes as no surprise that this love/hate relationship often produces indicative texts around objects of love that are never complete, and thus, they always leave the subject hanging perpetually from an illusion that Lacan names as the *objet petit a*. The mutilation is thus largely caused by the disappointment the subject suffers from first or repeated paranoiac (mis)encounters with the real, namely, in this case, that his imagined object of love is in fact devoid of romantic or sublime traits. It may be argued that *Dogville* can be interpreted simply as a work of bad conscience, yet, it seems that, at its unconscious core, it is a paranoiac work that *produces* this mis(encounter) by taking the agency of creating an image of cinematic America and attaining a kind of mastery over the creation to compensate for the unattainable imagined beloved which does not really exist—either as a perfect woman with no female *jouissance* or as a perfect universal home.

Notes

1. There is a female *jouissance*, as Lacan taught, that is "beyond the phallus" and it "belongs to that 'she' (*elle*) that doesn't exist and doesn't signify anything". It is an "enigmatic" *jouissance*. *On Feminine Sexuality, The Limits of Love and Knowledge: Encore, 1972–1973*, trans. with notes by Bruce Fink (New York and London: W.W. Norton & Company, 1998), pp. 74, 144. Frances Restuccia uses this Lacanian idea in her analysis of von Trier's *Breaking the Waves* to argue for the heroine's "hysterical/mystical faith in a (Lacanian) sexual relation [...] with God". 'Impossible Love in *Breaking the Waves*: Mystifying Hysteria', *Lacan and Contemporary Film*, eds Todd McGowan and Sheila Kunkle (New York: Other Press, 2004), p. 206.
2. Lacan defines the symptom as metaphor and desire as metonymy in his essay 'The Agency of the Letter in the Unconscious or Reason since Freud', *Écrits: A Selection*, trans. Alan Sheridan (London and New York: Routledge, 1989), p. 193.
3. For example, Horace Howard Furness Jr, in the *New Variorum Edition of Shakespeare: Macbeth* (New York: Dover Publications, 1963), p. 78.
4. Lacan states that "a letter always arrives at its destination" in his analysis of Baudelaire's translation of Edgar Allan Poe's *The Purloined Letter* because "the sender [...] receives from the receiver his own message in an inverted form". *Écrit: The First Complete Edition in English*, trans. Bruce Fink (New York and London: W.W. Norton and Company, 2006), p. 30.

Bibliography

Badley, Linda. *Lars von Trier*. Urbana, Chicago, Springfield: University of Illinois Press, 2010.

Brecht, Bertolt. *The Threepenny Opera*. Translated by Hugh MacDiarmid. London: Eyre Methuen, 1973.

Brecht, Bertolt. *The Good Person of Szechwan*. Translated by John Willett. London: Eyre Methuen, 1974.

Brecht, Bertolt. *The Resistible Rise of Arturo Ui: A Parable Play*. Translated by Ralph Manheim. London: Eyre Methuen, 1976.

Brecht, Bertolt. *Mother Courage and Her Children*. Translated by John Willett. London: Eyre Methuen, 1980.

Brooke, Nicholas. *The Tragedy of Macbeth—The Oxford Shakespeare*. Edited by Nicholas Brooke. Oxford and New York: Oxford University Press, 1990.

Conrad, Peter. *Imagining America*. London and Henley: Routledge and Kegan Paul, 1980.

Dickens, Charles, and Hablot Knight Browne. *The Life and Adventures of Martin Chuzzlewit*. London: Oxford University Press, 1951.

French, Marilyn. *Shakespeare's Division of Experience*. New York: Summit Books, 1981.

Freud, Sigmund. *The Origins of Religion*. Edited by Albert Dickson and translated from the German under the general editorship of James Strachey. Penguin Books, 1990.
Freud, Sigmund. 'The Character of Lady Macbeth'. *Macbeth*. Edited by Alan Sinfield. Hampshire and London: Macmillan, 1992.
Furness, Horace Howard, Jr. *A New Variorum Edition of Shakespeare: Macbeth*. New York: Dover Publications, 1963.
Gardiner, Michael. 'Bakhtin's Carnival: Utopia as Critique'. *Critical Studies. Vol. 3 No. 2—Vol. 4 No. 1/2*. Edited by Myriam Diaz-Diocaretz. Amsterdam and Atlanta, GA: Rodopi, 1993.
Hassan, Ihab. *Radical Innocence: Studies in the Contemporary American Novel*. Princeton, NJ: Princeton University Press, 1961.
Horkheimer, Max, and Theodor W. Adorno. *Dialectic of Enlightenment: Philosophical Fragments*. Edited by Gunzelin Schmid Noerr and translated by Edmund Jephcott. Palo Alto, CA: Stanford University Press, 2002.
Koutsourakis, Angelos. *Politics as Form in Lars von Trier: A Post-Brechtian Reading*. New York, London, New Delhi and Sydney: Bloomsbury, 2013.
Lacan, Jacques. *Écrits: A Selection*. Translated by Alan Sheridan. London and New York: Routledge, 1989.
Lacan, Jacques. *The Four Fundamental Concepts of Psycho-Analysis*. Edited by Jacques-Alain Miller and translated by Alan Sheridan. Penguin Books, 1994.
Lacan, Jacques. *On Feminine Sexuality, The Limits of Love and Knowledge: Encore, 1972–1973*. Translated and with notes by Bruce Fink. New York and London: W.W. Norton and Company, 1998.
Lacan, Jacques. *The Ethics of Psychoanalysis 1959–1960*. Edited by Jacques-Alain Miller and translated by Dennis Porter. London: Routledge, 1999.
Lacan, Jacques. *Écrit: The First Complete Edition in English*. Translated by Bruce Fink. New York and London: W.W. Norton and Company, 2006.
Lumholdt, Jan. *Lars von Trier: Interviews*. Mississippi, Jackson: University Press of Mississippi, 2003.
Lyon, James K. *Bertolt Brecht in America*. Princeton, NJ: Princeton University Press, 1980.
O'Connor, John. *Macbeth—William Shakespeare*. Harlow: Pearson Education Limited, 2003.
Restuccia, Frances L. 'Impossible Love in *Breaking the Waves*: Mystifying Hysteria'. *Lacan and Contemporary Film*. Edited by Todd McGowan and Sheila Kunkle. New York: Other Press, 2004.
Said, Edward W. 'The Other America'. *Al-Ahram Weekly Online*. Issue No. 630. 20–26 March 2003. Accessed 2 October 2005. http://weekly.ahram.org.eg/2003/630/focus.htm
Schepelern, Peter. 'The Making of an Auteur: Notes on the Auteur Theory and Lars von Trier'. *Visual Authorship: Creativity and Intentionality in Media*. Edited by Torben Grodal, Bente Larsen and Iben Thorving Laursen. Copenhagen: Museum Tusculanum Press, University of Copenhagen, 2005.

Shakespeare, William. *The Tragedy of Macbeth—The Oxford Shakespeare*. Edited by Nicholas Brooke. Oxford and New York: Oxford University Press, 1990.
Shakespeare, William. *Three Roman Plays*. Edited by Norman Sanders, Emrys Jones and G.R. Hibbard. London and New York: Penguin Books, 1994.
Shakespeare, William, and Kenneth Muir. *Macbeth*. London: Routledge, 1991.
Simons, Jan. *Playing the Waves: Lars von Trier's Game Cinema*. Amsterdam: Amsterdam University Press, 2007.
Sloterdijk, Peter. *Critique of Cynical Reason*. Translated by Michael Eldred. New York and London: Verso, 1988.
Sophocles. *Antigone; Oedipus the King; Electra*. Translated and edited by H.D.F. Kitto with an introduction and notes by Edith Hall. Oxford: Oxford University Press, 1994.
Stevenson, Jack. *Dogme Uncut: Lars von Trier, Thomas Vinterberg, and the Gang That Took on Hollywood*. California: Santa Monica Press, 2003.
Tocqueville, Alexis de. *Democracy in America*. Edited by J.P. Mayer and translated by George Lawrence. New York: HarperPerennial, 1988.
Villiers de l'Isle-Adam, Auguste, comte de. *Tomorrow's Eve*. Translated by Robert Martin Adams. Champaigne, IL: University of Illinois Press, 2001.
Walsh, Martin. *The Brechtian Aspect of Radical Cinema: Essays by Martin Walsh*. Edited by Keith M. Griffiths. London: British Film Institute Publishing, 1981.
Wood, Michael. *America in the Movies, or, "Santa Maria, It Had Slipped My Mind"*. New York: Columbia University Press, 1989.
Žižek, Slavoj. *The Plague of Fantasies*. London and New York: Verso, 1997.
Žižek, Slavoj. *Enjoy Your Symptom! Jacques Lacan in Hollywood and Out*. New York and London: Routledge, 2001.

Filmography

Breaking the Waves. Directed and written by Lars von Trier. Paris: Pathé, 2003.
Dogville. Directed and written by Lars von Trier. Hong Kong: Edko Films Ltd., 2005.
A Fistful of Dollars. Directed by Sergio Leone. Written by A. Bonzzoni, Victor Andrés Catena, Sergio Leone and Jaime Comas Gil. Los Angeles, CA: United Artists, 1964.
The Terminator. Directed by James Cameron. Written by James Cameron and Gale Anne Hurd. Los Angeles, CA: Orion Pictures, 1984.
Terminator 2: Judgment Day. Directed by James Cameron. Written by James Cameron and William Wisher, Jr. United States: Tri-Star Pictures, United Kingdom: Guild Film Distribution, 1991.
Terminator 3: Rise of the Machines. Directed by Jonathan Mostow. Written by John D. Brancato and Michael Ferris. Los Angeles, CA: Warner Bros, 2003.

CHAPTER 6

Manderlay: The Gift, Grace's Desire and the Collapse of Ideology

As a sequel to *Dogville*, von Trier's *Manderlay* deals primarily with what it perceives as American racism. It takes America's democratic ideal—that which is taught to the slaves of Manderlay by Grace—and reveals it as a "social fantasy", which is a notion that Žižek designates as a "necessary counterpart to the concept of antagonism". What illuminates this social antagonism, however, is Grace's personal experience with Timothy—her sexual fantasy fixing the racist divide in America's social structure, "masking its constitutive antagonism by the fullness of enjoyment" (*Interrogating the Real* 254). The enjoyment in (watching) *Manderlay* is precisely the enjoyment of the black body as a (cinematic) gift, as an object for the gaze. On this particular point, von Trier's film seems to be more or less in line with several Hollywood productions content-wise, regardless of its minimalist stylistics.

What is different about *Manderlay*, however, is that it takes the black body, through Grace's desire, on a Lacanian detour from sublime to soil, from fantasy to feces; in other words, from the Lacanian objet petit a to the gift. And, as a gift, the same black body loops back and transforms itself again into the objet petit a. It is at this point that the film goes beyond its racist discourse; even beyond gender difference. *Manderlay*, over and above dealing with the history of slavery in America and the black/white division, uses Grace's desire to reconsider the concept of human freedom through disturbing the viewer's common sense of the term in three particular scenes: the scene of Grace's dream in which we have no access to the dream images except through the narrator's voice; the scene in which

Timothy rapes Grace; and the scene in which Grace whips Timothy near the end of the film. In analyzing these three scenes, three notions will help to radically revise what we take as the common sense of freedom. These three notions are the gift, the object cause of desire, and fantasy. Accused of both misogyny and racism, it is particularly in the whipping scene that *Manderlay* paradoxically goes beyond both accusations, depicting the figure of Grace as ultimately a genderless subject perpetually hanging from an illusion that Lacan calls the objet petit a.

There seems little doubt about *Manderlay*'s hidden criticism with regard to America's policy of interventionism and 'democratization' in the Middle East, as many readers of the film perceive,[1] even though its director claims it has nothing to do with America's Middle Eastern policies.[2] But what is more interesting in Grace's personification of America in the film, over and above any political point, is the way the film plays ideology against the instinctual needs of the nether regions of Grace's body. Her restless sleep beside Wilma as she indulges in an onanistic fantasy is described by John Hurt's narrator in a way reminiscent of D.H. Lawrence's reading of Fenimore Cooper's character Eve Effingham who "had pinned herself down on the *Contrat Social*, and she was prouder of that pin through her body than of any mortal thing else. Her IDEAL. Her IDEAL of DEMOCRACY." America, in Lawrence's reading of it through its classical literature, just like Eve Effingham, "pushed a pin right through its own body, and on that pin it still flaps and buzzes and twists in misery" (49). Similarly, Hurt, explaining what the viewer sees on the screen, tells us that Grace "pressed herself onto the knot she had rapidly and instinctually formed by bunching her quilt. Whether it was pleasurable or painful is hard to tell, but she kept at it. It was beyond her control".

Initially, it can be argued that Grace's sexual fantasy does not seem to be about Timothy in particular. In the scene in which she passes by the public bath, Hurt's narrator exposes her secret thoughts about "black skin, male and black manhood" in its generality. It is precisely this generality that marks the phantasmal relationship between Grace and her object of desire as an imagined object. The situation is not simply that of an individual white woman admiring a 'proudly nigger' who displays a freedom of spirit usually attributed to free men, but that of a subject, in a Lacanian sense, and the objet petit a as the object-cause of desire. The subject, in Lacanian discourse, "has nothing to do with the subjective … nor does it have anything to do with the individual. The subject is in a strict sense an effect of the signifier". Grace's sexual fantasy is not only the site of an imagined object of desire but, more importantly, the site of a subjectivity whose very condition of existence is determined by nothing other than a linguistic gap, a void, that is there "before the individual, even before it exists as a living being" (*My Teaching* 79). A look at Grace's dream can help to elaborate this point.

In her dream, where her unconscious and the sexual urges of her lower body stratum take control, the viewer gets an interesting narrative description of her fantasy. Hurt's narrator tells us that Grace sees herself in "Southern climes" among listless men and women in exotic costumes and turbans and a "flock of Bedouin" who were "satisfying her with their noses". Even when Timothy appears in her dream, he is doubled; he is at once the "slave bearing wine, hands shaking" and the "Sheikh himself, whose authoritative hands tested the size of Grace's most intimate orifices". In a sense, Timothy appears in Grace's dream as both "Mansi" and "Munsi"; the slave who should properly tremble while serving his master, or "cry, shout and beg for mercy" while being flogged, and the authoritative Sheikh or master of the tribe whose authority, quite appropriately, does not and cannot exceed its only perceived function in Grace's dream, which is to "test the size of her most intimate orifices", in other words, to give her sexual pleasure just like all the other listless Bedouins and their noses.

Somehow, the phantasmal picture—made all the more powerful by narration without showing any part of Grace's dream on the screen—seems to be overwhelmed by exotic big hands and prominent noses. There can be either smudged faces or no faces in it. Even Timothy's face cannot but fade away in the presence of his shaky/authoritative hands. The Sheikh may be master in his own Oriental tribal world, but he is definitely no master in Grace's white and Western consciousness, even though the situation in the dream suggests that her desire is to be *enslaved* by a black Sheikh. For fantasy is not about the objectification of the Other; on the contrary, it is a "way for the subject to answer the question of what object they are for the Other" (Žižek, *Interrogating the Real* 58). This Other, in Grace's fantasy, assumes the place of the objet petit a in all its illusiveness and unattainability, hence, it has to be pinned down to something tangible yet not particular, personal, or detailed enough to assume an identity for itself and spoil the whole fantasy; it has to be somewhat general, somewhat undefined and unidentifiable. This 'something' in Grace's fantasy is "black skin" meticulously and elaborately framed as "black manhood".

The split in Timothy's image – slave and Sheikh, chameleon and proudly – serves to illustrate Grace's unconscious perception, which does not really care to distinguish between a slave and a Sheikh, provided they are both black. The ridiculous phonetic closeness between the two supposedly oppositional words, 'Mansi' and 'Munsi', seems to stress the point even further. Dr Hector, the cynical card shark, whom Grace greatly detests, seems to describe Grace's experience with Timothy in a "motto" that encapsulates it all: "They say the Mansi are better hung than the Munsi. Or, the Munsi are so up-stuck, but the Mansi, how they fuck!" It is as if Hector sees through her fantasy. It would be erratic to suggest that Grace desires Timothy, so she starts to fantasize about black manhood. It is her fantasy, in accordance with Lacan's definition of the concept, that "dominates the entire reality of desire" (*Other Side* 128–9). For the subject, insofar as he is dependent on the Other, "doesn't know what he wants, and it is the role of fantasy to tell him that, to 'teach' him to desire" (Žižek, *Interrogating the Real* 280).

In parallel with all the gifts that her unconscious presents to her in her dream—the exotic costumes, the dates, the hands and the noses—Grace's waking life experience in Manderlay is clearly marked by her perception of *herself* as a gift. She seems to "perceive herself as a gift to this Godforsaken place" (Mahmutovic). But one of *Manderlay*'s main questions is what to do exactly with a gift. Even the most basic of human rights, if perceived as a gift, immediately loses real value on account of assuming to be something it essentially cannot be. The gift is not just impossible; it is, according to Derrida, "*the* impossible" itself, "the very figure of the impossible" as it assumes a position in which it "must *keep* a relation of foreignness to the circle [of economics], a relation without relation of familiar foreignness" (*Given Time* 7). When Grace gives the blacks of Manderlay their freedom, they do not know what to do with it. They do know, however, how to express thanks, properly, by giving something in return; asking her to be their new Mam—a gesture that only means rejecting the gift of freedom, which, we can properly assert, is not there from the start.

The gift of freedom is not there from the start because, given and received as a gift, it is annulled by both the giver and receiver. As soon as the giver "intends to give, to pay himself with a symbolic recognition, to praise himself, to approve of himself, to gratify himself, to congratulate himself, to give back to himself symbolically the value of what he thinks he has given or what he is preparing to give", the gift is annulled. As soon as the receiver "perceives or receives it, if he or she keeps it as a gift, the gift is annulled" (14). The gift cannot be innocent; it cannot reside outside the law of symbolic exchange. That is why even Manderlay's blacks' rejection of the gift of freedom is expressed only through its return; by asking Grace to be their new Mam. So, whereas the gift is rejected, something is given in return as if it has been accepted. The symbolic exchange in this particular case makes the very acceptance/rejection of the gift of freedom indeterminable. The acceptance of it, which is evidenced by giving something in return, is immediately voided by nothing but the return gift itself, which carries the very rejection of the gift.

To Lacan, all gifts are "already symbols, in the sense that symbol means pact, and they are first and foremost signifiers of the pact they constitute as the signified; this is plainly seen in the fact that the objects of symbolic exchange […] are all destined to be useless" (*Écrits: The First Complete Edition* 225). That is why every gift in *Manderlay* seems to be functionless. Mam's notorious book as a "weighty written evidence" on the survival of slavery in the plantation is a useless gift. Freedom is a useless gift to Manderlay's blacks. Offering Grace the gift of being the new Mam only maddens her. In fact, Grace's problem with the concept of gift giving starts earlier than *Manderlay*; it starts at the end of *Dogville*. Her ultimate problem is that she does not really know what to do exactly with her father's gift of shared power. She is too anxious to use that power in a righteous way but discovers she simply can't.

Being the antithesis of the pragmatic gangster her father is—an antithesis of a politician on a larger scale—Grace does not know that the secret of power is to know that "power *does not exist*", as Baudrillard puts it (63). It is a secret which, according to Baudrillard, "also belongs to the great bankers, who know that money is nothing, that money does not exist; and it also belonged to the great theologians and inquisitors who knew that God does not exist, that God is dead. This gives them incredible superiority" (64). Grace's problem is that she recognizes the gift but does not recognize its emptiness, its nothingness; the fact that one can never use it satisfactorily in either a righteous or abusive way. The logic of the gift is extended further when the lawyer, Joseph, enforces it on the whites by drawing up "deeds of gift" for them to transfer the property to the former slaves in joint ownership. Joseph, literally, takes the gift from its pretentious position as something given outside the law of symbolic exchange or outside economic reason, which is impossible, to an exchange that is imposed. The assumption in all this is that the gift means or signifies sharing power, while in fact what *Manderlay* aims at from this work's perspective is to show that offering a gift and accepting a gift means that one is not at all questioning the assumed structure of power.

The question of what to do with a gift seems to reach even beyond the film's content to *Manderlay* itself as a cinematic production that leaves viewers at a loss as to what to do with it exactly, and how to react to it. Grace at one point declares with definite resolution: "Manderlay is a moral obligation", which means ending slavery in Manderlay, teaching the former slaves the principles of democracy, and putting whites and blacks on an equal footing constitute a moral obligation to her as one of the whites. Lars von Trier once said that "my main [female] characters are also built on my own person [...] this is my female side" (Badt).

Andrew Gordon even takes von Trier's identification with his female characters to the point of ruining the premiere of *Melancholia* at the Cannes Film Festival, at which his identification with the melancholic Justin compelled him to humiliate himself publicly by confessing to "sympathizing with Hitler" and declaring that he was a Nazi (Gordon). Therefore, adhering to the logic of the gift, it can be argued that von Trier himself also seems to claim that *Manderlay* is a moral obligation. While Grace wants to end slavery, he obviously wants the viewers to rethink America's history of black slavery and whether it still relates to its present. John Hurt's narrator at the end of the film says, "America was a many-faceted place, no doubt about it. But 'not ready' to accept black people? You really could not say that. America has proffered its hand, discreetly perhaps, but if anybody refused to see a helping hand ... he really only had himself to blame."

Yet, *Manderlay* is done in such a way as to destabilize any contented definition of what constitutes the moral, as well as impairing the viewer's common sense about certain master signifiers like freedom, power, democracy and civilization. The questions of 'What to do with freedom?', 'Who is free?' and 'Free from what?' are all problematic questions in *Manderlay* no matter from which main character's perspective they are posed. These questions apply to power as well. With all the power given to her, whatever changes Grace makes in Manderlay only lead her back to Mam's law, which has miraculously survived all her civilizing projects and finally transform Grace herself into a new Mam, with a whip. Her relationship with Timothy, from admiring his pride, to fantasizing about him, to letting him rape her in his own 'traditional' way, to flogging his black body mercilessly, only seems to establish her father's view that "however much [women] go on and on about civilization and democracy, sexy they ain't" and that "deep down inside, there isn't a woman alive who doesn't nurture these fantasies, whether they involve harems [or] being hunted through the jungle by torch-bearing natives".

The father's discourse, which gives no particularity to any 'native' as an individual, is obviously rejected by Grace, but it is also unconsciously repressed, entailing a Freudian return of the repressed in Grace's slips of the tongue, mistakes, fantasies and dreams. As Žižek puts it, "in our daily existence, we are immersed in 'reality' (structured-supported by the fantasy), and this immersion is disturbed by symptoms which bear witness to the fact that another repressed level of our psyche resists this immersion" (*In Defense* 329). Thus, Grace enthusiastically gives Jim a gift—another one of *Manderlay*'s gifts—to advance his painting talents but, embarrassingly, mistakes Jack for Jim, giving Timothy a chance to see through her white unconscious, which does not really care to differentiate much between the two brothers who are both black.

Even though Grace seems to expect words of thanks from the freed slaves in return for her gift, as her father shrewdly perceives, she does express her perception of freedom as no human-given gift, or, as common belief would put it, as a gift from God. Yet, freedom as a God-given gift still seems controversial if looked at from a Lacanian point of view. Perhaps the maxim of being 'born free' needs to be reconsidered. Is Man born free? And free from what? Isn't he born into a complete symbolic system that effectively shapes his destiny as Lacan asserts?[3] Doesn't he get raised thereafter by nothing but ideology? In her attempt to establish freedom, justice and democracy in Manderlay, Grace frees the slaves, imposes a communist ideal of wealth redistribution by drawing up "deeds of gift" for the whites to transfer the property to the former slaves in joint ownership, under the gun, and follows that with her lectures on the ideal of democracy. The two major political systems of modern history are applied, one after the other, in a rapid, righteous and, in a way, innocent manner to secure the founding principle of freedom.

The two political systems have precise definitions in Lacanian theory: communism is "a desire of/for the Other based upon justice in the redistributive sense of the word" and it requires "putting the desire of the Other in charge of a regime", while liberal democracy is "a desire of the Other based upon what they call freedom, resulting in talk with no effect" (*My Teaching* 48–9). The result of 'democracy', or, the "talk with no effect", is clear enough and it is criticized in writings as early as Shakespeare's *Coriolanus* whose hero defines political democracy as a "double worship ... where gentry, title, wisdom, cannot conclude but by the yea and no of general ignorance", resulting in a situation in which "nothing is done to purpose" (*Three Roman Plays* 567). It is unnecessary to say that both systems base themselves on principles which seem to be historically irreconcilable; namely, justice and freedom. What is interesting, however, is the implication of Lacan's "what they call freedom", which clearly points to being governed by a certain regime still.

Freedom is not only opposed to materialist, redistributive, authoritarian and communist justice; freedom itself is not free enough. Grace, for example, teaches the blacks how to vote as the first lesson in democracy's freedom of choice. It goes without saying, however, that the freedom of choice does not include choosing to be a racist, or, as actually happens in Manderlay, choosing to be a slave. As Žižek puts it, freedom of choice in liberal democratic societies is about "going on making our small choices, 'reinventing ourselves' thoroughly, on condition that these choices do not seriously disturb the social and ideological balance" (*On Belief* 122). Reminiscent of D.W. Griffith's *Birth of a Nation*, in which the freed blacks are shown as misfits in garments not their own at the height of their power in the South, *Manderlay* portrays the former slaves as people who do not know how to use the democratic ideal; they can only abuse it by literal identification with its general rules. Thus, they vote to execute old Wilma for stealing Claire's food at night, basing the death sentence on an assumption that, if not for the lack of food, the pneumonia-stricken child would have lived.

They have gone from being slaves lacking control over their own lives to free 'decision makers' in the Adornian sense of the word. Criticizing Heidegger's "freedom of decision" and Kierkegaard's "right living", which is "defined entirely in terms of decision" as what testifies to humanity or what constitutes its "authentic completion" in existential philosophy, Adorno shows how "the speakers for existence move toward a mythology, even when they don't notice it. Self-possession, unlimited and narrowed by no heteronomy, easily converges with freedom" (*Jargon of Authenticity* 104–5). At its best, freedom, in a "Deleuze-Hegelian formulation" suggested by Žižek, "is not simply a free act that, out of nowhere, starts a new causal link, but rather a retroactive act of endorsing which link/sequence of necessities will determine me" (*Organs Without Bodies* 100). The execution of Wilma is precisely that "retroactive act" by which the blacks of Manderlay 'choose' or make a 'decision' under the new democracy established by Grace and her father's gangsters in order to determine who they are or forge for themselves a new identity.

Freedom is not freedom from racism, and democracy does not guarantee freedom from racist ideologies. One of the most intelligent scenes in *Manderlay* is that in which Grace penalizes the whites by painting their faces in black and forcing them to serve the blacks—a penalty that is obviously more offensive to the blacks themselves, since it suggests that the color 'black' is a degradation, a punishment in itself. Again, the scene seems to be reminiscent of *Birth of a Nation*, a film that represents black Americans with hardly any black cast in it, since almost all the black characters are played by white actors with black-painted faces. As an anti-Hollywood figure, Lars von Trier's scene cannot be innocent of acute mockery of American cinema itself.

Though it belongs to a certain historical era that seems to have nothing to do with the present, Griffith's *Birth of a Nation*—with its racist content and an aesthetic form which favors the color white over the color black—does have a long-lasting ideologico-political effect that still manifests in the general, not-so-bright characterization of black Americans in Hollywood films. Films which do their best to put black and white on an equal footing by showing how the white hero cannot really save the day without his 'black brother'—like the *Die Hard* series, for example—still always put the black American in second place. Quentin Tarantino's *Pulp Fiction*, which might be Hollywood's best attempt to put black and white in the same melting pot (the black hero even appears in it as having more intellect, professionalism and composure than his white counterpart), had nevertheless to get the black gangster sodomized by the white cop in a mordant shot that seems to stand out in the film, no matter how quickly the black victim is saved by another white. So, the black is still both victimized and saved by the white.

On the other hand, the number of films and TV series produced in recent years with all-black casts seems to indicate that the white-black division somehow could not be cinematically bridged, after all, and had to be finally lived with or even reinforced by separating white films from black films. It can be argued, then, that *Birth of a Nation* is not just a film about the birth of a nation that needed to segregate black Americans in a certain way in a specific historical era. *Birth of a Nation* itself as a cinematic production seems to be the birth of a certain cinematic white America that is apologetic and racist at the same time towards black Americans. It is precisely that cinematic white America that is ridiculed by *Manderlay*'s scene in which an attempt to correct the wrong does nothing but more wrong.

In fact, the film's overall content also suggests that any attempt to correct the wrong done to the blacks by slavery through any kind of symbolic compensation or any 'gift'—including how blacks are portrayed in cinematic productions—will do nothing but more wrong. Mam's law survives.

There is something in it similar to Kafka's law in "Vor dem Gesetz" ("Before the Law") (*Metamorphosis* 197–8) in the sense that there can be no escape from it; it is prohibition and is itself prohibited. It prohibits a lot of things that shouldn't be done. It is itself prohibited by nothing but its imagined stature and by being too easily accessible and known to almost everyone.

On her deathbed, Mam requests that Grace burn the book in which Manderlay's racist law is written. Grace refuses to do so and, on her way out of Mam's bedroom, tells Wilhelm that "there is a weighty written evidence concealed in this very room", to be used when the former slaves press charges against Mam's family. How ridiculous this must sound to Wilhelm since he is the one who wrote Mam's law and it is hardly 'concealed' since most of Manderlay's inhabitants know about it. "The gate to the law remains open as ever" (197) and the staged prohibition is not prohibiting anything. Mam's law, or something like it, still survives no matter how many films are produced with an aim of symbolically compensating the blacks for what has been done to them, precisely because of the problems the notion of gift raises. The symbolic compensation in the form of films that glorify the blacks or tell the story of slavery by way of a critique of it, in any form or according to any school of thought, is accepted and rejected at once. Perhaps the difficulty von Trier faced in casting the black characters of *Manderlay* speaks for that.[4]

An early scene in *Manderlay* illustrates the importance as well as the ludicrousness of gift giving and symbolic exchange as such. After freeing the slaves, Grace waits in the car, and her father correctly guesses that she is expecting to be thanked for her gift of freedom to the slaves—implying that, since she expects something in return, she does not really believe freedom is their natural right, and that no gift is a free gift. The dialogue that follows between her and Timothy, however, is marked by his ingratitude and absolute coldness:

Timothy: When we were slaves, we were not required to offer thanks for our supper and for the water we drank and the air we breathed.
Grace: Nobody needs to say thank you, but …
Timothy: But what? You mean there is something you think we are to be thankful for?
Grace: I didn't mean 'but', I meant 'and'… There is no reason to be thankful to anything as natural as your freedom … I am the first to apologize for everything you and your people have been subjected to … See those gates: they should have been unlocked seventy years ago.

Timothy:	Only seventy years ago? But before that, of course, they were completely justified.
Grace:	No ... no, no, no, you misunderstand me ... Hm ... What can I say?
Timothy:	You need to say nothing at all.

This is a dialogue which shows the impasse that takes place when one participant in it does not adhere to the rule of symbolic exchange which decrees that "the symbolic debt has to be repaid" (Žižek, *Enjoy Your Symptom* 16). Grace's first unfinished sentence is meant to say 'nobody needs to say thank you but we have to keep the appearances of exchanging gifts, or empty words'. Its equivalent in America's political discourse with regard to freeing the Iraqis from their dictatorial oppressor is 'there is no reason to be thankful for anything as natural as your freedom but just give us the oil for free'. Grace's position in this dialogue is that of the subject of symbolic exchange whose symbolic act, in Žižekan thought, is "best conceived of as the purely formal, self-referential, gesture of the self-assertion of one's subjective position (*On Belief* 84). Timothy, clearly seeing how her position and the exchange she expects from him is meant to "conceal [...] the abyss of the Otherness that no sacrifice could appease – that is, with which no relationship of exchange is possible (Žižek, *Enjoy your Symptom* 58), does his best to cut it short.

When she stammers "no, no, you misunderstand me ... what can I say?" he tells her "you need to say nothing at all". Symbolic exchange is precisely about the human ability to mis(understand), to use the gift of pretense which humans, in fact, cannot communicate without. As Lacan puts it: "You are in the presence of a subject insofar as what he says and does—they're the same thing—can be supposed to have been said and done to deceive you, with all the dialectic that that comprises, up to and including that he should tell the truth so that you believe the contrary" (*Psychoses* 37). The problem that Timothy's last sentence poses for Grace in this 'dialogue'—if one can still call it that—is not human, graceful silence when one realizes that the wrong done cannot be in any way corrected, that is, silence which still carries a certain message, but the *inhuman* demand that nothing at all should be said or communicated in any form. Perhaps even color has nothing to do with this if one equates Timothy of *Manderlay* with Chuck of *Dogville*. In spite of the differences between the two characters, they seem to share the disbelief in gifts and symbolic exchange. They both believe only in the master-slave zero equation of power.

Out of *Manderlay*'s characters, however, it is Dr Hector who sees most clearly through the pretense of symbolic exchange. He tells Grace: "I do more than play, I cheat." Dr Hector is also a racist cheater; he cheats the Negroes to keep them indebted to the Whites. His statement is made in such a matter-of-fact way, as if cheating is the most normal business, since this is what humans do every day just by communicating via the medium of language. This is precisely why Lacan once stated that he prefers the word "colloquium" over "dialogue", since he saw that "being in dialogue is one of the most enormous pretensions of our times" (*My Teaching* 59), assuming erringly that "the essential effect of speech is to communicate, when in fact the effect of the signifier is to call forth in the subject the dimension of the signified" (*Anxiety* 285). Grace, however, arrives at the epitome of her personal repayment of the symbolic debt when she apologizes for "everything you and your people have been subjected to". This is the most ridiculous of all her statements. It is as if the experience she went through before, in Dogville, is repeating itself and, again, she makes herself responsible for a collective guilt—a Christ-like sacrifice which her father sees as sheer arrogance or as a sacrifice of herself primarily for herself in order to maintain some sort of ethical standards unattainable by others.

In spite of accusations of both misogyny and racism, which cannot but be true to a certain extent, von Trier's *Manderlay* problematizes both notions. Grace, unlike in *Dogville*, is in a position of power from the start to the end. Even though she ends up a prisoner in Manderlay, as she was in Dogville, this does not last for long and she manages to escape after giving Timothy a heated flogging. The flogging scene, which constitutes the film's denouement, is far more erotic than the one which features at its climax: the scene in which Timothy makes love to, or, perhaps, rapes Grace. The latter seems to stage more of a cultural racist encounter than a sexual one. The encounter in fact illustrates nothing but the disappointment in the exotic black body and black manhood as an imagined objet petit a. At the heart of this disappointment lies the problem of culture as a characteristically neurotic phenomenon, as the major sign which dominates the scene is nothing but a cultural message.

By displaying a cultural code, the subject sends a message to the other, which means that he turns *himself* into a signifier. Based on this, it can be argued that human culture is by definition neurotic, or, even more precisely, that neurosis is in fact the very condition of culture. Lacan says that the neurotic subject not only identifies himself in language, he loses his own being in the signifying chain; he transforms himself into a signifier and becomes language (*Psychoses* 155). The Neurotic phenomenon thus seems to be inherent in culture since the 'normal' human subject does transform himself or herself into a signifier on daily basis. Transforming oneself into a signifier maintains the whole system of symbolic exchanges that define one's daily life and regulate all one's relations with others.

Timothy's white handkerchief becomes that cultural code/sign; a cultural message—formerly unintelligible to the viewer and now appalling—that carries love and rape at once. Covering Grace's face is not only supposed to prevent her from seeing her object of desire—the black body; it also protects him from her gaze, cutting off the possibility of any communication with her as another human being and dealing with her only as a dehumanized white body to be penetrated with a vengeance. Whether her subsequent screams mean great pleasure, pain, fear, or all three of them, is left for the viewer to speculate on. What is certain, however, in this scene, is that Grace has got what she wished for, what she fantasized about, which is precisely to swap roles with Timothy and become a black man's sex-slave, or, to be enslaved by none other than someone who is perceived as a slave; in other words, to offer her body as a gift or, more precisely, to return the gift she perceives as the black body that has always already been offered by default as an object for the gaze by the effect of slavery.

Yet, the problem of her sexual intercourse with Timothy is that she comes face to face with the core of her dream, the real of her own desire to become his slave; and, as Lacan teaches, coming face to face with the real of one's own desire is traumatic. To illustrate this point, Lacan discusses Freud's analysis of the dream of the ill-fated father who saw his burning child in his dream only to wake up and discover that the corpse of his child was actually burning (Freud, *The Interpretation of Dreams* 652–4, 681–2, 725–6). The dream was the illustration of the guilt of the father who unconsciously wished for the death of the burdensome sick child; a wish he couldn't even admit to himself in waking life. Lacan concludes that the dream is "essentially [...] an act of homage to the missed reality—the reality that can no longer produce itself except by repeating itself endlessly, in some never attained awakening" (*The Four Fundamental Concepts* 58–9). A dream, thus, is a compensation for that which cannot be articulated or symbolized in waking life thanks to the metonymic structure of desire.

"The core of our fantasy is unbearable to us" (Žižek, *Organs Without Bodies* 88) because at the core of fantasy is the utter voidness of the subject, or, that which the subject cannot deal with on the level of consciousness, which is a domain marked by ideologies and political correctness.

The wish to become a sex-slave to Timothy is not only in discord with Grace's project of eliminating slavery, but also touches upon the Žižekan idea that "fantasy, at its most elementary, becomes inaccessible to the subject; it is this inaccessibility that makes the subject 'empty' ($)" (*Interrogating the Real* 108). Fantasy's inaccessibility is based upon its being an answer to the anxious "Chè vuoi?" (Lacan, *Écrits: A Selection* 345–6) question, by which the subject finds a way to relieve itself from the anxiety of the question, in other words, by creating a fantasy around the desire of the Other with regard to the subject; what the Other wants from the subject, or what it wants the subject to be.

Grace's fantasy inscribes "male and black manhood" as the unattainable objet petit a. She is unable to attain Timothy as her sexual partner, who is the Other to her, except inasmuch as 'Timothy', in the strict sense of "male and black manhood", is the cause of her desire. It is appropriate, convenient and poetically just to imagine that the desire of the Other, who happens to be a slave in this case, is to enslave the subject, who will of course gladly play at being the slave of the Other, since this seems to be a realization of the subject's fantasy; in other words, the Other's imagined desire (mis)read as the subject's own desire. The complication is that once the subject comes close to the realization of desire, (s)he comes face to face with the real of that desire, which is not only utter disappointment at the reality of the *other* as devoid of any sublime traits, but, over and above this disappointment, the realization that the desiring subject himself is a barred subject; a subject whose very intangibility is made out of the same fantasy that inscribes the Other as the object cause of desire; a fantasy whose Lacanian formula, according to Žižek, clearly illustrates the "relationship between the *empty, nonphenomenal subject* and the *phenomena that remain inaccessible to the subject*" (*Interrogating the Real* 108).

Black slavery is taken to its ultimate limits by showing a black man being whipped by a white woman. While *Dogville* ends by wiping out the mostly white inhabitants of the township, *Manderlay* 'properly' ends with flogging a black man. On the surface of it, while both American whites and blacks are demonized respectively, the whites seem to at least be afforded the respect of being killed by live ammunition, while the black slaves are portrayed as not even worth killing. It is enough to flog one of them and make an example out of him. No matter how much reviewers and critics praise *Manderlay* as thought-provoking art-house cinema, no matter how much its discourse can be argued to work against Hollywood's ideological racism, it remains an obvious fact for the common viewer that the ultimate 'gift' that *Manderlay* presents to the viewer is the black body itself as cinematic material, as an exotic body made different by cinema, or as a sexuality made either too monstrously potent or too impotently supine, or, figuratively speaking, as a massive yet semi-erect penis ("the lesser of two evils"[5]). What to do with it? The scene which stages the film's "apocalyptic denouement" (Cunliffe) seems to provide the only available answer from an acutely Hollywoodian position – flog it!—which is precisely in accordance with not only the history of slavery in America but the history of American cinema itself, which produced countless scenes in which a black body is flogged.

Manderlay's flogging, however, seems to disorient the torturer much more than the tortured. Playing Mam, or actually being a Mam, Grace decides to finally put the blacks of Manderlay where they seem to prefer:

> Timothy, you can stop being proud and silent. Cry and shout, and beg for mercy. Let the Mansi you are, be the Mansi who you despise so much. And it is that hatred, Timothy and the rest of you, that hatred against yourselves, that you will never make me accept. You are a cheat of the lowest kind, and Wilhelm and all of you who follow him are nothing but traitors to your race. I hope that your fellow Negroes one day discover your betrayal and punish you for it. You make me sick.

She drops the whip at this point and starts to leave. Timothy, however, ultimately dissatisfied with this conclusion, tells her: "Sure you got it right, Miss Grace. Most likely, it is impossible to revile us Negroes enough. But what I don't get is why it makes you so angry ... Aren't you forgetting something? You made us."

This last statement, in which Timothy quotes what she herself says at an earlier stage in the film, infuriates her, so, she picks up the whip again and starts lashing his black body frantically. It is clear that it is at this moment—and not at any other, either in *Manderlay* or in *Dogville*—that Grace's power and self-confidence totally and unequivocally collapse, taking down with them all the ideological fantasies of freedom, equality, democracy and sacrifice. Timothy's affront is in its essence a Baudrillardian challenge, a "challenge to power to be power, power of the sort that is total, irreversible, without scruple, and with no limit to its violence". Baudrillard states that "it is in facing this unanswerable challenge that power starts to break up" (60-1). In fact, power has already begun to break up earlier when she orders Timothy to "cry and shout and beg for mercy", like Verdi's Egyptian princess, Amneris, giving her Ethiopian captive, Aïda, the impossible order to tremble as the slave she is: "Trema! o rea schiava!" (Tremble! O thou slave!) (*Aïda*), which is categorically an impossible demand. Grace's physical answer to Timothy's "unanswerable challenge" to power—her violent whipping of him, watched by her smiling father and mistaken for a real change in her nature that finally enables her to put the gift of power to some use—is clearly powerless.

Her frantic acting-out seems to foresee another equally important scene in von Trier's *Melancholia* in which the heroine mercilessly yet *helplessly* beats her horse in order to vent her anger over trying to change a situation that cannot be changed. This outrageous acting-out should not be understood in terms of 'Grace transgressing over her own ethics and belief in the equality between the races'. If that were the case, the scene of whipping Timothy would have been shot differently, with a different attitude (perhaps more like inflicting punishment with a matter-of-fact abandonment as, for example, when she shoots Tom in the head in *Dogville*). Grace, in *Manderlay*, does not undergo the kind of elemental change she undergoes in *Dogville's* final chapter. Her transgression here is effectively a demonstration on her *inability to transgress*.

She is exposed by Timothy because he is the one slave who showed her, practically, that she, like other whites, is incapable of really loving black people. What she loved in him is his pride, the fact that he already acts like a free man. Marc De Kesel writes that "what Grace loves in Timothy is first of all that he is, so to say, of her kind. He is free like she is free. And he, too, is willing to fight for it" (15). She did not love him as one of the blacks. It is not only that Grace's earlier perception of Timothy was distorted by her desire to see him as number one (proud and admired) while he was never actually anything but seven (chameleon and despised). One and seven are precisely the same in her unconscious. Her dream clearly shows that.

What happens in the flogging scene, therefore, is much more disturbing to her, the torturer, than to Timothy, the tortured, since it is at this moment that her dream comes true for the second time, and she actually sees out there what is hidden in her unconscious, namely, that Timothy the Mansi and Timothy the Munsi are one and the same; the moment he is exposed as a chameleon is the moment in which he demonstrates real pride and takes the whipping stolidly without any trembling. It is not surprising that, out of Mam's, or more precisely Wilhelm's, seven descriptive categories of slaves, it is the chameleon, who can transform himself into exactly what the beholder wants to see, that describes the human condition as such, since the ideal ego is based on nothing but anxiously posing and imaginatively answering the "Chè vuoi?" (Lacan, *Écrits: A Selection* 345–6) question with regard to the desire of the Other (what does the

Other want of me?), which signals an incomprehension on the part of the subject as to the desire of the Other. In short, the moment of Timothy's exposure as a chameleon *exposes Grace* as a chameleon.

Over and above her desperation, which comes out of knowing too well that her flogging of Timothy only throws her own failure in Manderlay into sharp relief, Grace's flogging is at a deeper level directed to the phantasmal object cause of desire, which, at a moment of clarity, seems less than what she previously imagined it to be. As a slave, Timothy's only truth, in Grace's unconscious, corresponds with that of the hysteric in Lacan's discourse who "has to be the object a in order to be desired" (*Other Side* 176). What Grace is angry about—to risk an answer to Timothy's question—what she is helplessly whipping, is the very inaccessibility of her own fantasy, the un-attainability of the objet petit a; the black body symbolizing male and black manhood, a different kind of sexuality as she imagined it; in other words, something which does not exist. The scene can in fact be seen as a visual transliteration of Lacan's famous statement: "I love you, but, because inexplicably I love in you something more than you—the *objet petit a*—I mutilate you" (*Four Fundamental Concepts* 268).

And, because fantasy "does not only conceal the horror of the real, it also creates what it purports to conceal" (Žižek, *Žižek Reader* 92), what is at stake for Grace is not only an unattainable object, but her own subjectivity, since it is around that illusive object that the subject always seeks to know *itself* beyond what is mandated by the symbolic order; beyond being an "effect of the signifier" (Lacan, *My Teaching* 79). Grace, in the flogging scene, may be punishing one of the blacks who flatly rejected her gift of freedom and democracy, but more importantly, she is also hitting out at the very nothingness of her own subjectivity. It is a moment in which she realizes that her previous sexual fantasy about Timothy was not only simply her personal scenario through which she imagined fixing America's historical social antagonism. It was not even her personal scenario, by which she imagined attaining an unattainable or nonexistent object. It was always already what *she* as a subject is made of, the very core of her being as nonbeing, namely, a scenario which inscribes the Other as the object cause of desire. In this scenario, it is not simply that the objet petit a is the subject's illusive creation; it is the subject itself, in all its fictitiousness, that hangs perpetually from the illusion that the petit a is; therefore, the subject's very existence becomes questionable. The creator diminishes in front of her creation and perceives herself as a mere side effect of it. It is precisely at this moment that von Trier's *Manderlay* goes beyond its own racist discourse and that the figure of Grace herself, as a desiring, genderless subject, becomes the very collapse of ideology.

Like *Dogville*, which ends with a series of photographs presumably pointing to America's social injustices, *Manderlay* ends in the same way with photographs particularly about Black American misery. The series of images ends beautifully with an image of a black man cleaning the gigantic white marble statue of Abraham Lincoln, which fades out with the last sound. Commenting on the first scene of Chaplin's *City Lights*, Žižek writes:

> The tramp assumes [...] a role of stain in the picture: in front of a large audience, the mayor of the city unveils a new monument; when he pulls off the white cover, the surprised audience discovers the tramp, sleeping calmly in the lap of the gigantic statue [...] the tramp is thus an object of a gaze aimed at something or somebody else [...] as soon as the audience becomes aware of the mistake—he turns into a disturbing stain one tries to get rid of as quickly as possible. (*Enjoy Your Symptom* 4)

The last image of *Manderlay* shows a black man in a more or less similar situation to the tramp. Here, however, he is overshadowed by a gigantic white statue that particularly connotes American ideology, symbolizing America's greatest moral turning point, its abolition of slavery, the modernization of its economy, and assassinated tolerance all at once. But, whereas Chaplin's tramp sleeps calmly in the lap of the statue, offering nothing to society and tarnishing its ideological image with his "disturbing" presence, the black American worker adds a new dimension: *he cleans the very image that he stains with his presence*. Without his presence, without this black 'stain', American ideology would immediately lose its bearings and collapse. The legacy of Lincoln himself would be less significant. The black body, as an American cinematic gift, functions in the same way. Gazed at, often admired, often humiliated, occasionally flogged, oversexed and undersexed all at once, it is just as imagined and "impossible" (Derrida, *Given Time* 7) as the gift.

Notes

1. Like Adnan Mahmutovic in 'Lars von Trier's Gift', *Under the Midnight Sun*—Reviews, accessed 2 January 2014, http://undermidnightsun.wordpress.com/2009/01/21/lars-von-triers-gift-by-adnan-mahmutovic, Eric Hynes in 'Manderlay: Examination in 9 Parts', *Reverse Shot*, accessed 30

March 2014, http://www.reverseshot.com/article/manderlay, Tim Grierson in 'Manderlay: American Racism is Alive and Well', *The Simon*, accessed 14 February 2014, http://www.thesimon.com/magazine/articles/bias/01079_manderlay_american_racism_alive_well.html, and Jesse Hicks in 'Manderlay (2005)', *PopMatters*, accessed 30 March 2014, http://www.popmatters.com/review/manderlay-2006.
2. Lars von Trier mentions that he wrote the film before the Iraq War in an interview with Stefan Grissemann entitled 'Torture is Fine', *Film Comment*, accessed 10 January 2014, http://www.filmcomment.com/article/lars-von-trier-interview-manderlay.
3. In what seem to be his most fatalistic statements, Lacan asserts that symbols "envelop the life of man with a network so total that they join together those who are going to engender him 'by bone and flesh' before he comes into the world; so total that they bring to his birth, along with the gifts of the stars, if not with the gifts of the fairies, the shape of his destiny". 'The Function and Field of Speech and Language in Psychoanalysis', *Écrit: The First Complete Edition in English*, trans. Bruce Fink (New York and London: W.W. Norton & Company, 2006), p. 231.
4. Lars von Trier mentions that casting American actors for *Manderlay*'s black parts was "extremely difficult" in his interview with Stefan Grissemann, 'Torture is Fine', *Film Comment*, accessed 10 January 2014, http://www.filmcomment.com/article/lars-von-trier-interview-manderlay. Mette Hjort writes that the "ideas that [*Manderlay*] communicates [...] through its narrative [and] its acting styles and costumes were seen by actors as likely to give offense. This was the case for those actors who declined roles in the film (Sydney Poitier and Harry Belafonte) as well as for those who ultimately agreed to be in it". 'The Problem with Provocation: On Lars von Trier, Enfant Terrible of Danish Art Film', *Kinema: A Journal for Film and Audiovisual Media*, accessed 2 December 2013, http://www.kinema.uwaterloo.ca/article.php?id=492andfeature.
5. Wilhelm, one of the main black characters in *Manderlay* and the actual writer of Mam's law, which guaranteed the prolongation of slavery on the plantation for 70 years after its official abolition, describes the blacks' choice of slavery over freedom in a society that is "not ready" to accept them as free men as the "lesser of two evils".

Bibliography

Adorno, Theodor W. *The Jargon of Authenticity*. Translated by Knut Tarnowski and Frederic Will. London and New York: Routledge Classics, 2003.

Badt, Karin. 'At War with Myself: A Word with Lars von Trier at Cannes 2005'. *Bright Lights Film Journal* 49 (August 2005). Accessed 1 April 2014. http://brightlightsfilm.com/49/trieriv.php#.UzrATUewrDc

Baudrillard, Jean. *Forget Foucault*. Translated by Nicole Dufrense. Los Angeles, CA: Semiotext(e), 2007.
Cunliffe, Philip. 'Manderlay: The Danger of Do-gooding'. *Spiked-culture*. Accessed 21 February 2014. http://www.spiked-online.com/Articles/0000000CAFF9.htm
Derrida, Jacques. *Given Time. I, Counterfeit Money*. Translated by Peggy Kamuf. Chicago: University of Chicago Press, 1992.
Freud, Sigmund. *The Interpretation of Dreams*. Edited by Angela Richards. Translated and edited by James Strachey with the assistance of Alan Tyson. London and New York: Penguin Books, 1991.
Gordon, Andrew. The Bride of Melancholia. *Psy Art*, 7 September 2012. Accessed 20 July 2013. http://www.psyartjournal.com/article/show/gordon-the_bride_of_melancholia
Grierson, Tim. 'Manderlay: American Racism is Alive and Well'. *The Simon*. Accessed 14 February 2014. http://www.thesimon.com/magazine/articles/bias/01079_manderlay_american_racism_alive_well.html
Grissemann, Stefan. 'Torture is Fine'. *Film Comment*. Accessed 10 January 2014. http://www.filmcomment.com/article/lars-von-trier-interview-manderlay
Hicks, Jesse. 'Manderlay (2005)'. *PopMatters*. Accessed 30 March 2014. http://www.popmatters.com/review/manderlay-2006
Hjort, Mette. 'The Problem with Provocation: On Lars von Trier, Enfant Terrible of Danish Art Film'. *Kinema: A Journal for Film and Audiovisual Media*. Accessed 2 December 2013. http://www.kinema.uwaterloo.ca/article.php?id=492andfeature
Hynes, Eric. 'Manderlay: Examination in 9 Parts'. *Reverse Shot*. Accessed 30 March 2014. http://www.reverseshot.com/article/manderlay
Kafka, Franz. *Metamorphosis and Other Stories*. Translated by Michael Hofmann. London and New York: Penguin, 2007.
Kesel, Marc De. 'Journey between Mirrors'. Accessed 11 February 2014. http://marcdekesel.weebly.com/uploads/2/4/4/4/24446416/made_-_on_lars_von_trier_manderlay.pdf
Lacan, Jacques. *Écrits: A Selection*. Translated by Alan Sheridan. London and New York: Routledge, 1989.
Lacan, Jacques. *The Four Fundamental Concepts of Psycho-Analysis*. Edited by Jacques-Alain Miller and translated by Alan Sheridan. Penguin Books, 1994.
Lacan, Jacques. *The Psychoses 1955–1956*. Edited by Jacques-Alain Miller and translated by Russell Grigg. New York and London: W.W. Norton and Company, 1997.
Lacan, Jacques. *Écrit: The First Complete Edition in English*. Translated by Bruce Fink. New York and London: W.W. Norton and Company, 2006.
Lacan, Jacques. *The Other Side of Psychoanalysis*. Translated and with notes by Russell Grigg. New York and London: W.W. Norton and Company, 2007.
Lacan, Jacques. *My Teaching*. Translated by David Macey. London and New York: Verso, 2008.

Lacan, Jacques. *Anxiety*. Edited by Jacques-Alain Miller and translated by A. Rae Price. Cambridge: Polity Press, 2014.
Lawrence, D.H. *Studies in Classic American Literature*. Harmondsworth: Penguin Books, 1977.
Mahmutovic, Adnan. 'Lars von Trier's Gift'. *Under the Midnight Sun*—Reviews. Accessed 2 January 2014. http://undermidnightsun.wordpress.com/2009/01/21/lars-von-triers-gift-by-adnan-mahmutovic
Shakespeare, William. *Three Roman Plays*. Edited by Norman Sanders, Emrys Jones, and G.R. Hibbard. London and New York: Penguin Books, 1994.
Verdi, Giuseppe, and Antonio Ghislanzoni. *Aïda: In Full Score*. New York: Dover, 1989.
Žižek, Slavoj. *The Žižek Reader*. Edited by Elizabeth Wright and Edmond Wright. Oxford and Malden, MA: Blackwell Publishing, 1999.
Žižek, Slavoj. *Enjoy Your Symptom! Jacques Lacan in Hollywood and Out*. New York and London: Routledge, 2001.
Žižek, Slavoj. *On Belief*. London and New York: Routledge, 2001.
Žižek, Slavoj. *Interrogating the Real*. Edited by Rex Butler and Scott Stephens. London and New York: Continuum, 2006.
Žižek, Slavoj. *In Defense of Lost Causes*. London and New York: Verso, 2009.
Žižek, Slavoj. *Organs Without Bodies: On Deleuze and Consequences*. London and New York: Routledge Classics, 2012.

Filmography

The Birth of a Nation. Directed by D.W. Griffith. Written by Thomas F. Dixon, Jr, D.W. Griffith and Frank E. Woods. Los Angeles, CA: Epoch Film, 1915.
City Lights: A Comedy Romance in Pantomime. Directed and written by Charles Chaplin. Burbank, CA: MK2 Editions, 2003.
Die Hard. Directed by John McTiernan. Screenplay by Jeb Stuart and Steven E. de Souza. Los Angeles, CA: 20th Century Fox, 1988.
Die Hard 2: Die Harder. Directed by Renny Harlin. Screenplay by Steven E. de Souza and Doug Richardson. Los Angeles, CA: 20th Century Fox, 1990.
Die Hard with a Vengeance. Directed by John McTiernan. Written by Roderick Thorp and Jonathan Hensleigh. Los Angeles, CA: 20th Century Fox, 1995.
Dogville. Directed and written by Lars von Trier. Hong Kong: Edko Films Ltd., 2005.
Manderlay. Directed and written by Lars von Trier. Delmar, CA: IFC Films, Distributed by Genius Entertainment, 2005.
Melancholia. Directed and written by Lars von Trier. Hong Kong: Edko Films Ltd., 2011.
Pulp Fiction. Directed and written by Quentin Tarantino. Burbank, CA: Miramax Home Entertainment, 1994.

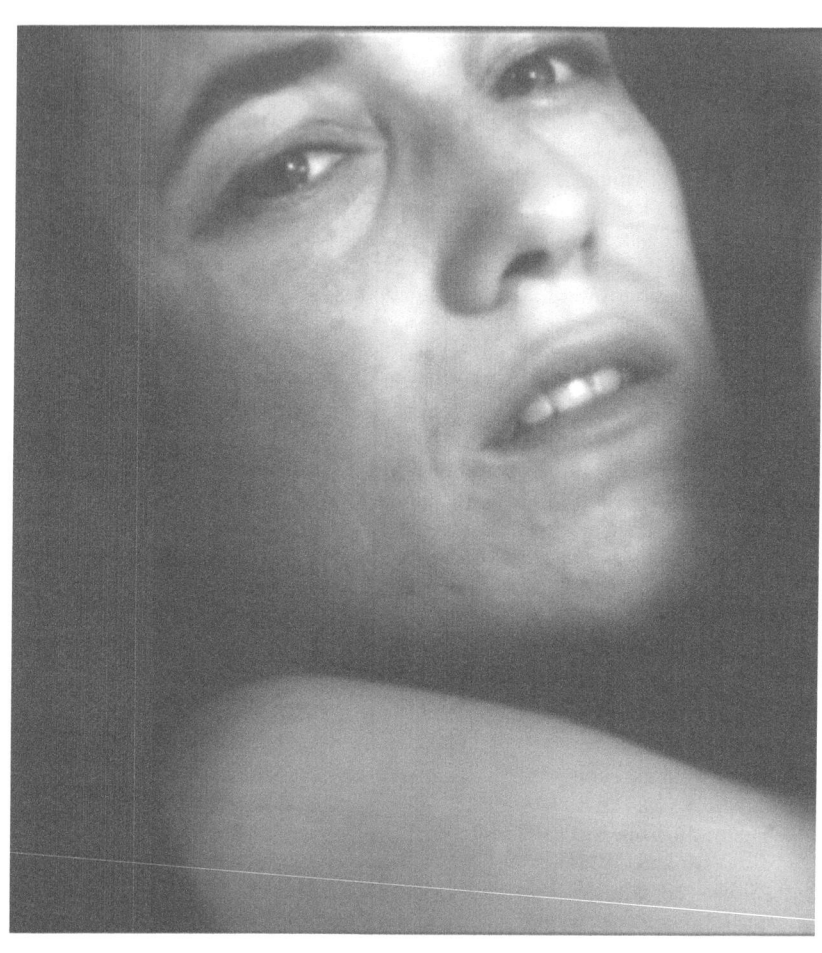

CHAPTER 7

The Deployment of the Impossible ~~Woman~~ in *Antichrist*

In a press conference at Cannes 2009, Lars von Trier was asked by a journalist to justify the making of *Antichrist*. He rejected the idea of justifying his film *tout court*. When the journalist insisted that the director should justify making the film, von Trier replied: "It is the hand of God, I am afraid. And I am the best director in the world. I am not sure God is the best god in the world." Von Trier's cinematic art has always been seen by many as at odds with his provocative stance, to the extent that some writers even see him as "less of an artist than he could be, on account of his consistent gravitation, in his films and in his public pronouncements, toward provocation" and feel that the "stance of the provocateur, as adopted by von Trier, … [is] inappropriate, irresponsible, disingenuous, and incoherent" (Hjort, *Kinema*).

With a shot of hard-core pornography, images of physical and sexual violence, explicit masturbation and genital mutilation, there is no doubt that *Antichrist* is one of the most provocative films ever made in the history of cinema. On top of its graphic violence, the film is also commonly seen as the epitome of von Trier's perceived misogyny, even though this is an accusation he flatly denies. The worst possible stance with regard to von Trier's work—and unfortunately the most popular one—is to suggest that, even though he may be a misogynist, his beautiful and enjoyable cinematic art should be separated from his personal traits, whatever these are.

This is similar to what Žižek sees as the awkward and "totally unconvincing compromise" of those people who enjoy Wagner's music immensely, know the "anti-Semitic and proto-Fascist dimension of Wagner's art", and somehow try to distance themselves from Wagner's fascism. Or, on the other hand, those who adopt the "standard aestheticist" position, which suggests that "'Wagner as a private person had his defects, but he wrote music of incomparable beauty, and in his art, there is no trace of anti-Semitism ...'"(*In Search of Wagner* xxvii), which is simply a monumental lie. Wagner's music *is* Wagner, and it is both beautiful and fascist; therefore, it has to be dealt with in all of its beauty as well as its fascism. By the same token, Lars von Trier's cinema *is* Lars von Trier. Enjoying it and detaching oneself from it cannot be combined unless with a kind of fundamental pretense. Its artistic beauty seems to be intrinsically mixed with its perceived misogyny. As far as *Antichrist* is concerned, accusations of misogyny, as Rob White suggests, seem to be nothing but "an opt-out from serious engagement".

Perhaps the best critical responses to *Antichrist* are the ones which try to avoid the "simplistic dichotomies of the discussions" (Koutsourakis, *Pop Matters*), or the ones which attempt serious analysis of the film in order to understand the human condition; in other words, which try to answer questions like: why do we enjoy it? Why do we find it repulsive? Where is the line that demarks cheap provocative cinema from thought-provoking art-house cinema? This essay will neither look for positive traits in *Antichrist* nor dismiss it as an entirely harmful film. To put it quite bluntly, content-wise, there is nothing positive in *Antichrist* and, in terms of stylistics, everything is employed to stress an ultimate fundamental failure to think about the human condition in any optimistic way—which is, of course, nothing new to von Trier's cinema.

However, in the imaginary, nightmarish world of *Antichrist*, in its ultimate negativity and perceived identification with the idea that women may be evil by their very nature, the film takes an already established historical discourse of female marginalization and identifies with it to the very point of that discourse's self-destruction. Moreover, it is precisely what is seen by some viewers as the film's "clumsy climactic sequence during which Gainsbourg's character takes inspiration from her studies on genocide and comes to embody all the evils done to woman throughout history" (Page) that marks the film's deepest insight into the human condition as such, beyond gender politics. Two stylistic traits in *Antichrist* play major roles in communicating its unsettling message: the employment of voices and sounds, and the employment of the sexual scenes.

When Willem Dafoe (he) discovers that Charlotte Gainsbourg (she) always made their son, Nic, wear his shoes on the wrong feet by looking closely at photographs of the boy, he crosses out the word 'Satan'—which earlier in the film replaced a crossed-out 'Nature'—as the supposed source of her fear and writes his final therapeutic discovery: 'ME'. 'ME' refers to her own self as the primary reason behind her fear. Precisely at this point she starts hitting him with a log of wood, after which a cycle of vicious violence plays out until he finally strangles her to death and burns her body on a pyre. When he has sex with her for the first time in the film, he seems to regret it right after the act out of a sense of duty, believing that the therapist should not have sex with the patient. He stages his professionalism as dead serious, yet somehow manages all the time to draw a suppressed titter from the viewer. His confident low voice, slow and articulate speech, his patient listening to his patient, and his occasional note jotting are somehow presented in a way that only evokes the viewer's distrust in him. Dafoe, the actor, is playing a character *playing* a therapist and, as such, everything the character says sounds hollow. He *seems* to have sex, with a touch of unwillingness, as if only to satisfy her desire. Yet, Dafoe's brilliant performance leaves the viewer in no doubt that this pseudo-therapist is immensely enjoying the sexual breaks in between the therapy sessions.

The ludicrousness of playing the therapist gets mocked occasionally by her in different parts of the film. When he criticizes her doctor's method of overmedication in the hospital, she tells him "trust others to be smarter than you" and "you are not a doctor". When he tells her that she needs to know the source of her fear and suggests writing a list of things she is afraid of, she asks "Can't I just be afraid without a definite object?" She gets angry at one point and yells at him "you shouldn't have come here, you are just so damn arrogant, but this may not last. Have you thought of that?" But it is in that scene, in which he concludes his therapeutic exploration with 'ME', that his ludicrousness reaches its climax, as we realize that, even after discovering she deformed their son's feet on purpose, he still goes on playing his idiotic therapeutic game. Earlier in the film she accuses him of having been distant from her and their son, that he became interested in her only when she became his patient, and tells him "you're indifferent to whether your child is alive or dead". Now, her statement suddenly sounds true.

Her subsequent attack, then, can be viewed in two different ways. On the surface of it, it seems to be an early reactionary attack as she now realizes that he must eventually leave her after her viciousness with Nic is exposed. Gainsbourg does shout "you're leaving me, you bastard!" as she hits him. At a deeper level, however, her attack is in its essence an attack on pretense, on his arrogant position of assuming the place of the "subject supposed to know" (Lacan, *Four Fundamental Concepts* 230–43 and Žižek, *For They Know Not* 109), and on his deliberate slighting of her identification with the medieval and early modern ideas of demonizing some women and considering them evil by nature. It is an attack on his notion of 'therapeutic truth' or, indeed, on 'truth' as such. This view is confirmed by what happens next. She manages to overpower him on the floor and he, exhausted or playing submissive, lets her grab his penis. She gets on top of him and copulates with him frantically. But he spoils it by saying the most politically correct, culturally correct, misread, and misreading statement, "I love you", to which she replies, with a screaming, ferocious voice, "I don't believe you!"

Gainsbourg's "I don't believe you!" is not simply about distrusting her husband's expression of love. On one level, it is about disbelieving that he can still utter such an ideological message of love, which, at this point, sounds not only pretentious, politically and culturally correct, but downright unethical and irresponsible. On another level, his "I love you", located precisely where it is located in this scene, ultimately contains an underlying patronizing disrespect for her conscious identification with the mythical yet historical and real image of woman as evil in witchery texts. Her line might as well go like this: 'I do not believe that you have the audacity—or the idiocy—to hold on to your belief in both of our constructed narrative identities as modern subjects against my chosen identification to such a ridiculous and incredible limit'. Her yelled statement, "I don't believe you!", also seems to purge what the viewer always wanted to say out loud with regard to Dafoe's therapy sessions.

In his seminar on feminine sexuality, Lacan designates "the object of sucking, the object of excretion, the gaze, and the voice" as "substitutes for the Other" and argues that it is in their condition as substitutes for the Other that these objects "are laid claim to and made into the cause of desire" (*On Feminine Sexuality* 126). One of the most important features of *Antichrist* is that the voice in it functions, in an almost perfect accordance with Lacanian psychoanalysis, precisely as an excess, as a foreign remainder that goes beyond both the visual and the spoken word or, to put it in Žižekan terms, as "an object, an objectal remnant, a meaningless leftover" (*Sublime Object* 103). However, it is this meaningless leftover, from the present work's point of view, which elevates von Trier's *Antichrist* above the accusation of being a cheap film of sexual violence as well as elevating the director himself above the accusation of being a mere irresponsible provocateur.

If there is one major stylistic element of cultural politics in *Antichrist* it is, par excellence, the way von Trier employed the idea of both voice and sound in the service of subverting patriarchal power. Aside from his own rational voice in the therapeutic sessions, all other voices and sounds in the film seem to work against Willem Dafoe. His wife's mocking voice often renders his therapeutic efforts meaningless. Her voiced disbelief in the usefulness of his methods challenges his arrogant belief in them. The sound of falling acorns at night disturbs him, the fox announces "chaos reigns" against his attempt to rein in the chaos in his wife's mind, the dead crow becomes alive, it seems, for the single reason of emitting a screech in order to expose his hiding place inside the fox hole. Gainsbourg's screams while she is searching for him contrast with his complete silence. She discovers where he is hiding and, at this dreadful moment, he resists and kicks against her shovel without emitting any sound.

On the other hand, in her world—and through her, to the viewer—the voice takes on a completely different role. In the scene in which she hears Nic's voice crying in the forest, even though he is nowhere to be seen, the voice literally functions as a "ghost-like apparition which can never be pinned to a definitive visual object" or as a "foreign body, as a kind of parasite introducing a radical split" (Žižek, *Enjoy Your Symptom* 1–2). She, as well as the viewer, learns later that the child is happily playing with a piece of wood inside the cabin. This separated voice, which has nothing to do with the visual, becomes a bone of conflict later when her husband insists that what she experienced was just panic and that "the scream wasn't real". His idea that the spectral voice she heard wasn't real maddens her and she tries to attack him. Later, she explains to him how the acorns keep falling on the roof and dying and that "now I [can] hear what I couldn't hear before; the cry of all the things that are to die". He characteristically dismisses what she says as "very touching if it was in a children's book". The separated voice thus operates on various levels. On one level, it is nothing but the imagination of a disturbed woman. On another, it is a symbol; it may symbolize anything depending on the argument, from the sheer cruelty of nature to "the cry of a cosmic Christ, suffering for the sins of the world" (Beattie) from a theological point of view.

On the most important level, however, the separated voice is nothing but an expression of the very foreignness of voice as such, or, voice as "the remainder of the signifying operation, i.e., the meaningless piece of the real which stays behind once the operation of 'quilting' [capitonnage] responsible for the stabilization of meaning is performed". Nic's crying voice, which literally assumes in the film the status of the "living dead" or the "spectral apparition which somehow survives its own death" (Žižek, *Interrogating the Real* 195), does not only stand, content-wise, for the voice of "all the things that are to die" but also, stylistically, for the employment of voice as an alienated object in many scenes of *Antichrist*, including that of the talking fox, as well as Gainsbourg's own voice, which, in many parts of the film, seems to deliberately go beyond its 'proper' measure—the measure needed for the articulated word—into passionate screams, as in the case of "Where are you?" when she is searching for Willem Dafoe in the forest and "I don't believe you!" when she is responding to his "I love you"—all statements that seem to mark the survival of the physical voice beyond meaning or on account of the death of meaning.

Above all, it is the sounds and the voices that we do not hear during a typical von Trier prologue, aestheticized by slow-motion, black-and-white cinematography and Handel's aria 'Lascia ch'io pianga', which provide "the exemplary case of the voice *qua* object".[1] What the viewer de facto hears is Handel's aria, which, if presented with the voice of a soprano, would in itself contain a "climax of the (feminine) operatic aria" or a moment at which "the singing voice 'runs amok', cuts loose from its anchoring in meaning, and accelerates into a consuming self-enjoyment" (Žižek, *Interrogating the Real* 198). That moment corresponds with Gainsbourg's orgasmic facial expression as Nic's body approaches its fatal collision with the ground beneath the open window.

In the prologue, what Dafoe primarily hears is presumably his own and her love-making sounds, made all the more erotic, perhaps, by the accompanying rhythmic sounds of the shower and the dryer as well as the chaotic sounds of falling objects (a glass with a toothbrush inside it and a bottle of vodka). Larry Gross argues that "the tempo of the clothes whirling in the dryer matches that of the erotically linked bodies, in a particularly delicious touch". A brief shot of Dafoe's facial expression, mouth half-open and eyes shut, right after Nic's misstep outside on the windowsill, reveals his obliviousness to what is happening to his son.

Yet, it is precisely the sounds that are heard neither by Dafoe nor by the viewer (but can only be imagined, of course) and which can only be heard by the sensitive ear of the mother at night that count here; the toddler getting out of his cot, pushing a chair against the table beneath the window so as to be able to climb on to it, pushing the three figurines out of his way and causing them to fall off the table, et cetera. It is these unheard sounds, paving the way to Nic's death, that constitute the horror that builds up and precedes the moment of experiencing the muted orgasmic scream of Gainsbourg as the "voice *qua* a dark spot of non-subjectivizable remainder, the point of the eclipse of meaning, the point at which meaning slides into *jouis-sense*" or "enjoyment-in-meaning" (Žižek, *Interrogating the Real* 197–8).

It is neither her id nor her ego that is in control at this moment. What is in control during the muted orgasmic scream of Gainsbourg is precisely the superego, which, "in its intimate imperative", to Lacan, "is indeed 'the voice of conscience,' that is, a voice first and foremost, a vocal one at that, and without any authority other than that of being a loud voice" (*Écrits: The First Complete Edition* 573). As far as stylistics are concerned, it is precisely the absence of voices and everyday-life sounds in the prologue, which more or less indicates the perceived subtlety of female *jouissance* and its relation to what is mystic and incomprehensible, that renders the prologue of *Antichrist* almost inexplicable to most viewers who "can only accept its shockingly contradictory message of beauty and death" (Christie). It is no coincidence that Lacan associates the "voice of conscience" or the superego with the "voice that [...] the Bible tells us was heard by the people parked around Mount Sinai" in *Écrits* (573), while in *Encore*, he clearly sees female *jouissance* in terms of a "relationship to God" (*On Feminine Sexuality* 83).

To fully grasp what exactly happens at the moment of Nic's fall, his mother's final gaze upon him, and her perceived orgasm at that moment, what is needed is a closer look at the sexual scenes in the film with no prior convictions that they are just there to either provoke the viewer or give him the measure of pornography needed for the cinematic voyeur's satisfaction. It does not take much to see that Gainsbourg is playing a woman who neither believes in her husband's abilities as a therapist nor seems to give much weight to his presence as a sexual partner. She seems to be mainly enjoying herself, yet her urge, her occasional violence, and her frantic ways seem to reflect some sort of, again, *disbelief* on her side that this is actually enjoyable. Her performance seems to connote the idea of meaningless repetition. Her "I don't believe you!" seems to be inscribed in her sexual behavior, as if what is unbelievable is that this meaningless repetition constitutes any kind of enjoyment—an inner belief that copulation as such does not lead to real enjoyment. Something is missing in it.

More accurately, there is always something else that is beyond it; something that leads to a *jouissance* of a completely different nature.

It is as if, while he enjoys the flow of signifiers between them in the therapeutic sessions, his interpretation of her symptoms, and what he *thinks* to be a sexual relationship between him and his wife, she, on the other hand, seems to be immersed in a play of signifiers all the time, during the therapy talk and during having sex. And since, as Lacan puts it, "signifiers are not made for sexual relations" (*Other Side* 33), they seem to be always in the way, and not only between her and her partner but, more importantly, between her and her own body. In other words, Gainsbourg in *Antichrist* somehow manages to *show* the viewer, with several scenes of copulation, not only that "there's no such thing as a sexual relationship" (Lacan, *On Feminine Sexuality* 144), but that sexuality as such has a certain limit in the kind of *jouissance* it promises or provides.

Anna Kornbluh argues that Lacan's assertion that "what makes up for the sexual relationship is, quite precisely, love" (Lacan, *On Feminine Sexuality* 45) "can mean that love is an imaginary lure that conceals sexual antagonism, or it can mean that, when in love, the subject is willing to live with the antagonism" (Kornbluh 128). This is, of course, true. That is to say: true if we talk about love precisely as a lie. But it does not quite get to the depth of the Lacanian statement, which, perhaps, should be taken literally without overloading it with too many meanings. In other words, it is love that is thought to establish some kind of relationship between two people of different sexes because, in the realm of the sexual, there is none, there is only the onanistic fantasy and either the "perverse" *jouissance* of the male or the "crazy and enigmatic" *jouissance* of the female.[2] Sexual antagonism in Lacanian thought, on the other hand, has more to do with the perceived *jouissance* of the Other, which, definitely, "is not the sign of love" (Lacan, *On Feminine Sexuality* 4) and, one might add, cannot be tolerated or lived with in the name of love.

True love, on the other hand, as Lacan puts it, "gives way to hatred" (146). When love is true it neither conceals antagonism nor lives with it; it opens up to hatred. This is, *precisely*, the kind of love the female character in *Antichrist* is capable of. In an acute Lacanian sense, it is a character that senses that the "'I' is not a being, but rather something attributed to that which speaks"—hence the importance of the representation of voice as a foreign alien element in *Antichrist*—and that this speaking body manages to reproduce "thanks to a misunderstanding regarding its jouissance" (120). Lacan further explains this by saying that the speaking body "reproduces thanks to missing what it wants to say, for what it wants to say [...] is its effective jouissance. And it is by missing that jouissance that it reproduces—in other words, by fucking. That is precisely what it doesn't want to do, in the final analysis" (121).

In all of the scenes of copulation in the film, Gainsbourg brilliantly manages to show the viewer a woman who seems to possess a voracious sexual desire, yet, at the same time, is fucking voraciously because this is exactly what she doesn't want to do. The repetitive act seems to merely express desperation over something else that is always already undone or, more precisely, always already unsaid—the speaking body's "effective jouissance". That is why the horror of the mother who commits infanticide in *Antichrist*, from this work's perspective, goes well beyond the idea of gender antagonism—she would let a female baby plunge to its death just the same—as what is at stake in it is the realization that reproduction as such, or that which ensures the survival of the human species, is achieved only through what the speaking subject doesn't want to do, which in itself is nothing but a desperate repetitive expression of missing what it wants to say. It would have been much more to the point, much more effective and in line with the character, if Gainsbourg had cut her own tongue with the scissors and lost the ability to speak instead of mutilating her clitoris. For on the level of a *jouissance* that is "beyond the pleasure principle",[3] the organ that fails the most in fulfilling its function is the tongue and not the sexual organ. Above all desires, it is precisely the "desire to communicate" that "doesn't live up to expectations" (Lacan, *Anxiety* 286).

In the disturbing world of *Antichrist*, her identification is an "identification with a sinthome" (Žižek, *Sublime Object* 124). Žižek defines Lacan's neologism *le sinthome* as a "particular signifying formation which is immediately permeated with enjoyment—that is, the impossible junction of enjoyment with the signifier" (123). Nothing in the film summarizes this in a single shot better than the black-and-white, slow-motion scene in the film's prologue in which Gainsbourg's orgasm seems to coincide precisely with the moment of her son's death—a moment, we learn later, towards the end of the film, that is preceded by her "merciless gaze" (White) upon her son moving towards the open window.

The scene is not simply that of a woman who, in her orgasmic moment, decides not to interrupt her enjoyment by any intruding event, even if that event is her son's certain death. The issue is much deeper than that. Gainsbourg in *Antichrist* is playing a woman whose identification with the medieval and early modern image of the witch happens to mark her "*passage à l'acte*" or "'passage to the act'", which "entails an exit from the symbolic network, a dissolution of the social bond" (Žižek, *Žižek Reader* 33), and with it the dissolution of motherhood. Against a human history of female subordination and dependence, she identifies with that historical moment in which a certain female was perceived as a real threat to society, religion, patriarchy and universal order. Her enjoyment in the prologue, therefore, is not simply sexual, but an enjoyment that is intrinsically woven with a "particular signifying formation", which, for her, functions as "the ultimate support of [her] consistency" (30) as a subject while, for the viewer, constituting the idea of the malignant mother who fulfills her wish of committing infanticide—a chilling reminder that mothers in particular are in a position to practically end humanity's existence.

She mocks her husband's therapeutic inquiry because she knows he is looking for some kind of 'truth' about her psyche. Her occasional outbursts remain, for him, within the realm of the hysteric, "determined by the coordinates of truth", while she is already beyond any truth graspable to him, as her passage to the act, represented by letting her son plunge to his death while she watches and copulates at once, "suspends the dimension of truth" (33)—the social truth of the mother as the ultimate provider of unconditional love. While he remains caught in the symbolic network from the start to the end, observing symptoms and interpreting them, she becomes increasingly committed to her "psychotic kernel", which "can neither be interpreted (like a symptom) nor 'traversed' (like a fantasy)" (31). As Žižek puts it, "in so far as truth has the structure of a (symbolic) fiction, truth and the Real of *Jouissance* are incompatible" (33).

After discovering her reading/writing material in the attic, Willem Dafoe has a discussion with her about female nature and evil in a scene in which she appears to believe in the evil nature of women while he appears to defend female nature. He tells her "the literature that you used in your research was about evil things committed against women, but you read it as proof of the evil of women? You were supposed to be critical of those texts; that was your thesis. Instead, you're embracing it. Do you know what you're saying?" He, the modern subject, conveniently assumes a position that is critical of the historical persecution of women by the Catholic Church inquisitions, which is, of course, part and parcel of modern gender politics.

She, on the other hand, seems to identify with witchery texts. But her identification takes an important turn when she mentions that "women are not in control of their bodies". On one level, her statement can be understood as referring to the menstrual cycle and ovulation in which women have no hand. On a deeper level, it can also be understood in terms of female sexuality and woman's mystic *jouissance*. It is at this point that her discourse goes beyond gender politics—since there is a third party in female *jouissance* that constitutes its mysticism, which will be referred to later here—and, therefore, becomes completely ungraspable to him.

Seen from the position of radical identification with the figure of the malignant mother or the 'ultimate witch', her "Real of *Jouissance*" is not only beyond his imagination, which circles within his limited therapeutic 'truth', but beyond anything bearable even to *herself*. When she commands him to hit her while they are having sex, he refuses. She then goes out to nature, lies down at the base of a gigantic tree and masturbates frantically. He copulates with her at the base of the tree and hits her to fulfill her wish. At this point she says, "the sisters from Ratisbon could start a hailstorm," referring to two women described in Heinrich Kramer and James Sprenger's *Malleus Maleficarum*—a fifteenth-century treatise on witchery—as witches who could invoke "a violent hailstorm" that "destroyed all the fruit, crops and vineyards in a belt one mile wide, so that the vines hardly bore fruit for three years".

It would be simplistic to suggest that she finally manages to extort some sadomasochistic fantasy from him and is now referring to his violence as a hailstorm. The hailstorm is hers and the filmic image is completely dominated by her onanistic fantasy in which his presence makes little or no difference. In fact, her radical identification with the "sisters" obliterates her own presence as well. To put it in Lacanian language, she "makes [herself] the instrument of the Other's *jouissance*". This, though, should be thought of more in terms of perversion than in terms of sacrifice, and it certainly leans more to male phallic *jouissance*, which seems more relevant to that particular scene in *Antichrist*, which stages mainly a masturbatory fantasy. Lacan explains how the formula of fantasy ($ \$ \lozenge a $) in the case of perversion helps to bring out the fact that the subject makes himself the instrument of the Other's *jouissance*, as Φ (the symbolic phallus, the signifier of *jouissance*) makes the male sex the weaker sex with regard to perversion (*Écrit: The First Complete Edition* 697). Gainsbourg's masturbation scene, then, stages her literal enjoyment *for the 'sisters', on their behalf*, offering her *jouissance* to them, and in doing so, in her imagination, she manages to start their resurrection from the dead. The human arms that materialize at the base of the tree seem to constitute von Trier's stylistic expression of that imagination.

Her death at the end of the film marks the completion of their resurrection, which is represented by the faceless mass of women among which Dafoe completely disappears. The fact that her *jouissance* is offered to the dead confirms the Žižekan idea that the "*sinthome* is a certain signifier" that is "merely a mute attestation bearing witness to a disgusting enjoyment, without presenting anything or anyone". Žižek offers an example of this "meaningless enjoyment" (*Sublime Object* 76) from Kafka's short story *A Country Doctor*, in which Kafka describes a deadly wound on a child's body as "gapingly obvious as a mine-shaft ... Worms, the length and thickness of my little finger, roseate and also coated with blood, are writhing against the inside of the wound, with little white heads, and many many little legs" (Kafka, *Metamorphosis* 189). Žižek argues that "this nauseous, verminous aperture [is] the embodiment of vitality as such, of the life-substance in its most radical dimension of meaningless enjoyment" (*Sublime Object* 76). Kafka's "wound", then, like von Trier's artistic scene of making love among the dead at the base of the tree, embodies both life and death at once. It is nature that enjoys itself, and in doing so, it generates life eternally and threatens it with death at the same time.

In her comparison between Dafoe's and Gainsbourg's characters and their relationship to the animals in the film, Nina Power perceptively argues that "he may get the identifiable animals, but she gets everything that swarms, those things that make the ecology feel unsafe and excessive: the acorns, the burning ground, the ants crawling on the runt chick ...". This unsafe excessiveness is as much about her melting in nature—visually represented in the film by the scene in which she actually melts into the green landscape of Eden—as it is about her "*jouissance* beyond the pleasure principle" (Lacan, *Four Fundamental Concepts* 184) or beyond the metonymic structure of desire; a *jouissance* in which neither he nor she exists in any identifiable form except the "life-substance in its most radical dimension of meaningless enjoyment" (Žižek, *Sublime Object* 76).

At her most psychotic moment, the moment she gazes upon Nic before he plunges to his death, the signifier 'being a mother' is overshadowed, not by female *jouissance*, as some might think, but by Nic himself, albeit as a completely different signifier that has nothing to do with 'being a son', but with being the product of the very failure of the speaking body to speak its *jouissance*. If there is any female character in the history of cinema that comes close to presenting the viewer with the clearest possible image of Lacan's "Woman" who "cannot be said", whom "nothing can be said of [her]" (*On Feminine Sexuality* 81), who is outside the system of symbolization yet defined as its very subversion, it is Gainsbourg's character in *Antichrist*. Her relationship to the "sisters" can be viewed as one form of relationship to the divine. She, in accordance with Frances Restuccia's reading of Lacan's ~~Woman~~—which she mentions in the course of analyzing another von Trier film (*Breaking the Waves*), yet which seems to be much more relevant here—is a mystic ~~Woman~~ who "enters into a *à trios*, making God the third party in the business of love" (Restuccia 190) where man, to her, functions only as a "fantasmatic place-holder" (194).

It is in this sense that her unforgettable gaze upon Nic before his death should be understood. The most erratic reading of it is to suggest that this is the gaze of a disturbed woman who is taking revenge upon man or a woman whose sexual voraciousness at the moment of female orgasm overshadows her motherhood. Gainsbourg's gaze, which we meet not in the prologue that stages Nic's death but later in a flashback towards the end of the film, is not the gaze of a woman at all, but the gaze of ~~Woman~~ who "falls into the hole of the Other"; a woman who is, literally, having a "sexual relation with God" (206)—and it is the God of "all the things that are to die".

God, in the world of *Antichrist*, has none of the attributes given to him in the language of religion(s). He is a Lévinasian God. He is:

> other than the other [*autre* qu'autrui], other otherwise, other with an alterity prior to the alterity of the other, prior to the ethical bond with another and different from every neighbor, transcendent to the point of absence, to the point of a possible confusion with the stirring of the *there is*. (Lévinas, *Collected Philosophical Papers* 165–6)

To put this in Lacanian language, God, like female *jouissance*, is "radically Other"[4] and cannot be talked about except in terms of complete mystery. Hence the foreclosure of God in the real, the one, in Lacan's words, who "has not yet made his exit" (*On Feminine Sexuality* 84), and the creation of God in language, the God of cultural interpretations. And, it is precisely the God of cultural interpretations in whose name all of the historical atrocities of religion have been committed, including those committed against women. The "sisters" in *Antichrist*, to whom Gainsbourg decides to belong, represent the foreclosed part of the divine—that which is equivalent to female *jouissance*—and it is this foreclosure itself that creates the God of the soul, that of love, the spiritual God, in other words, that which has nothing to do with the body, *of woman*. Lacan's explanation of this divine split accurately describes how woman came to be literally the historical enemy of culture and established religions:

> So that the soul may come into being, woman is differentiated from it right from the beginning. She is called woman *(on la dit-femme)* and defamed *(diffâme)*. The most famous *(fameux)* things that have come down to us about women in history are, strictly speaking, what one can say that is infamous *(infamant)*. (*On Feminine Sexuality* 85)[5]

Yet, in Lacanian psychoanalysis, it is precisely this infamous being, this enemy of culture and religion, who can be said to have any relation to God *that is not mediated by language*. The story of *Antichrist* is not only the story of a woman who "perceives her body as a material existence that escapes her subjectivity" (Koutsourakis, *Pop Matters*); it is the story of a woman who couldn't retreat from the borders that define the dangerous territory her female *jouissance* occasionally glimpses; a woman who completely transforms into a ~~Woman~~. The "things that are to die", from the falling acorns to herself, are the things that are unable, or *unwilling*, to continue living in the facade that language created—the world, its cultures, its ideologies, its religions, et cetera.

Gainsbourg in *Antichrist* clearly evokes the figure of Lacan's phallic mother:

> As very precious as an object is for her, inexplicably, she will be dreadfully tempted *not to hold onto it in a fall*, expecting goodness knows what miraculous outcome to such a catastrophe, and [she would declare] that the *most beloved child is precisely the one that one day she inexplicably dropped* (all emphases mine). (Lacan, *Anxiety* 122)

In this sense, letting Nic fall and die may be the sign of ultimate love, and her gaze upon him may not be as "merciless" (White) as it seems. For her violence against him clearly belongs to a Benjaminian "divine violence" that is "law-destroying ... boundlessly destroy[ing boundaries] ... without warning, without threat ... expiatory" and ultimately questioning with regard to the position of those thinkers who profess the "doctrine of the sanctity of life" as well as the general "dogma of the sacredness of life" (Benjamin 297–9). In its appalling violation of all kinds of laws—natural and man-made—her act, like divine violence, "is an expression of pure drive, of the undeadness, the excess of life, which strikes at "bare life" regulated by law and "elevates [love] over mere unstable and pathetic sentimentality" (Žižek, *Violence* 198, 204).

Her gaze, which is directed to Nic, as well as the *viewer*, who will eventually die, too, is precisely Lacan's "objet a *in the field of the visible*" (*Four Fundamental Concepts* 105), or, as Todd McGowan puts it, the point at which "the subject loses its subjective privilege and becomes wholly embodied in the object" (7); in other words, the point that marks the death of the subject as such, who instantly loses the subject position and becomes *subjected* to the gaze. It is the point where *Antichrist* changes its position from a filmic object and, strictly speaking, "looks back at [the spectator]" (164) who trembles at being exposed to a gaze which seems to transcend the character played by Gainsbourg; a gaze which the "Other cannot embody" (87), an impossible blank point which knows the secret of the subject, its truth and its future, beyond the knowledge of the Other; an all-knowing unknowable and all-seeing unseen. Nic's deformed feet—a deformation caused by his distorted mother—may be thought to prove Kramer and Sprenger's statement that women constitute a "structural defect rooted in the original creation" (*Malleus Maleficarum*). Yet, the deformed feet and the distorted mother also remind us that *we* are a "distortion in being", and that "the direct encounter with the gaze exposes us as this distortion and uproots every other form of identity to which we cling" (McGowan 210).

In his seminar on feminine sexuality, Lacan discusses the structure of female subjectivity in terms of its connection to the notion of woman who "does not exist" and "is not-whole", even though she may initially take the same detour as man within a discourse that is predominantly written in the Name of the Father:

> ~~Woman~~ cannot be said (*se dire*). Nothing can be said of Woman. Woman has a relation with S($A̸$), and it is already in that respect that she is doubled, that she is not-whole, since she can also have a relation with Φ. (*On Feminine Sexuality* 81)

In other words, the subjectivity of the female relates to woman who does not exist in the system of symbolization yet exists at the level of *jouissance* where she, as well as the big Other itself, are crossed out. She is not symbolized but she is defined as the very collapse of the system of symbolization. Her relation with the big Other is not marked by any symbolic exchange since that relation exists only as pure *jouissance* where meaning does not count. Her lack becomes the sign of her ultimate being as real beyond reality.

This split nature of woman becomes clearest when we look at *Antichrist*'s simultaneous deployment of the mother who commits infanticide and the mother who grieves for her son's tragic death—Woman and woman; the impossible Woman who is capable of love in its truth, the kind of love which "gives way to hatred" (146), and the human being who is not made for this kind of love; in other words, who is capable of love only insofar as it is a social lie, and therefore regrets departing from the safety of social identity for the dangerous domain of the real. Without this Lacanian connection between Woman and woman, it becomes impossible to think about any link between the woman who gazes upon her son's fatal fall while having an orgasm and the woman who collapses under the weight of an unbearable grief at losing her child.

Notes

1. The exemplary case of the voice *qua* object according to Žižek is "a voice which remains silent, i.e., which we do not hear". 'Why Does the *Phallus* Appear?' *Enjoy Your Symptom! Jacques Lacan in Hollywood and Out* (New York and London: Routledge, 2001), p. 117.
2. Lacan states that, in the case of the male, "one's jouissance of the Other taken as a body is always inadequate—perverse … insofar as the Other is reduced to object a"; in other words, the Other is not really involved in one's phallic *jouissance* since what constitutes it is the awareness of one's own body, while the Other serves only as the phantasmal object-cause of desire. In the case of the female, on the other hand, *jouissance* is mystic and more radical in its dissociation from the Other, "The rat in the maze". *On Feminine Sexuality, The Limits of Love and Knowledge: Encore, 1972–1973*, ed. Jacques-Alain Miller and trans. with notes by Bruce Fink (New York and London: W.W. Norton & Company, 1998), p. 144.
3. Freud discusses the pleasure of repetition beyond the pleasure principle in terms of the child's fort-da game by which he plays at mastering the experience of displeasure due to the mother's occasional disappearances. 'Beyond the Pleasure Principle', *On Metapsychology: The Theory of Psychoanalysis*, ed. Angela Richards and trans. from the German under the general editorship of James Strachey (Penguin Books, 1991), pp. 275–349. Lacan explains how a *jouissance* that is beyond the pleasure principle is realized at a certain

stage where the subject realizes "that his desire is merely a vain detour with the aim of catching the *jouissance* of the other". A *jouissance* that is beyond the pleasure principle thus seems to fall outside the metonymic structure of desire. 'The Transference and the Drive', *The Four Fundamental Concepts of Psycho-Analysis*, ed. Jacques-Alain Miller and trans. Alan Sheridan (Penguin Books, 1994), p. 184.
4. Lacan states that "it is insofar as her jouissance is radically Other that woman has more of a relationship to God than anything that could have been said in speculation in antiquity following the pathway of that which is manifestly articulated only as the good of man". God and female *jouissance*, therefore, belong to the realm of the mystic or what cannot be articulated or talked about. 'A love letter *(une letter d'âmour)*', *On Feminine Sexuality, The Limits of Love and Knowledge: Encore, 1972–1973*, ed. Jacques-Alain Miller and trans. with notes by Bruce Fink (New York and London: W.W. Norton & Company, 1998), p. 83.
5. Bruce Fink notes that "*dit-femme* and *diffâme* are homonyms in French; the latter also contains *âme* which means 'soul'", while *infamant* means both "infamous" and "defamatory". He also notes that, in French, "phonemically speaking, *fameux* and *infamant* both contain *femme*, 'woman'". Jacques Lacan, 'A love letter *(une letter d'âmour)*', *On Feminine Sexuality, The Limits of Love and Knowledge: Encore, 1972–1973*, ed. Jacques-Alain Miller and trans. with notes by Bruce Fink (New York and London: W.W. Norton & Company, 1998), p. 85.

Bibliography

Beattie, Tina. '*Antichrist*: The Visual Theology of Lars Von Trier'. *Open Democracy*. Accessed 23 November 2013. http://www.opendemocracy.net/article/antichrist-the-visual-theology-of-lars-von-trier

Benjamin, Walter. *Reflections: Essays, Aphorisms, Autobiographical Writings*. Edited by Peter Demetz and translated by Edmund Jephcott. New York: Schocken Books, 1986.

Christie, Ian. 'All Those Things That Are to Die: *Antichrist. The Criterion Collection*'. Accessed 15 October 2013. http://www.criterion.com/current/posts/1650-all-those-things-that-are-to-die-antichrist

Fink, Bruce. *On Feminine Sexuality, The Limits of Love and Knowledge: Encore, 1972–1973*. Translated and with notes by Bruce Fink. New York and London: W.W. Norton and Company, 1998.

Freud, Sigmund. *On Metapsychology: The Theory of Psychoanalysis*. Edited by Angela Richards and translated from the German under the general editorship of James Strachey. Penguin Books, 1991.

Gross, Larry. 'The Six Commandments of the Church of Lars von Trier's *Antichrist*'. *Film Comment*. Accessed 4 December 2013. http://www.filmcomment.com/article/the-six-commandments-of-the-church-of-lars-von-triers-antichrist

Hjort, Mette. 'The Problem with Provocation: On Lars von Trier, Enfant Terrible of Danish Art Film'. *Kinema: A Journal for Film and Audiovisual Media*. Accessed 2 December 2013. http://www.kinema.uwaterloo.ca/article.php?id=492andfeature

Kafka, Franz. *Metamorphosis and Other Stories*. Translated by Michael Hofmann. London and New York: Penguin, 2007.

Kornbluh, Anna. 'Romancing the Capital: Choice, Love, and Contradiction in *The Family Man* and *Memento*'. *Lacan and Contemporary Film*. Edited by Todd McGowan and Sheila Kunkle. New York: Other Press, 2004.

Koutsourakis, Angelos. 'The Illusion of Identity in Lars Von Trier's *Antichrist*'. *Pop Matters*. Accessed 11 November 2013. http://www.popmatters.com/column/124428-the-illusion-of-identity-in-lars-von-triers-antichrist/

Kramer, Heinrich, and James Sprenger. *Malleus Maleficarum*. Accessed 20 July 2013. http://www.malleusmaleficarum.org/part-ii-question-i-chapter-xv/

Lacan, Jacques. *The Four Fundamental Concepts of Psycho-Analysis*. Edited by Jacques-Alain Miller and translated by Alan Sheridan. Penguin Books, 1994.

Lacan, Jacques. *On Feminine Sexuality, The Limits of Love and Knowledge: Encore, 1972–1973*. Translated and with notes by Bruce Fink. New York and London: W.W. Norton and Company, 1998.

Lacan, Jacques. *Écrit: The First Complete Edition in English*. Translated by Bruce Fink. New York and London: W.W. Norton and Company, 2006.

Lacan, Jacques. *The Other Side of Psychoanalysis*. Translated and with notes by Russell Grigg. New York and London: W.W. Norton and Company, 2007.

Lacan, Jacques. *Anxiety*. Edited by Jacques-Alain Miller and translated by A. Rae Price. Cambridge: Polity Press, 2014.

Lévinas, Emmanuel. *Collected Philosophical Papers*. Translated by Alphonso Lingis. Dordrecht, the Netherlands: Nijhoff, 1987.

McGowan, Todd. *The Real Gaze: Film Theory After Lacan*. Albany: State University of New York Press, 2007.

Page, Nicholas. 'The Last Temptation of Von Trier: *Antichrist*'. *The Big Picture Magazine*. Accessed 10 October 2013. http://thebigpicturemagazine.com/index.php?Option=com_contentandview=articleandid=127:the–last–temptation–of–von–trier–antichristandcatid=34:film–reviewsand-Itemid=60

Power, Nina. '*Antichrist*: A Discussion'. *Film Quarterly* 63, no. 2 (Winter 2009). Accessed 7 October 2013. http://www.filmquarterly.org/2009/12/antichrist-a-discussion/

Restuccia, Frances L. 'Impossible Love in *Breaking the Waves*: Mystifying Hysteria'. *Lacan and Contemporary Film*. Edited by Todd McGowan and Sheila Kunkle. New York: Other Press, 2004.

White, Rob. '*Antichrist*: A Discussion'. *Film Quarterly* 63, no. 2 (Winter 2009). Accessed 7 October 2013. http://www.filmquarterly.org/2009/12/antichrist-a-discussion/
Žižek, Slavoj. *The Sublime Object of Ideology*. London and New York: Verso, 1989.
Žižek, Slavoj. *The Žižek Reader*. Edited by Elizabeth Wright and Edmond Wright. Oxford and Malden, MA: Blackwell Publishing, 1999.
Žižek, Slavoj. *Enjoy Your Symptom! Jacques Lacan in Hollywood and Out*. New York and London: Routledge, 2001.
Žižek, Slavoj. *For They Know Not What They Do: Enjoyment as a Political Factor*. London and New York: Verso, 2002.
Žižek, Slavoj. 'Why is Wagner Worth Saving?' *In Search of Wagner*. Translated by Rodney Livingstone. London and New York: Verso, 2005.
Žižek, Slavoj. *Interrogating the Real*. Edited by Rex Butler and Scott Stephens. London and New York: Continuum, 2006.
Žižek, Slavoj. *Violence: Six Sideways Reflections*. New York: Picador, 2008.

Filmography

Antichrist. Directed and written by Lars von Trier. Irvington, NY: Criterion Collection, 2010.
Breaking the Waves. Directed and written by Lars von Trier. Paris: Pathé, 2003.

CHAPTER 8

Besides Melancholia and Beyond Gender: *Melancholia*

Let us approach the topic of melancholia through von Trier's cinematic take on it in his film *Melancholia*, a film seen by many as a sort of deviation from those of his works usually perceived as misogynistic, and even hailed by some as particularly feminist. The argument that follows will show that, even though the film deals primarily with melancholia, its focus radically shifts from the category of the melancholic to the category of the hysteric towards its end. By taking a close look at certain scenes in von Trier's film, the present work seeks to show that, in *Melancholia*, there is something else besides melancholia that remains with the viewer long after experiencing the film, which, even though still related to the film's melancholic stasis (both content and stylistics-wise) and what some of its readers see as its nihilistic drive, is fundamentally situated in the desiring, living, hysterical subject as such as what constitutes the human condition in general.

To put it in simple language, von Trier's *Melancholia*, regardless of what the director's intentions may be in terms of what he really wants to communicate to the viewer, shows that while melancholia may be regarded as an illness afflicting certain people (Lars von Trier himself is known to have experienced severe bouts of depression), being a desiring subject is itself an incurable illness that can be traced back to the subject's very inscription into the symbolic order—an inscription that is melancholic by its very nature since it is based not on a gain but on a certain fundamental loss within the psyche. In the course of this, it will also be shown that nothing hinders coming to grips with a filmic text like *Melancholia* and trying to fully grasp the scope of its radical implications more than feminist readings of it.

Melancholia begins with an overture of 16 shots that introduce some of the film's visual leitmotifs, accompanied by a soundtrack that plays the famous prelude to Wagner's opera *Tristan und Isolde*, and which later complements all the film's defining moments. The film is set in an unnamed country and consists of two parts. In the first part, entitled "Justine", newlyweds Justine and Michael arrive late to their own reception at the estate where Justine's sister, Claire, and her husband, John, reside. Justine happens to notice a bright red star in the twilight sky, which John identifies as Antares, and, in spite of being two hours late already, she makes sure to visit her horse, Abraham, in the stables before meeting her wedding guests. Over the course of the evening, Justine's mother, Gaby, delivers a verbal downer on the idea of marriage in a toast which triggers Justine's melancholic withdrawal from the whole affair. Her boss repeatedly harasses her to write better ad copy. Her sister becomes frustrated with her and chastises her for not reacting to the reception as a happy bride. Justine seems increasingly cut off from her surroundings; she drifts away from the party several times, falls asleep, pisses in the open on the estate's golf court, insults her boss and loses her job irrevocably, brushes off her husband's sexual advances and goes walking in the grounds where she fucks a stranger she has been introduced to only a few minutes before. At the end of the party, Michael abandons her. At dawn the next day, Justine reluctantly goes horseback riding with her sister. Justine's horse, Abraham, stops at a certain bridge and refuses to move any further. At this point, Justine notices the disappearance of the Antares from the sky.

In the second part, entitled "Claire", Justine becomes severely depressed, moving in with Claire and John where she becomes almost catatonic, unable even to take a bath on her own. Meanwhile, John explains that the reason for Antares' disappearance is the rogue planet Melancholia, which blocks the star from view. Melancholia, a large blue planet formerly hidden behind the sun, becomes visible in the sky as it approaches ever closer to Earth. John is excited about the planet and looks forward to the "fly-by" predicted by scientists. Claire becomes gripped by fear that the end of the world is imminent in spite of her husband's reassurances that Melancholia will not collide with Earth. The melancholic Justine, on the other hand, welcomes Melancholia's approach and even seems to gradually recover from her melancholia. Justine and Claire go horseback riding again. Abraham stops again at the bridge and Justine beats him violently and repeatedly with the riding crop until he collapses to the ground. The rogue planet is now visible in the sky. Justine goes out at night, sprawls naked on a river bank and gazes upon the blue planet in adoration. She claims to possess a kind of clairvoyance and tells Claire that life on Earth is evil and that Melancholia is here to bring it all to an end. On the night of the fly-by, Melancholia merely passes very near without colliding with Earth then starts to move away from it. The next day, however, Claire realizes that the planet is circling back and will collide with Earth after all. She searches for John and finds him dead of an apparent suicide. Faced with the impending collision, Claire becomes distraught and suggests getting together on the terrace with wine and music. In response, a surprisingly calm and upbeat Justine dismisses her idea before going to comfort Claire's son, Leo. She makes him a protective magic teepee on the lawn of the estate. Justine, Claire and Leo enter the rickety wooden shelter as the rogue planet looms large and approaches fast. In the final seconds of the film, a shockwave of fire overcomes the characters as the planet Melancholia destroys Earth.

Most of the critical responses to *Melancholia* seem to suggest that viewers identify with the melancholic Justine (Kirsten Dunst) in her rebellion against social customs, the phoniness of marriage rituals, the patriarchal order, capitalism and all forms of control, as well as in her melancholic strength and almost militant resignation, through which she totally commits to the destructive force of the rogue planet, Melancholia, and the end of the world. These views seem to assume that identification with Justine is an absolute one, since she clearly represents the drive's ultimate goal, which is death. According to these views, at no time would the viewer identify with the other sister, Claire (Charlotte Gainsbourg). Who would identify with Claire's ridiculous schedules and strict order, dependence on and subordination to her ultra-rich husband, or her clinging to her bourgeois life to the extent of suggesting meeting death and the end of the world on her terrace with a glass of wine and some music? It is Justine's melancholia that reflects our desire to be absolved of the burdens of being, to be freed from the illusions of 'reality' and daily life's agonies, from ideologies and false identities, and from the absurdities of society and its ridiculous conventions.

That is why, for example, in her all-encompassing essay 'Freedom in Oblivion: Post-Feminist Possibilities in Lars von Trier's *Melancholia*', Kim Nicolini reads *Melancholia* as a "radically feminist" film in which Justine "intentionally annihilates the systems that would like to contain her, and in their annihilation she breaks free from her gender and the systems that want to trap her", and that "this liberation is represented by the planet

Melancholia, which promises to put an end to every form of cultural, economic and political bondage by annihilating the Earth itself". Justine, to Nicolini, "is not the one subjugated in this film as women are in earlier von Trier films. Instead, she subjugates everyone to her depressive will and her emotional resistance" (3–6).

There seems to be little doubt that the film aims at making the viewer identify with Justine in the first part of it, in which she is a formidable figure of non-conformity. The husband can't consummate his sexual relationship with her. The boss can't get his tagline out of her. No one can get a real smile out of her. The only one who gets something is the viewer: total identification with her and total fascination with her melancholic passivity. Yet this identification, from the present writer's point of view, gets seriously destabilized in the second part of the film. For, in it, Justine does not only become a "de-gendered deity of disorder" (14); she clearly attains some kind of *control*; she tells Claire "the earth is evil, we don't need to grieve for it" and "I know we are alone". When Claire expresses doubt about her sister's omniscient knowledge, Justine tells her the correct number of beans in the bean lottery competition, which nobody guessed, and "when I say we are alone, we are alone. Life is only on Earth, and not for long". It is at this point that Justine is transformed from one state to another.

Nina Power argues that Justine's nihilism can be seen as a "model of knowledge far more apt than the neurotic position held by Claire" (Power). This cannot be free of problems, though, as Justine's position effectively changes from the melancholic subject to the "subject supposed to know" (Lacan, *Four Fundamental Concepts* 230–43 and Žižek, *For They Know Not* 109), the one who is supposed to have answers and presumed to have some knowledge about the desire of the big Other—a position previously occupied in the film by Claire's arrogant husband and, therefore, immediately questioned. It is at this point, from this essay's point of view, that the viewer experiences some kind of alienation from Justine or the end of unequivocal identification with her melancholic position.

The issue of knowledge in itself should be looked at more closely. For the viewer's presumed identification with Justine is based on the notion that she *knows* about the phoniness of our ridiculous reality, and so is unwilling to participate in it. She rejects the world. But the viewer may also notice that Justine can afford the consequences of her melancholic transgressions. She can afford to ruin a marriage that hasn't taken shape yet and lose a job she hates as her sister and her rich brother-in-law are taking care of her. Justine can *afford* being strong and melancholic. Now, let us assume that, in spite of her tight schedules, time-keeping, ridiculous attention to detail, presumed happy marriage and bourgeois life, Claire also *knows* about the phoniness of all that. Who is truly melancholic? It is no coincidence that the second part of the film, which takes us through Justine's almost catatonic experience, her later sublime submission and dalliance with Melancholia—the illness and the planet—and finally her living up to Leo's expectations as "Aunt Steelbreaker" with her melancholic calmness and composure in face of the end of the world, is entitled *Claire*.

At the end of the sisters' first ride, Justine's horse, Abraham, refuses to cross the bridge. Justine looks up into the sky and tells Claire: "The red star is missing from Scorpio. Antares is no longer there." In one of her essay's most perceptive moments, Nicolini states that "at this moment, Justine's face is infused with a sense of calm and wonder while her sister Claire circles on her horse looking anxiously up into the sky. Claire and Justine begin to switch places" (50). Nicolini then writes about the sisters' second ride in which Abraham again stubbornly refuses to cross the bridge, Justine beats him, looks up into the sky and sees the blue planet Melancholia. In her essay, Nicolini confuses Claire's reaction to the disappearance of the red star (the first ride) with her reaction to the first actual appearance of Melancholia in the sky (the second ride). She writes:

> Claire circles on her horse, her body hunched and taught with anxiety as she looks with dread at the rogue planet in the sky. The terror, beauty and emotion of the film all converge in that one moment. (51)

This actually happens in the first ride (not the second) when the sisters realize that Antares is missing. At this time, the rogue planet is not yet visible in the sky. Nicolini perceptively stresses the importance of the scene in which Claire anxiously circles on her horse, but unfortunately displaces it. The displacement is unfortunate because the location of this scene is as important as the visual itself.

Justine tells Claire that the Antares is no longer there. Her voice is calm, but her face at this moment obviously reflects more disenchantment than wonder, as she is witnessing the disappearance of the red star that fascinated her on her arrival at John's estate, and not the appearance of Melancholia. The camera then cuts to Claire, circling on her horse, "her body hunched and taught with anxiety as she looks with dread at the" (51) *empty place of the Antares in the sky*. Gainsbourg's performance at this moment is particularly brilliant. The moment she hears that the Antares is no longer there she looks up to the sky, then nervously left and right *around herself* as if she is missing something much more personal, then again back to the sky with an ashen and apprehensive face. The scene fades out on her and her horse's restless movements to a black screen followed by the appearance of the intertitle "PART TWO: CLAIRE".

It is during these cinematic moments in von Trier's movie that not only "Claire and Justine begin to switch places" (50) but the viewer begins to identify more with the restlessness of Claire than the self-assuredness of Justine. It is true that the film's stylistics as a whole is mainly employed to present to the viewer Justine's melancholia. As Judit Pintér puts it, *Melancholia* "is the phenomenon of melancholy itself" as its "slow pace, its recurring leitmotif-like sentences and images in place of a narrative, offer the viewer a condition rather than a story". Yet, it is Claire's sense of loss at this particular moment that, over and above Justine's melancholic condition, becomes instantly more at home with the restlessness of the human condition as such, with the instability of the subject, with the subject's imaginary unified image falling back into primary fragmentation and, backhandedly, with the instability of von Trier's images themselves and his handheld camera.

Claire is the remainder that leaves the viewer restless after everything seems to have been settled by Justine's melancholic identification with the drive towards death. Charles Bukowski seems to touch upon the idea of that inexplicable remainder as something that is fundamentally out of order in the human psyche and which is clearly distinguishable from what we name as melancholia (302–3), the implication of which is that it shouldn't be assumed melancholia itself is a disorder; on the contrary, it may be the very sign of normalcy, while the remainder is this incurable illness without which there is no perceivable psyche in the first place. It is precisely this human remainder that distorts us beyond melancholia. And, it is this remainder, from the present work's point of view, that problematizes defining the state of melancholia as an illness often marked by a desire to annihilate the self.

In its strange relation to melancholia, this remainder, this (in)significant leftover, is no less than a Derridean "supplement" which "produces no relief" and resists settling the drive's dalliance with the idea of death through identification with the melancholic position. By its very definition, the supplement, in Derrida's words, "adds only to replace. It intervenes or insinuates itself *in-the-place-of*; [...] Compensatory [*suppléant*] and vicarious, the supplement is an adjunct, a subaltern instance which *takes-(the)-place* [*tient-lieu*]" (Derrida, *Of Grammatology* 145). What I call here the remainder is, like the supplement, neither a subtraction nor an addition, but effectively a shadowy substitute; another point of identification which is always already a threat to the melancholic position, making identification with it not only inconsistent (comes and goes) but ultimately uncomfortable with itself.

From the presumed point of identification with melancholia, the remainder is perceived to be in some kind of subaltern position to melancholia (just as Claire's hysterical position is perceived by feminist as well as non-feminist readers of the film as subaltern to Justine's melancholia, or as Gainsbourg's role itself may be perceived as subaltern to Dunst's as the main heroine who presents melancholia to the viewer). Yet, it is precisely the supplementarity of the remainder that threatens its subalternity to the state of melancholia; in other words, melancholia itself, in its clinical definition as a certain illness, can never be consistent with its own definition because the melancholic, as a human subject, must be aware of the existence of this contingent replacement, which, even though it seems no match to melancholia's identification with its perceived ultimate destination, which is death, is nevertheless what constitutes the human subject's desire to perpetuate herself as a desiring subject even if the final destination is death. The remainder, in other words, is a supplement which supplants melancholia itself. Claire's seemingly inexplicable sense of loss at that moment when she circles nervously on her horse as she realizes the disappearance of the Antares corresponds precisely with the melancholic position; for the melancholic, as Jacques Hassoun argues, "is tormented not by a loss, but by the lack of possibility for naming and designating this loss" (29).

It is precisely this remainder which urges us to repeat the experience of watching the film—and perhaps in particular the end scene—from the safety of our surrounding reality. What we really enjoy is not the orgasmic collision and the end of the world, but the notion that this can always be played again, because it is this repetitive gesture that corresponds with the idea of our survival as desiring subjects even while/after watching the world coming to a catastrophic end. We can watch again the melancholic calm composure of Justine as she sits inside her 'magic cave'—a calmness she transfers to her nephew, Leo—and the traumatic experience of Claire as the shockwaves of Melancholia's wind and fire cause her body to flutter like thin paper before the world disappears. How can this act of repetition be described if not as a conscious reconstitution of a spectacular traumatic moment—*from the position of Claire*—that is to be enjoyed? Identification with Justine at this moment may reflect a philosophical position, a theoretical satisfaction, but it cannot constitute any erotic enjoyment.

Justine may be "'saner' than the rest of her family" (Power) but the problem is that she loses her privileged position as a resistant melancholic once she becomes "sane", once we realize this sanity, or once her weakness is transformed into omnipotence and her melancholic defiance in the first part of the film becomes omniscience in the second. The viewer identifies with the insane. In fact, in her composed acceptance of death, Justine is not far from being a model of religious and eschatological conformity, even if she appears to be the opposite of that. It is Claire who dies while still posing the erotic question 'why is this happening?'; in other words, who still has the apprehension of the subject and its total confusion before the mandates of an imagined, incomprehensible power. Identification with Justine, at this point, assumes a philosophical position that declares with assurance, but not without some sort of triumphalism, that it knows this world is worthless, that it has to end in some violent catastrophe, and that this is a logical and acceptable end.

The beauty of *Melancholia* is that its stylistics negates its content, and vice versa, at crucial points. Certain that the end of the world is coming soon, Claire suggests meeting death on her terrace with a glass of wine. Against this attempt at being joyous while meeting death, Justine mocks her sister's idea by replying contemptuously: "How about a song? Beethoven's Ninth?" Rob White argues that "Beethoven's work comes out of the same barbarous 'high culture' (and high Science) that produced industrial capitalism and industrial mass murder. What's to be joyous about?" (White). However, a minor adjustment to the film's dialogue here would produce a highly self-critical and almost comical effect: 'How about a song? Wagner's Tristan Chord?'

Wouldn't the film and Justine's melancholia have a much lesser impact on the viewer without Wagner's music, "with its characteristic stasis, its unwillingness to develop freely" (Pintér)? It is precisely what Justine holds in contempt—making music and listening to it in general—that presents her melancholia to the viewer. And, it is Wagner's music in particular that happens to be historically connected to barbarism and mass murder due to Wagner's known anti-Semitic tendencies. In perfect parallel with this, Justine's "refusal to exit the world aesthetically (sitting drinking wine and listening to music with Claire)" (Power) is, however, marked by precisely exiting the world aesthetically thanks to the graphics. The last scene of the film definitely needs no music. The visual contains enough music for the eyes.

Stefan Bolea states that *Melancholia* "could be interpreted as a logical consequence of the history of European nihilism" and that "perhaps the Danish director is expressing our deepest unconscious desire to be absolved of existence: he's expressing the mysterious *will to die*, the instinct of death, which has its roots in the core of our civilization" (Bolea). Bolea's statement in fact reveals the complication of the notion of the drive towards death; however, one has to suggest that there is a certain difficulty in defining the state of melancholia itself as an illness in relation to it. Lacan states that "the drive is precisely that *montage* by which sexuality participates in the psychical life, in a way that must conform to the gap-like structure that is the structure of the unconscious" (*Four Fundamental Concepts* 176). The drive thus is sexuality's tool by which it creates an aim for itself within the intricacies of the unconscious. That aim is not the drive's final destination. As Žižek puts it:

> The real purpose of the drive is not its goal (full satisfaction) but its aim: the drive's ultimate aim is simply to reproduce itself as drive, to return to its circular path, to continue its path to and from the goal. The real source of enjoyment is the repetitive movement of this closed circuit. (*Looking Awry* 5)

Justine's full satisfaction, then, cannot represent the aim of the drive but rather its imagined final goal—death—which is not really its purpose. It is inevitable here to conclude that the melancholic position may not be exactly free of a certain pretense. In other words, I totally agree with Bolea that "*Melancholia* could be interpreted as a logical consequence of the history of European nihilism", yet, "our deepest unconscious desire to be absolved of existence" (Bolea) can only be thought of in terms of enjoyment. It is symbolic existence that is involved here. The drive to non-existence is nothing but a drive towards the level of *jouissance* where "truth is simply inoperative" (Žižek, *For They Know Not* LXVII) and where both the subject and the big Other disappear. This is the only nihilism that *Melancholia* could be the logical consequence of.

A lot of things happen in the few moments that precede Melancholia's collision with Earth. Wagner's music stops. Logically, Wagner's music gains more importance precisely when it stops; in other words, when it returns to where it came from. As Daniel Barenboim puts it, "the prelude to *Tristan und Isolde* is an obvious example of the sound evolving out of silence" (9). Wagner's first note "creates a situation of being in no-man's-land" (19). This is not just the situation of the melancholic; it is the situation of the human subject as such, regressing to a state of primary fragmentation that precedes subjectivity. It was Adorno who first noticed that "the radical process of integration" in Wagner's work as a whole "is already no more than a cover for the underlying fragmentation" (*In Search of Wagner* 93). The characters sit silently inside Justine's magical cave—Justine and Leo entirely calm, Claire non-sonorously panicking. The sonorous element in the film changes radically; there are no more human voices or human-made sounds. We hear only the "roiling undertone of the end of the world, an emotional and physical evacuation" (Nicolini 61).

Yet, the main idea that the present work is trying to stress here is that we come to know that this stylistic "undertone" marking the melancholic "emotional and physical evacuation" the film ends with is traumatic and *deafening* through no one but Claire, as she is the only character who performs that natural reaction of covering her ears with her palms to try to protect her hearing while Justine and her disciple—little Leo—seem to be unaffected by that deafening noise. Nicolini states that "even though Claire and Leo are present, we ultimately experience the end of the world through Justine" (61). Is that true? Won't most viewers in fact enjoy experiencing the end of the world through Claire, whose senses seem to be more alert to what's happening at that moment? Claire may not be holding us "captive inside her head" (61) like Justine, yet all the eroticism of the moment is concentrated around her trembling body. And, when the moment of collision comes, it is Claire's swaying body being violently consumed by the shockwaves of Melancholia's wind and fire that holds the viewer's gaze.

If we are to choose between Justine and Claire, at this particular moment, as a figure to replace the homunculus in Edvard Munch's painting *The Scream*, that figure has to be Claire. The homunculus, with its mouth open in a traumatic scream (unheard and only imagined by the onlooker), its hands covering its ears (or the earless sides of its featureless head) in a clear gesture of trying to protect its senses from great, calamitous noise, and its slender body swaying with the colorful spirals of a visual yet unidentified ongoing catastrophe, remarkably resembles Claire in the last few frames of *Melancholia*'s visual. If *The Scream* is, in Fredric Jameson's words, "a canonical expression of the great modernist thematics of alienation, anomie, solitude, social fragmentation, and isolation" (11), it is the trembling figure of Claire that condenses all of these thematics at the end of *Melancholia*, even if they are monopolized by the melancholic Justine during most of the film.

In his description of the colorful loops that dominate Munch's painting, Jameson writes:

> Such loops inscribe themselves on the painted surface in the form of those great concentric circles in which sonorous vibration becomes ultimately visible ... in an infinite regress which fans out from the sufferer to become the very geography of a universe in which pain itself now speaks and vibrates through the material sunset and landscapes. (14)

As the "daughter of chaos" (Nicolini 27), it can be argued that Justine indeed "has turned the world upside down, emptied herself of structure, systems and containment, and now, ironically, she has built a structure to lead Claire, Leo, and the audience to the cataclysmic yet beautiful end" (59–60). Justine at that moment indeed seems to prove Jacques Hassoun's point that "clinical practice teaches us that at the height of distress, melancholics are free of anxiety" (67). The beautiful end, however, seems to place all of its beauty in the anxious and suffering figure of Claire. *Melancholia*'s last spectacle, like Munch's *The Scream*, "subtly but elaborately disconnects its own aesthetic of expression" (Jameson 14), but in its own case, it does that, first, by the discontinuation of Wagner's musical notes which mark all the outstanding scenes in the film and, second, by totally muting Claire's traumatic scream—for there must be one.

Claire's muted scream, which is also ours if we have the courage to abandon the pretentious position of being melancholic and truly enjoy masochistically the moment that precedes the orgasmic collision, translates immediately into the loops and spirals of Melancholia's wind and fire, the power of which can only be evidenced by the final violent vibration of Claire's body before the screen goes black. Thus, identification with Justine in the final scene, though easily assumed and more or less established by various critical responses to the film, requires a kind of philosophical reflection that is devoid of Lacan's object of fantasy or object-cause of desire, the objet petit a[1]—a position that is phantasmal in itself no doubt, if not downright pretentious.

To illustrate this point further, let us reflect on the scene in which Justine sprawls naked on the river bank at night and gazes adoringly upon the blue planet in the sky. By "looking awry" (Žižek, *Looking Awry* 11–12) at this approaching danger, Melancholia becomes so beautiful precisely because Justine's gaze upon it is distorted by her desire. She sees something in the planet "more than itself".[2] The planet at a distance is the shape the objet petit a assumes for the eyes of Justine, who imagines herself as "the bride of Melancholia" (Gordon). Justine in this scene is clearly making love to her object of fantasy, which is 'materialized' by the blue planet. The appearance of the planet, to Justine, literally becomes constitutive of the moment of "melancholic passion" that Hassoun, in his analysis of melancholy, defines as:

> A moment of the sudden surfacing of a phenomenal object that is the cause of all desires, an object that will mold itself onto some chosen being whose appearance captivates the subject and draws it into an experience of radical desubjectivization. (7)

Her solid calmness at the end, however, suggests that she actually got something in the place of the nothing that the object of fantasy actually is. In other words, the objet petit a no longer exists for her. While identification with the naked Justine on the river bank conforms to the (ab)normality of the human psyche, identification with the "daughter of chaos" (Nicolini 27) at the end of the film is a false position that pretends the subject—melancholic or not—can afford to confront the real of desire or "psychic reality" (Žižek, *Looking Awry* 16) in a direct way, or can deal with the utter void, the very nothingness beyond being that the subject approaches in a nightmare before *waking up, terrified, in order to continue to dream*. Lacan uses Freud's analysis of the dream of the unfortunate father and his burning child in the *Traumdeutung* (Freud, *The Interpretation of Dreams* 652–4, 681–2, 725–6) to show that—contrary to Freud's idea that this is a dream whose function is to satisfy the need to prolong sleep—there is another kind of reality in the dream, a "missed reality" or the "reality that can no longer produce itself except by repeating itself endlessly, in some never attained awakening". This reality is psychic reality or the real of desire, which causes the dreamer to wake up literally in order to escape from psychic reality into the reality of waking life, which in this case is nothing but a dream in which there is no real awakening (Lacan, *Four Fundamental Concepts* 58–9).

The film then shows that the melancholic, to put it in Lacanian language, can afford *not to wake up*, to continue the nightmare to its end, to face the real of desire to the point of the subject's destruction and disappearance. The question that poses itself here, of course, is: is this at all possible? And if it is cinematically possible, can the viewer truly identify with it? The answer is: yes, but by the means of some sort of 'pure' philosophy that can repress the notion of the objet petit a. As Lacan puts it, "Cet objet est celui qui manque à la considération philosophique pour se situer, c'est à dire pour savoir qu'elle n'est rien" (*Cahiers pour l'Analyse* 9) (This object [a] is what philosophical discourse lacks in order to situate itself, in other words, to know about its own fallibility.) The stark proof that identification with Justine in the final scene can only take place through this kind of philosophical reflection, which may belong to the mind but not the psyche, is the sheer anxiety that we experience in watching the scene.

In his essay 'From Reality to the Real', Žižek argues that "it is not the lack of the object that gives rise to anxiety but, on the contrary, the danger of our getting too close to the object and thus losing the lack itself. Anxiety is brought on by the disappearance of desire" (*Looking Awry* 8). In light of this, it can be argued that, while the objet petit a no longer exists for Justine in the final scene—in which she lacks everything and nothing at once—the viewer enjoys the scene precisely because s(he) *does not and cannot* identify with Justine's position (which involves looking the real in the face without flinching) and, hence, can still get anxious by "getting too close to the object"; in other words, by being merely *threatened* with "losing the lack" that defines him as a desiring subject and becoming totally immersed in a state of passive desire-less-ness as the position of the melancholic Justine assumes.

It is crucial to understand, though, that this anxiety *cannot* be transferred to the viewer through Justine but *only* through Claire who, by all psychoanalytic and/or philosophical accounts, if we can really imagine the moment the world comes to an end, does not and cannot be simply clinging to "the world around her—the golf course, John's estate, her role as mother, as wife, as woman" (Nicolini 60) as the feminist reading of Nicolini suggests. Claire, in the final scene, goes far deeper than that. She clings to her position—our position—as a *desiring subject*, regardless of her gender.

It is the erotic play with the idea of the end of our own eroticism that urges us to enjoy watching the climactic scene of *Melancholia* over and over again. The problem with a feminist reading of *Melancholia* is thus the fact that it stakes too much on the idea of questioning or overcoming sexual difference when the film is clearly more concerned with the idea of total disappearance and death—something sexual difference simply cannot get to grips with. As Derrida puts it, "sexual difference does not count in the face of death. Sexual difference would be a being-up-until-death" (*Gift of Death* 45).

After all the aforesaid, it should not come as a surprise to the reader when I suggest that, among the several scenes staging Justine's delightful melancholic transgressions, which cause her to lose her marriage and career in a single night, it is the scene which appears to be the least transgressive of all, the one with no serious consequence whatsoever, that stands out as a summing-up of all of these transgressions as well as an indicator of the very *impossibility* of transgression. On the surface of it, the scene in which Justine frantically beats her horse, Abraham, might be taken as the least transgressive. After all, what's beating a horse compared to abandoning her wedding guests and sleeping at the wrong time, pissing on John's expensive golf course, insulting her boss and irrevocably losing her job, refusing her husband's sexual advances and fucking a stranger instead? Yet, it is in the scene of beating Abraham—who totally refuses to cross the bridge at the limits of John's estate (where the whole film takes place)—that the idea of transgression itself, through both content and form, is seriously questioned at the very moment it is staged.

We should be clear first that Justine loves Abraham. Arriving so late to her wedding party, she makes sure nevertheless to visit him before doing anything else. She tells him softly in an apologetic voice that she is now married, as if she were talking to a best friend or an old boyfriend who should mind her new status. Justine and Abraham have obviously known each other for a very long time. They understand each other well. When Abraham stops at the bridge on the first ride, Justine spurs him knowingly: "Come on Abraham, come on!" as if she knows beforehand that he will stop at this point. It is as if Abraham never crossed that bridge and his behavior at it is expected by Justine. However, when Abraham stops again at the same bridge on the second ride, Justine, this time, beats him violently and repeatedly. Justine *knows* that Abraham will never cross that bridge. She gets angry but she is not surprised. She does not try to get off the horse and lead him across. She does not cross the bridge on foot and wait for him on the other side. She does not give way to Claire's horse so it can cross over first and show Abraham an example of good equine behavior. She only beats him desperately, fully aware that the beating will not result in his crossing the bridge.

Justine might also have contemplated beforehand beating Abraham if he refused to cross the bridge this time. Earlier, while saddling the horses just before the ride, she stands reluctantly beside him causing Claire to shout at her: "Justine, take him out!" as if Justine wanted to avoid the ride altogether, knowing she will eventually come to the bridge, Abraham will eventually stop at it yet again and, this time, she will beat her beloved horse mercilessly. If Justine knows that Abraham will never cross the bridge, what does it mean to beat him? If Abraham is known to be that obstinate horse who always stops at the bridge, shouldn't we then conclude that Justine is beating him not just because of his behavior at this particular moment but because of *who he is*?

The question of who Abraham is poses itself at the very point at which "fantasy does not only conceal the horror of the real, it also creates what it purports to conceal" (Žižek, *Žižek Reader* 92). What Justine wants to cross is not just the border of John's estate but the phantasmic border between reality and the real, the delicate screen which stands between the subject's symbolic world and the utter void the screen conceals. In her drive towards total destruction—her "passion for the real" (Žižek, *Welcome to the Desert* 6)—Justine not only wants to "empt[y] herself of the feminine" (Nicolini 13) or "break free from her gender and the systems that want to trap her" (4), but to commit to the oblivion of the real, not in a suicidal sense, but in the sense of the ultimate transgression of coming face to face with the very nothingness of her own being.

Crossing the bridge thus assumes, in Justine's mind, the gigantic status of knowing the self beyond the identity given to her by narrative, which, in Žižek's words, "does not stage the suspension or transgression of the Law, on the contrary, it is the very act of its installation" (*Žižek Reader* 94). Like writing literature, phantasmic narrative is that realm where the self tries its utmost to touch upon its own core, ultimately to no avail. Justine's transgressive act of beating Abraham is precisely Pierre Klossowski's "image" of the "act to be done" (Klossowski 41), or, the image of the transgressive act which remains always already undone. Klossowski's "act to be done" would be an act that is unmediated by narrative and cannot be represented by language. It is always foreclosed. Klossowski writes:

> 'Foreclosure' means that something remains outside. That which remains outside is ... the act to be done. The less it is perpetrated the more it raps on the door—the door of literary vacuity. (41)

The impossible transgressive act, which cannot be done, remains forever sequestered by language, submerged by literature or concealed by narrative that can only illuminate its *image*. Justine's repetitive beating of Abraham is *Melancholia*'s radical form of that image. That is why Lacan states that "we don't ever transgress" (*Other Side* 19). The less the transgressive act of crossing over to the real is perpetrated by Justine, the more she madly beats Abraham who symbolizes, not the least by his proper name, phantasmic vacuity.

Klossowski's analysis of the phenomenon of monotonous repetition in Sade's work points to the monotonous repetition of the act of writing itself, which can also apply to the act of creating art (or, in von Trier's case, the act of making movies)—a continuous attempt at the impossible transgressive act of knowing the self, which, at its most reaching limit, would be an encounter with the real—the very nothingness on which the human self is based. Justine's monotonous repetition of beating Abraham is precisely the image the film gives to that impossible act of transgression which *cannot be done*.

For we cannot cross over to the real by an act of will. For the real to live up to its Lacanian definition as a "hole in the symbolic" (Lacan, *Psychoses* 156), it has to attack us at a moment it chooses. Yet, because of her "passion for the real" (Žižek, *Welcome to the Desert* 6), Justine can't wait to cross over and, when she isn't able to, takes it out violently on Abraham in an act which, *to her*, must be the most transgressive of all, yet which, at the same time, stands as a stark indicator of the very impossibility of transgression. Justine cannot leave John's estate, Kirsten Dunst cannot leave von Trier's film setting, Lars von Trier cannot but continue to make movies, we cannot but enjoy them, and the rapping on the door of *our own vacuity* just continues.

Justine, in the scene of beating Abraham, is much more than "the abused becoming the abuser" and Abraham is much more than "the last man standing" (Nicolini 50). Justine is the human subject as such, genderless, at the very limits of its symbolic existence, and Abraham stands for identity as such; that which is based on that tacit process of imaginary identification, the foundation of a subjectivity that is fated never to find its own tangibility. Abraham is based on nothing but literature, or, Abraham *is* literature; that which "voids itself in its limitlessness" (Derrida, *Acts of Literature* 177), saying everything and nothing at once. Stopping at the bridge every time he comes to it, Abraham stands at Kafka's gate to the Law, which "remains open as ever" (Kafka, *Metamorphosis* 197) but virtually inaccessible, "deferr[ing] forever till death … entry into the law itself, which is nothing other than that which dictates the delay" (Derrida, *Acts of Literature* 205). Justine beats Abraham because, in his symbolization of the inaccessibility of what is beyond reality, his own truth, just like Justine's, in a Kafkaesque way, is "made of literature"; he, as well as Justine, is "nothing else, and cannot be anything else" (Kafka, *Letters to Felice* 304). The Law does not allow any other form of being.

Abraham, like religion, is so defining yet so irrelevant at once, and like religious eschatology, cannot come to grips with what he believes in or what he obeys. Like human imagination, Abraham always falls back helplessly on what Lacan describes as "the realm of what is considered acceptable or, in other words, the realm of prejudices" (*Ethics of Psychoanalysis* 251). Abraham is civilization, whose history is the history of "the introversion of sacrifice" (Horkheimer and Adorno 46) in the form of the ultimate guilt of betraying humanity itself in the name of duty, for "absolute duty demands that one behave in an irresponsible manner (by means of treachery or betrayal) while still recognizing, confirming, and reaffirming the very thing one sacrifices, namely, the order of human ethics and responsibility" (Derrida, *Gift of Death* 67).

Abraham is the "sign of Abraham, of Father Abraham, the absolute patriarch" (Derrida, *Acts of Religion* 414) who is also the ultimate symbol of the "culture of hospitality", which is, in Derrida's view, "culture itself" (360–1). And because culture is neurotic by definition, Father Abraham is history's most prominent symptom of neurosis, or, transforming the self into a signifier,[3] while Justine, unable to cross the bridge on her horse's back—which bears the symbolic name of Abraham—and unable to break free from reality, instantly experiences a psychotic moment and becomes madly against signification itself. Neuroses, like Abraham, remain inside the symbolic order, precisely because erotic relations with the other, or, that which is a reflection of the self, remain in them. Transforming oneself into a signifier maintains the whole system of symbolic exchanges that define one's life and relations with others. In her psychotic moment of beating Abraham, Justine declares war against culture, religion, language, identity, and the chain of signification itself, yet ultimately shows us, clearly and unequivocally, that there is no way out.

Father Abraham is, de jure, through intention and firm determination, the slayer of his own son in the name of duty. Abraham, in *Melancholia*, stands for Father Abraham himself, who is "faithful to God only in his absolute treachery, in the betrayal of his own" (Derrida, *Gift of Death* 68). Like Father Abraham, who betrays his son in order to remain faithful to God, Abraham betrays Justine but remains absolutely faithful to his role in the film, his duty, and what he is supposed to do once he reaches the bridge. Abraham is the exemplification of absolute responsibility and absolute irresponsibility at once. In his absolute integrity as himself, in accordance with himself, in his truthfulness to himself, he betrays and sacrifices *primarily himself*; he destroys his legacy at the very moment in which he claims it. Abraham, like Father Abraham, is "at the same time the most moral and the most immoral ... because he responds absolutely to absolute duty" (72). He is thus "paradox, scandal, and aporia [which] are themselves nothing other than sacrifice, the revelation of conceptual thinking at its limit, at its death and finitude" (68).

Abraham is the Abrahamic; that which "harangue[s] us toward a prophetic and messianic future that, more often than not, comforts because it presents, destroys, or steals no more than the images of the other" (Anidjar 9). Justine's rebellion is not simply a feminist one. It is not just about Abraham, the patriarch, it is about the Abrahamic itself, which, in its own turn, is not just religious narrative or eschatology but narrative as such as the ambiguous source of both religion and eschatology. Eschatology is comforting precisely because it is a fantasy by which the Abrahamic deceptively answers the Lacanian anxious question "Chè vuoi?" (what does the Other want of me?) (Lacan, *Écrit: The First Complete Edition* 690) with regard to the desire of God, even though—or precisely because—"God keeps silent about his reasons" behind "demand[ing] of Abraham that most cruel, impossible, and untenable gesture: to offer his son Isaac as a sacrifice" (Derrida, *Gift of Death* 58). Justine's psychotic repetitive beating of Abraham is a fervent questioning of the Abrahamic. It is an act of cruelty that questions cruelty.

Above all, Abraham is fantasy; "the imaginary scenario which, with its fascinating presence, screens off the lack in the Other, the radical inconsistency of the symbolic order" (Žižek, *Žižek Reader* 30). In his standoff against Justine's radical desire—to cross the bridge, to escape the imaginary, to leave the film's claustrophobic setting, to leave the world, or to break free from language—Abraham stands for "*desire itself* [as] *a defence against desire*", which is explained by Žižek as "the desire structured through fantasy" as "a defence against the desire of the Other, against this 'pure', trans-phantasmic desire (i.e. the 'death drive' in its pure form)" (*Sublime Object* 118). Abraham is the fantasy which "constitutes the frame through which we experience the world as consistent and meaningful— the a priori space within which the particular effects of signification take place" (123). It is this deceptive consistency and meaningfulness of the world that Justine is totally against. Abraham is deception itself, yet, he is also the only truth allowed to us. He is nothing and everything.

What is "wrong with [us] besides melancholia" (Bukowski 303) is something that melancholia as an illness does not and *cannot* have an answer for, because what is wrong with us relates to melancholia not as an exception but as the human condition as such, which *must* be by definition melancholic by virtue of the castrating gesture of the subject's very inscription into the symbolic order. That is why Julia Kristeva sees the sorrow of the narcissistic depressed as the "signaling of an incomplete, empty, and wounded primitive ego" that is not simply "injured but stricken by a fundamental lack, by a congenital deficiency"; a sorrow which "hides neither the guilt nor the failure of a secretly hatched vengeance against the ambivalent object", and instead is itself the melancholic's "only object", which could be the "most archaic expression of a narcissistic wound" that is "impossible to symbolize or name" (*New Formations* 7). This lack, to Kristeva, is constituted by the child's separation from the mother, which makes him "irremediably sad before uttering his first words" and which engenders in him a human imagination that is always already "manifestly or secretly, melancholic" (5).

Melancholia can only reject reality, but cannot deal with what is beyond reality. It may result in suicide, which can be nothing but the subject's "suicide '*in* reality'", which "remains caught in the network of symbolic communication" (Žižek, *Enjoy Your Symptom* 43), like putting a note in a bottle and throwing it into the sea in an attempt to "send a message to the Other" (44). However, what remains with us after watching *Melancholia* and its beautiful end (the blue planet colliding with Earth and ending the history of the human species) is not the category of the melancholic (Justine) or the "unconscious desire to be absolved of existence" (Bolea) but the category of the *hysteric* (Claire) or that which erotically enjoys being the victim of, and at the same time is tormented and ultimately destroyed by, an incomprehensible power, after having to live its whole life under incomprehensible mandates.

Nina Power argues that Justine's mother's ironic exhortation at the wedding—"enjoy it while it lasts"—seems far truer of Justine's own "dance of death" with Melancholia than it does of her own marriage". Let me add that Gaby's "enjoy it while it lasts" would seem truest if it were addressed to the viewer of *Melancholia*: 'Enjoy the film while it lasts, enjoy the two beautiful sisters, enjoy the approaching beautiful blue planet of orgasmic digital destruction, and above all, enjoy your postmodern identification with melancholy and the idea of the sublime from the comfort of your seat in front of the cinema screen, or, better still, in your 'melancholic' solitude in front of your DVD player. However, there will always already be the question of 'what to do next?' What else is there besides *Melancholia*? Is it a coincidence that Lars von Trier's next film is entitled *Nymphomaniac*?

Notes

1. Lacan explains how this object, symbolized by the cotton-reel of the Freudian fort-da game, "is a small part of the subject that detaches itself from him while still remaining his", marking a "Spaltung" (split) in the subject that is caused by the "repetition of the mother's departure" and "overcome by the alternating game, *fort-da*". It is this object which marks the distortion of the gaze by desire. 'Tuché and Automaton', *The Four Fundamental Concepts of Psycho-Analysis*, ed. Jacques-Alain Miller and trans. Alan Sheridan (Penguin Books, 1994), pp. 62–3.
2. Lacan summarizes this relationship between the subject and the object of desire by his famous statement "*I love you, but, because inexplicably I love in you something more than you—the* objet petit a—*I mutilate you*". 'In you more than you', *The Four Fundamental Concepts of Psycho-Analysis*, ed. Jacques-Alain Miller and trans. Alan Sheridan (Penguin Books, 1994), p. 268.
3. In his discussion 'On the rejection of a primordial signifier', Lacan explains how the neurotic subject, "instead of using words, uses everything at his disposal ... he gets completely inside himself, with the signifier, it's he who becomes the signifier. His real, or his imaginary, enters into the discourse". *The Psychoses 1955–1956*, ed. Jacques-Alain Miller and trans. Russell Grigg (New York and London: W.W. Norton & Company, 1997), p. 155.

Bibliography

Adorno, Theodor W. *In Search of Wagner*. Translated by Rodney Livingstone. London and New York: Verso, 2005.

Anidjar, Gil. '"Once More, Once More": Derrida, the Arab, the Jew'. *Acts of Religion*. Edited by Gil Anidjar. New York and London: Routledge, 2002.

Barenboim, Daniel. *Everything Is Connected: The Power of Music*. Edited by Elena Cheah. London: Weidenfeld and Nicolson, 2008.

Bolea, Stefan. 'Melancholia'. *Philosophy Now*. No. 91. July/Aug. 2012. Accessed 20 July 2013. http://philosophynow.org/issues/91/Melancholia

Bukowski, Charles. *The Pleasures of the Damned: Poems, 1951–1993*. Edited by John Martin. Edinburgh, London, New York and Melbourne: Canongate, 2010.

Derrida, Jacques. *Acts of Literature*. Edited by Derek Attridge. New York and London: Routledge, 1992.

Derrida, Jacques. *The Gift of Death*. Translated by David Wills. Chicago and London: University of Chicago Press, 1995.

Derrida, Jacques. *Of Grammatology*. Translated by Gayatri Chakravorty Spivak. Baltimore and London: Johns Hopkins University Press, 1997.

Derrida, Jacques. *Acts of Religion*. Edited by Gil Anidjar. New York and London: Routledge, 2002.

Freud, Sigmund. *The Interpretation of Dreams*. Edited by Angela Richards. Translated and edited by James Strachey with the assistance of Alan Tyson. London and New York: Penguin Books, 1991.

Gordon, Andrew. 'The Bride of Melancholia'. *Psy Art*, 7 September 2012. Accessed 20 July 2013. http://www.psyartjournal.com/article/show/gordon-the_bride_of_melancholia

Hassoun, Jacques. *The Cruelty of Depression: On Melancholy*. Translated by David Jacobson. Reading, MA: Addison-Wesley, 1997.

Horkheimer, Max, and Theodor W. Adorno. *Dialectic of Enlightenment: Philosophical Fragments*. Edited by Gunzelin Schmid Noerr and translated by Edmund Jephcott. Palo Alto, CA: Stanford University Press, 2002.

Jameson, Fredric. *Postmodernism, or, The Cultural Logic of Late Capitalism*. London and New York: Verso, 1991.

Kafka, Franz. *Letters to Felice*. Edited by Erich Heller and Jürgen Born and translated by James Stern and Elisabeth Duckworth. London: Secker and Warburg, 1974.

Kafka, Franz. *Metamorphosis and Other Stories*. Translated by Michael Hofmann. London and New York: Penguin, 2007.

Klossowski, Pierre. *Sade My Neighbour*. Translated by Alphonso Lingis. London: Quartet Books, 1992.

Kristeva, Julia. 'On the Melancholic Imaginary'. *New Formations*. No. 3, Winter 1987. London: Lawrence and Wishart Ltd, 1987.

Lacan, Jacques. *The Four Fundamental Concepts of Psycho-Analysis*. Edited by Jacques-Alain Miller and translated by Alan Sheridan. Penguin Books, 1994.

Lacan, Jacques. *The Psychoses 1955–1956*. Edited by Jacques-Alain Miller and translated by Russell Grigg. New York and London: W.W. Norton and Company, 1997.

Lacan, Jacques. *The Ethics of Psychoanalysis 1959–1960*. Edited by Jacques-Alain Miller and translated by Dennis Porter. London: Routledge, 1999.

Lacan, Jacques. *Écrit: The First Complete Edition in English*. Translated by Bruce Fink. New York and London: W.W. Norton and Company, 2006.

Lacan, Jacques. *The Other Side of Psychoanalysis*. Translated and with notes by Russell Grigg. New York and London: W.W. Norton and Company, 2007.

Lacan, Jacques. 'Résponses à des étudiants en philosophie'. *Cahiers pour l'Analyse* 3. May–June 1996, Paris. Accessed 20 September 2014. http://cahiers.kingston.ac.uk/pdf/cpa3.1.lacan.pdf

Nicolini, Kim. 'Freedom in Oblivion: Post-Feminist Possibilities in Lars von Trier's Melancholia'. Accessed 20 July 2013. http://www.Kimnicolini.Com/wp-content/uploads/2012/04/Melancholia_KN-4-5-12.pdf

Pintér, Judit. 'The Lonely Planet: Lars von Trier's *Melancholia*'. Translated by J. Tucker. *Senses of Cinema*. No. 61, December 2011. Accessed 20 July 2013. http://sensesofcinema.com/2011/feature-articles/the-lonely-planet-lars-von-triers-melancholia

Power, Nina. 'Lars von Trier's Melancholia: A Discussion'. *Film Quarterly* 65, no. 4 (Summer 2012). Accessed 22 July 2013. http://www.filmquarterly.org/2012/01/lars-von-triers-melancholia-a-discussion

White, Rob. 'Lars von Trier's Melancholia: A Discussion'. *Film Quarterly* 65, no. 4 (Summer 2012). Accessed 22 July 2013. http://www.filmquarterly.org/2012/01/lars-von-triers-melancholia-a-discussion

Žižek, Slavoj. *The Sublime Object of Ideology*. London and New York: Verso, 1989.

Žižek, Slavoj. *Looking Awry: An Introduction to Jacques Lacan through Popular Culture*. London and Cambridge: MIT Press, 1992.

Žižek, Slavoj. *The Žižek Reader*. Edited by Elizabeth Wright and Edmond Wright. Oxford and Malden, MA: Blackwell Publishing, 1999.

Žižek, Slavoj. *Enjoy Your Symptom! Jacques Lacan in Hollywood and Out*. New York and London: Routledge, 2001.

Žižek, Slavoj. *For They Know Not What They Do: Enjoyment as a Political Factor*. London and New York: Verso, 2002.

Žižek, Slavoj. *Welcome to the Desert of the Real! Five Essays on September 11 and Related Dates*. London and New York: Verso, 2002.

CHAPTER 9

Conclusion, or, Desire as Law: The Loneliness of *Nymphomaniac* between Pornography and Narrative

The world of pornography has always sustained itself through a particular dependence on two fundamental ideas: the complete removal of the idea of rejection (that women—and occasionally men—are always willing and happy to have sex, even in a rape situation) and the sheer number and heterogeneity of the women and men that pornographic material usually offers. In other words, the business of pornography sustains itself through fantasy and the law of desire. With regard to women in particular, the fantasy of the pornographic world answers the famous Freudian question "Was will das Weib?"[1] with one word: sex. At the same time, it plays on the metonymic structure of desire, which makes sure the subject always misses the object of desire; it remains forever unattainable. So first, all women are available and, second, none of them remains the object of desire for long. Or, if there is one starlet and many men, all the men are available, but none of them really satisfies her voracious sexual appetite. The same applies to the viewer addicted to watching pornographic films: scopophilic desire renews itself perpetually on the false promise that the next film will be different from, and more gratifying than, all the previous ones. The law of desire decrees that, in order for desire not to die out, the object of desire must remain forever outside its reach.

The following argument approaches the question of desire through Lars von Trier's *Nymphomaniac*, a film that can quite justifiably be seen as the director's most pornographic film – yet. *Nymphomaniac*'s pornography, however, seems to serve as the most effective tool by which the film *departs from* one of the fundamental pornographic rules, namely the play on the metonymic structure of desire, in order to effectively replace the law of desire with the Lacanian idea of *desire as law*, which Lacan discusses in his 'Kant with Sade' (*Écrit: The First Complete Edition* 645–68), in which he shows how those two seemingly irreconcilable figures meet at the very limits of moral law where Sade's *Philosophy in the Bedroom* "yields the truth" (646) of Kant's 'Critique of Practical Reason' in spite of the Kantian elevation of the Law above "pleasure ... pain, happiness ... abject poverty ... the love of life—in short, everything pathological" (662). Moreover, *Nymphomaniac* does this in a particularly Sadean fashion; by telling the story of her various sexual exploits, which by all means could have been written by the Marquis de Sade himself, the heroine *becomes* Sade in the sense that Simone de Beauvoir makes out of the Marquis as mainly a corpus of literature or as one long erotic narrative. And, when everything is said, once the heroine becomes able to regard herself as narrative, she, like Sade, becomes "afraid of the reality of the world" (Beauvoir 7).

On the surface, it is easy to accuse von Trier's *Nymphomaniac* of being nothing but a cheap pornographic film, even an immoral one. Seligman, an elderly, withdrawn and overeducated bachelor finds Joe, a self-diagnosed nymphomaniac, beaten up and lying on the floor of an alleyway near his house. He takes her to his apartment where Joe recounts the stories of her sexual life in eight chapters while Seligman connects those stories with what he has read in various books. She starts from early childhood when she first discovered clitoral sensation, then goes on to relate different episodes of her life such as losing her virginity casually to a random young man, having sex with strangers on a train, experiencing feelings of love for the first time, which she dismisses as "lust with jealousy added", having ten or more sexual intercourses with different men on daily basis, ruining families and households on the way, sleeping with several workers at the hospital where her father eventually dies and lubricating in front of his corpse, trying to engage in a sexual ménage à trois with two Africans, neglecting her son while seeking the sadomasochistic services of a stranger, K, who gives her brutal beatings, and engaging in organized crime and becoming a debt collector after realizing she has no place in society. In the end, Joe feels at peace after unburdening herself to Seligman and asks to go to sleep. As she starts to doze off, Seligman returns with his pants off and attempts to have sexual intercourse with her. She wakes up, realizes what he is trying to do, says "no" and reaches for her gun. As she racks the gun the screen cuts to black. In the dark, an astonished Seligman says in an unbelieving, reluctant voice, "but you … you've fucked thousands of men", after which a gunshot is heard, then sounds of Joe hastily grabbing her things and fleeing the apartment.

Taking Joe's sensuality thoroughly "beyond the pleasure principle" (Freud, *On Metapsychology* 275–349 and Lacan, *The Four Fundamental Concepts* 184) (see the discussions of this notion in Chapters 1 and 7), von Trier's *Nymphomaniac* can be thought of as a critique of sensuality as much as its promoter. In chapter seven, which is entitled "The Mirror", and which seems to stand out as it deploys the only episode in the film without any male characters in it, Joe's clitoris starts to wear out and bleed. A doctor tells her to see a psychologist who conducts group therapy sessions. When Joe introduces herself to the group as a "nymphomaniac", the therapist objects and tells her to use "sex addict" instead of "nymphomaniac" because "here, everyone's the same". When the others leave, Joe and the therapist have a dialogue in which they discuss the impossible idea of removing one's sexuality. While Joe wonders how the psychologist can base her treatment on a one-in-a-million chance of success, the latter just gets down to business and tells Joe that the most important thing is to "remove incentives and to reduce exposure".

The psychologist's chillingly rational, calculative and scientificist language is precisely the kind of language Michael Miller criticizes in his Foreword to Jacques Hassoun's *The Cruelty of Depression* as a language which "not only reflects but also contributes in small ways to our general decline of civility". Miller compares the continued French interest in the lively intellectual debate that psychoanalysis gives ground to, enabling theorists to "talk without embarrassment about […] gross portion[s] of anatomy", "ponder the contours of both body and soul", "consider early human development", and maintain a "close collaborative relationship between therapist and patient" and American psychiatry, in which language seems to be limited to discussing "chromosomes and neurotransmitters", reducing the states of mind to "waxing and waning hormonal tides" and emphasizing "short courses of behavioral and cognitive engineering topped off with drug treatment" as a systematic or scheduled set of procedures tailored for "managed care", which Miller describes as "one of the more sinister bureaucratic tropes of our era" (xvii–xviii).

So, in an unforgettable scene, Joe removes, cuts, covers and hides everything that makes her think about sex, including the phone, books, the shower head, brushes, plungers, water taps, door knobs, edges of pieces of furniture, windows and, above all, mirrors. She laboriously removes her own hand from her sucking mouth with her other hand as her own limbs remain as the only sexual "incentives" left uncovered in her house. In her final (and perhaps only the second) group therapy session, she tries to adopt the same ridiculous calculative language of the psychologist: "My name is Joe … and I'm a sex addict, but I haven't had sex for three weeks and five days." The group claps (von Trier's way of ridiculing those numerous Hollywood scenes in which, for example, fellow alcoholics clap for the one who announces that he or she has finally managed to abstain from drinking). Joe takes out notes to read from in order to explain how she managed to achieve this triumph over her sexuality. She reads: "Dear everyone, don't think it's been easy, but I understand now that we are all alike." When she lifts her eyes up from the paper after reading her first written statement, she sees an image of herself as a child in a stand mirror that is kept close to the group and their therapist (clearly as one of the indispensable tools for treatment).

This image of young Joe sitting on a bench and looking directly at mature Joe reading her statement profoundly disrupts her show of abstinence and the façade group psychotherapy is trying to make out of her. Seeing her reluctance to read, the sympathetic therapist asks her "would you rather share another time?" A silent answer to the question seems to come to Joe directly from the stern face of the child in the mirror, disallowing peaceful withdrawal from the group, as if even a peaceful withdrawal still amounts to self-betrayal. True to herself, rebellious Joe does not only stick to her nymphomania, and to her views about her nymphomania, but must speak them out loud and throw them cavalierly in the face of society. So she replies, "no, I would like to speak", tearing her paper notes to pieces. And, right after one of von Trier's signature image jumps, which suggest either an (un)intentional frame repetition or an (un)intentional erratic/clumsy edit, Joe says:

> Dear everyone, don't think it's been easy, but I understand now that we're not and never will be alike. I'm not like you, who fucks to be validated and might just as well give up putting cocks inside you. And I'm not like you. All you want is to be filled up, and whether it's by a man or by tons of disgusting slop makes no difference.

Then, addressing the psychologist:

> And I'm definitely not like you. That empathy you claim is a lie because all you are is society's morality police, whose duty is to erase my obscenity from the surface of the earth, so that the bourgeoisie won't feel sick.

Then, finally:

> I'm not like you. I am a nymphomaniac, and I love myself for being one, but above all, I love my cunt and my filthy, dirty lust.

How can this steely position be understood? What Joe seems to take for granted underneath her unshakable principle of sticking to her nymphomania can be reconstructed in the following manner: she knows after a lifetime of doing mainly nothing but looking for men to satisfy her uncontrollable lust that there are various structures that her impetuous sexual powers take on in their insurgent and menacing movement. In some of the structures that these powers have grown under the pressure of a world of institutionalized relationships, accepted and unaccepted sexualities, disciplined as well as forbidden desires, false individualities that seek nothing but the same thing, group psychology and its assumed 'norms', etc., she seems also to have developed an excessively conscious position in her very apathy towards others ("you can't make an omelette without breaking a few eggs").

Tolerating the intolerable exigencies of the psychologist whose first demand is to replace "nymphomaniac" with "sex addict"—in other words, to replace the sense of 'natural deformity' with the sense of 'acquired illness'—literally displaces Joe's sense of self; it threatens her very subjectivity. In other words, the psychologist assumes that what lies behind her patient's abnormally excessive sexual activities (the repetitive nymphomaniac gestures) is simply an insistent pathological pursuit of pleasure, while to Joe, in a particularly Lacanian sense, "what necessitates repetition is *jouissance*". The difference is crucial, as Lacan further explains that "it is because there is a search for *jouissance* as repetition that [...] what interests us qua repetition, and which is registered with a dialectic of *jouissance*, is properly speaking what goes against life" (*Other Side* 45); in other words, the death instinct.

What the psychologist sees in Joe's repetitive abuse of her vagina is a vicious cycle of need and satisfaction, as if the behavior dictates the life of the organ. What Joe finally comes to learn, however, is the Lacanian lesson that "repetition is not only a function of the cycles that life consists of, cycles of need and satisfaction, [...] it is a function of a cycle that embraces the disappearance of this life as such, which is the return to the inanimate" and, consequently, "the function [does not] create the organ. On the contrary, one makes use of the organ as best one can" (46–7).

The point of normativity that the psychologist assumes and aims at, that is, a point at which Joe's psyche would be at peace with itself in terms of believing that there is an illness called 'sex addiction' which afflicts some people, that those people are all the same, and that they can all be cured using the same methodology, is nothing but one ingredient in modern psychotherapy's encompassing idea that man can aim at "being whole" or at possessing a "total personality", which Lacan sees as "deviant premises" (*Écrit: A Selection* 318) or as a total miss.

On the other hand, seeing the challenge posed by her own image in the mirror as a defiant child, Joe immediately realizes that conforming to the demands of the psychologist by reading the notes she has prepared on how she presumably defeated her nymphomania is an act of *censorship* by the very forces that incriminate nymphomania and forbidden sexualities in general. In other words, she realizes that transgressive sexuality always already incorporates the idea of censorship; in fact, censorship is the most essential drive for it. Joe also realizes that the false show of remorse demonstrated under the public eye of group psychotherapy, with all the loud announcements and the loud clapping, might be nothing but a kind of lassitude caused by some bodily damage—like her own clitoral bleeding, for example—and not by a newly acquired sense of morality or an awakened conscience.

Can remorse be public? Isn't remorse, like prayer in a particularly Derridean sense, an "absolutely secret"[2] act? Joe realizes that the bond between her nymphomania and the idea of censorship which "society's morality police" represents is itself the Lacanian "tight bond between desire and the Law" (Lacan, *Ethics of Psychoanalysis* 177). Any act of transgressive sexuality first and foremost appears as a promise of *jouissance* precisely because its imagined reification is particularly sickening. Moreover, if the drive to repeat the act "beyond the pleasure principle" eventually eradicates any sense of ethicality, this eradication happens by virtue of the same forces of ethicalism provoking the same transgression. From this point of view, *Nymphomaniac* is not simply about a woman enjoying herself to the point of abuse and bodily damage; it is about a woman whose politically incorrect position with regard to society voids her nymphomania of its supposed worth, *jouissance*. It is not surprising that, in the course of this, she sometimes experiences the loss of her sensuality altogether when her clitoral feeling completely disappears, or, no less significant, that she eventually seeks the sadistic 'services' of K.

There seems to be a reference to Kafka in the figure of K, who bears the same initial as Kafka's famous hero in *The Trial* and *The Castle*. Yet here it is Joe who is playing the masochistic subject—Kafka's hero who is totally at the mercy of the big Other's incomprehensible mandates. Kafka's hero, in spite of his suffering under the yoke of the law, can still be enjoying a certain kind of eroticism in his relation to the law—the masochistic enjoyment of playing the victim of an ideological big Other. In fact, this seems to be one of the reasons why readers of Kafka enjoy his works immensely. K's role is always to enact a role for the big Other. The fact that he does not even know what role exactly he is supposed to enact adds to the arbitrariness of the big Other's mandate, its capricious demands.

Yet it must be made clear that K's being-for-the-Other can also be a form of being for himself. K can fit in the structure of hysterical neurosis in which the subject, according to Žižek, "is himself already symbolically identified with the gaze for which he is playing his role" (*Sublime Object* 106). At the outset, K tells Joe the rules that will define their subsequent relationship: "the first rule is that I don't fuck you [...], the second rule is that we have no safe word [...], third rule: if I choose to let you in, you have to be sitting out here. In other words, you won't know when." K fits perfectly into the category of the pervert who "fully acknowledges the obscene underside of the Law, since he gains satisfaction from the very obscenity of the gesture of installing the rule of Law" (Žižek, *Žižek Reader* 117). He is precisely this figure who "purports to violate all the rules of 'normal', decent behavior", yet, "effectively longs for the very rule of Law" (118).

The question Joe poses to him – "what do you get out of it?" – is precisely the Lacanian "Che vuoi?" (*Écrits: A Selection* 345–6) question, "What does the Other want of me?" It is the fact that this question never gets answered by K that maintains the highly erotic relationship between them. Joe is left virtually helpless with all the fantasies she can come up with in her mind with regard to K's mysterious desire and what exactly constitutes his *jouissance*. Lacan maintains that the pervert himself "doesn't know what jouissance he is serving in exercising his activity" and that "in any case, [it is not] in the service of his own jouissance" (*Anxiety* 150). Masochistic Joe, on the other hand, (mis)recognizes the way to her own *jouissance* as an answer to the "Che vuoi?" that is never satisfactory.

She does not realize that what she is seeking is not really K's *jouissance*, but his anxiety or that which constitutes her own *jouissance*, for "what escapes the notice of the masochist [is that] he is seeking the Other's anxiety" (151–2). Watching the sadomasochistic scenes between Charlotte Gainsbourg and Jamie Bell, the viewer is also left hanging between what seems to be the subtle promise of sexual intercourse that never takes place—like that other sexual intercourse that never takes place in Wong Kar-wai's deliciously tortuous *In the Mood for Love*—and the tense and highly erotic exhortation of their meetings. Von Trier's camera deploys those scenes in an uninhibited gut-wrenching fashion that is meant to extort an amalgamation of contradictory feelings.

In acting upon Joe's body, K is not only fulfilling his own sadistic desire to torture her but at the same time meeting Joe's explicit desire to be tortured. K's sadistic act, therefore, is in its essence an indeterminable one; it cannot be appropriately located. It is an act of ultimate brutality and impersonal detachment from the other (masochistic Joe), *yet*, at the same time, it also seems to be an act of limitless compliance with the desire of the other—an acquiescence which can take place only in an intense love relationship. In his analysis of the act of parricide in Rossellini's *Deutschland im jahre null (Germany, Year Zero)*, Žižek comes across the same idea of this "coincidence of opposites" which marks a "point at which every 'foundation' of acts in 'words', in ideology, fails" (*Enjoy Your Symptom* 35). Joe's nymphomania eventually leading her to K is nothing but the subject's repetitive failed attempts to access its own being through being in control of others, eventually leading it to being under the control of another. It is as if she comes to the conclusion that masochism is the "only access to being" (Žižek, *Žižek Reader* 118).

The philosophical implications of such an idea should not be missed. Žižek locates it across Kant's, Adorno's and Horkheimer's, as well as Lacan's, thought. In Kant, it is "correlative with the advent of modern Kantian subjectivity, with the subject reduced to the empty point of self-relating negativity". In Adorno and Horkheimer, it is the "perfect metaphor of the fate of Reason based on the repression of nature", which marks the "revenge of nature for our domination over it: unknowingly, we are our own greatest victims, butchering ourselves alive" (118). In Lacan, it is the idea of the "'barred' subject of the signifier [...] lacking a support in the positive order of Being", thus, "what [masochistic] fantasy stages is precisely the subject's impossible being lost owing to the subject's entry into the symbolic order" (119). This "only access to being", however, should not be understood outside the specific Lacanian formula of fantasy.

The function of this fantasy is that it deceptively relieves the subject of the anxiety of the "Che vuoi?" It is not accidental that the formula of fantasy ($ ◊ a), in Lacan's completed graph of desire (*Écrit: The First Complete Edition* 692), brings the subject back in the direction of—but not at all in—the imaginary realm. Therefore, it is not surprising that Lacan draws this resemblance between the "economy of masochistic pain" and the "economy of goods". The masochist aims at reducing himself or herself to this "nothing that is the good, to this thing that is treated like an object, to this slave whom one trades back and forth and whom one shares" (*Ethics of Psychoanalysis* 239). In their intense relationship, it is indeed hard to distinguish between K and Joe strictly as 'sadist' and 'masochist', for they are both using each other as well as being used by each other at once. Lacan maintains that "the sadist himself occupies the place of the object, but without knowing it, to the benefit of another, for whose *jouissance* he exercises his action as sadistic pervert" (*Four Fundamental Concepts* 185).

Joe is not only simply acted upon; she has some subtle agency, as she is in effect using K to explore the limits of her sexuality. Joe manages to break one of K's rules when she intrudes on his session with another woman and insists on taking her place and making her wait. K complies with Joe's demand, privileging her in a way the viewer can assume he never has anyone before. Yet her agency becomes most obvious when she experiences an intense orgasm while being delivered K's "original Roman maximum of 40 lashes". Such orgasm can be thought of as a "jouissance beyond the pleasure principle" (Lacan, *Four Fundamental Concepts* 184). Joe learns, even though in an ultimately violent and humiliating way, that it is not the filling up of her holes she needs to reach such a powerful *jouissance*; the kind of eroticism experienced beyond the pleasure principle has nothing to do with sexual intercourse because it requires communication with the Other on a much higher level (an intellectual level, for example).

In the case of Joe and K, it is about finding sexuality in her own way and through the awareness of her own body without the intervention of the body of the other and under the law of the big Other's capricious and unpredictable mandates—a pleasure so great because most hardly won. Again, the implications of a *jouissance* experienced in the midst of torture and ultimate humiliation should not be missed. In the discussion of what he sees as the "uncanny absolute proximity of trauma and fantasy", Žižek argues that, in a traumatic experience of suffering and humiliation, the subject identifies "resonances in [its] deepest disavowed fantasies", and that is why, "after being compelled to undergo such a horrible ordeal, the subject, as a rule, feels 'irrationally' guilty, or at least besmirched", which is an "ultimate proof of an unbearable *jouissance*" (*For They Know Not* lxvii).

Roman Polanski's *Death and the Maiden* seems to make a good case for it. A prominent lawyer (Gerardo) brings home a stranger (Dr Miranda) on a stormy day. The lawyer's wife (Paulina) is convinced that the stranger is the sadistic doctor who tortured and raped her repeatedly while she was blindfolded when she was a prisoner of a former fascist regime. She recognizes her torturer only by his voice. She takes him captive, tries to convince her unbelieving husband that this is the man who tortured and raped her, and demands a confession of guilt from the doctor in exchange for his life. Dr Miranda conspires with Gerardo to stage a false confession, which enrages Paulina further. Deemed unrepentant by Paulina, she leads him blindfolded outside the house to the edge of a cliff.

Faced with the prospect of being pushed off the cliff, Dr Miranda finally confesses that he really was the doctor who tortured and raped her. He also admits that he enjoyed doing this immensely and that he was sorry the fascist regime fell because its fall eventually stopped his secret pathological enjoyment. Paulina accepts this confession and lets him live. In the final scene, Paulina and Dr Miranda cast uncomfortable glances at each other in the middle of a concert of Schubert's *Death and the Maiden* quartet—the same music Miranda used to play while brutalizing her. Polanski's two final scenes seem to raise a number of important queries: why is the victimized heroine ultimately satisfied with only a confession of guilt from her torturer? How can repeated torture and rape be weighed against, and forgiven in exchange for, an oral but unequivocal confession of guilt? And, most important of all, what makes the heroine so attached to listening to a piece of music that is tied to the memory of her traumatic experience?

A Lacanian/Žižekan reader of the film would reduce all of these queries to one fundamental question. The question is: *how many times did Paulina experience a guilty orgasm, an "unbearable jouissance", during her torture and rape by Miranda? How many times has she witnessed the "possibility of an orgasm occurring at the height of an anguishing situation"* (all emphases mine) (Lacan, *Anxiety* 239). It is her own sense of guilt that she finally gets rid of by accepting Dr Miranda's confession. Killing a Dr Miranda who hasn't confessed would not relieve her sense of guilt. Killing a Dr Miranda who *has* confessed would not only amplify her sense of guilt, but would perhaps lead to her own suicide as a result of it. It is only the confession of the guilt of sadistic *jouissance* that can make her tolerate her own guilt of masochistic *jouissance*.

In Polanski's film, nothing of Paulina's traumatic experience is shown on the screen. In *Nymphomaniac*, on the other hand, the raw physicality and brutality of the flagellation scene adds another dimension to the idea of "unbearable jouissance". The viewer gets to see the immediate graphic effects of flogging on Joe's body; the cat-o'-nine-tails makes bloody red and blue marks on her backside, shredding her dress to pieces in the process. In his analysis of the erotic practice of flagellation, Lacan asserts that "the enjoying adopts the very ambiguity by means of which it is at its level and no other that the equivalence between the gesture of making a mark and the body, object of jouissance, can be reached" (*Other Side* 49). In other words, the gesture of marking the skin by flogging becomes equivalent with the body itself as the object of *jouissance*.

What is equivocal in this equivalence, however, is that *jouissance* itself becomes highly ambiguous. In flagellation it becomes ultimately indeterminable to ascertain *who* is enjoying *what*. In a sadomasochistic situation the distinction between the self and the other becomes blurred on either side of the relationship. That is why when Lacan talks about *jouissance* in this particular context he assigns it to "whosoever carries what [he calls] the glory of the mark", precisely because it is a context in which the "Other enters one's world" in an "irrefutable" way; yet, this entrance/presence of the Other is problematized by the "mark's affinity with *jouissance* of the body" (49), which indicates that the relation with the object at this point enters a narcissistic stage of non-being where the self *is* the other. It is significant that Joe uses some books to elevate her buttocks to the desired level for K to exact the torture. And though she relates to Seligman that she could sexually benefit from the friction of her clitoris against the books, the shot in which she experiences her most powerful orgasm under the lashes of the whip is indeed difficult to comprehend without reading all of those books by Lacan, Žižek and Kafka.

Seligman himself seems, to Joe, to be nothing but a book against which she can rub her clitoris in a metaphorical sense, that is, to whom she can talk about her nymphomania unreservedly without worrying about the presence of another with a sexuality. On the other hand, Joe's accidental intrusion into Seligman's asexual life can be likened to the introduction of radical otherness to his self-centered universe. In his essay 'The Subject and the Other in Lévinas and Lacan', Paul-Laurent Assoun discusses Lévinas's "'passion for alterity'" as a "return of Eros to [the] solipsistic thought" (84) of philosophy. Lévinas's critique of philosophy is that it is:

Produced as a form in which the refusal of engagement in the other ... the waiting preferred to action, indifference with regard to others [...] is manifest. Philosophy's itinerary remains that of Ulysses, whose adventure in the world was only a return to his native island—a complacency in the Same, an unrecognition [*méconnaissance*] of the other. (*Collected Philosophical Papers* 91)

Assoun argues that, contrary to the philosophical tradition which "reduc[es] the Other by 'saving' the identity of the thinking subject", Lévinas's intervention is a "question of awakening the 'pleasure' of the Other and of providing the means for 'recognizing' the Other" (84). In the context of *Nymphomaniac*, Seligman stands for philosophy in the sense of "solipsistic thought", while Joe is precisely the Lévinasian erotic intervention of the Other. Seligman is unfortunate, though; the Other that he happens to encounter is not only a woman—that which he has never been with—it is a nymphomaniac, a woman whose whole life consists of nothing but a perpetual search for female *jouissance*. Joe is effectively the representation of the feminine in its most radial form as the "Law of the Other" or as "'the Other forever in its *jouissance*'" (97).

The film's atmosphere is one of loneliness and melancholy. In spite of the fact that Joe makes use of thousands of men, her nymphomania sets her apart from everyone around her. The theme of loneliness is referred to several times by her as well as by other characters in the film. Yet, it is in the powerful image of her facing the solitary, tilted and leafless tree on top of the mountain, at that moment when she finally finds her "soul tree", that the idea of loneliness finds its most effective deployment. The loneliness—that of Joe as well as that of the tree—is beautifully emphasized by the stillness of the shot; an immobile and gazing Joe on one mountain facing an odd-looking and perfectly still tree on another mountain; both are distortions in nature, both are lonely, both are in an elevated position above the world beneath them, both seem to carry a steely character and a hardened appearance, both are in the world yet outside it, both sublimated by von Trier's camera, yet there is nothing sublime about them and, above all, both seem to be already dead long ago in a sense, yet physically standing steadfastly on the ground.

The theme of loneliness in *Nymphomaniac* is not presented as the romantic condition of the solitary subject and it would be a fatal mistake to understand von Trier's late art-house cinematic productions in this sense. Joe's loneliness meets with Seligman's at the very point which defines von Trier's *Nymphomaniac* itself as a work of art, which is, in a Heideggerian sense, "alien and uncommunicative, external to the world" (Bruns 57). According to Gerald Bruns, the work of art to Heidegger, as well as to Blanchot, exists in an "essential solitude" (56), communicating nothing but its own existence in a state of "pure passivity" or a "passivity whose purity consists in its exteriority, that is, in the fact that it is outside the alternatives of action and repose", which Bruns describes as an "existence without being" (57).

The experience of viewing *Nymphomaniac* as well as all of von Trier's other films on the subject of woman and female sexuality feels like the experience of being before a tableau, which is essentially inaccessible, even to its own creator. The space in which this tableau exists is the space in which the "solitude of the work occurs" and it is a space that is defined "neither by Being as presence nor by the presence of beings" but by being "'the opaque, empty opening onto that which is when there is no more world, when there is no world yet', as if in an interval (*entre-temps*) or interruption of being" (58). Solitude, in the world of *Nymphomaniac* as a von Trier film—thus a film about the film industry in a fundamental sense—is solitude of the work, since solitude of the human being, understood in Marcuse's sense as the "very condition which sustained the individual against and beyond his society, has become technically impossible" (Marcuse 74).

In other words, *Nymphomaniac* does not only deploy a form of feminine sexuality that is insatiable, non-conformational and dangerous through the figure of Joe; it does something far more important: it presents itself to the viewer as an interruption of mainstream cinema, not in the sense of its pornographization but in the sense of mainstreaming pornography itself by presenting it as more problematic and thought-provoking than entertaining. This is not to say, however, that it tries to intellectualize female sexuality, since intellectualizing female sexuality through the bookish Seligman is thoroughly mocked; he is not only a man—which is bad enough—he is a man who has never been with a woman, who gets killed immediately at the moment he attempts to rectify that.

The presentation of female sexuality in *Nymphomaniac* thus suggests that it cannot to be understood or interpreted because the bearer of interpretation cannot escape the economy of signs or the economy of desire as a metonymic structure. Female sexuality is something that can only *be*, not *mean*, whereas Seligman is trying to make it mean something for Joe. In his failed attempt to rid her of her guilt he does not get the point that it is precisely her present unbearable sense of guilt and shame—taken as a sign of repentance and abstinence—that has always already constituted her enjoyment as such beyond the *jouissance* of the body.

The idea of woman in *Nymphomaniac* is that which bears a sexuality that is not and cannot be symbolized. More importantly, by presenting what seems to be a deviant form of female sexuality and misreading it constantly through the character of Seligman, the film neither consciously denies it nor unconsciously represses it, but rather forecloses it completely as something that can only be imagined but never represented—thus the odd congruities that Seligman tries to draw between Joe's sexual experiences and his readings, as well as the stark contrast in the alternation between Joe's stormy sexual exploits in brightly lit scenes and the sterile dialogue she is having with Seligman in his dimly lit house, which hardly sees any sun.

The function those Joe-Seligman dialogue scenes play as mediatory communicators or explanatory negotiators by which the viewer is supposed to understand what went on or what is going on in Joe's sexual life is presented by von Trier in a highly complicated yet playful way so as to appear both philosophical and idle at once. Subjects like literature, anatomy, melancholy, delirium, musicology, mathematics, love, politics, religion, history, pedophilia and murder are all presented in a dialogue between two people as "Gerede" or "idle talk" in an acutely Heideggerian sense of "average intelligibility"; in other words, the viewer may have a general sense of the communicated discourse without having a "primordial understanding of it" or may not "understand the entities which are talked about" yet can still fathom "what is said-in-the-talk as such" (Heidegger 211–12). For example, the viewer may not have read Poe's *The Fall of the House of Usher*, know nothing about Roderick Usher's or the narrator's hallucinations or about the apparition of the "lofty and enshrouded figure of the lady Madeline of Usher" (Poe 49), yet can still fathom Joe's sense of fear and anxiety as she approaches the hospital in which her beloved father is interned suffering from delirium tremors. Or, the viewer may not necessarily know Thomas Mann's *Doctor Faustus* in order to understand that the uncanny image of Joe's laughing newborn is supposed to be a satanic omen.

This communication, then, between Joe and Seligman is not only a presentation of a problem (Joe, a repentant woman in great agony who is seeking some kind of expiation through vocal admonition from a man of letters who constantly refuses to vilify her), but also a problematization of the presentation itself; Seligman's analogies between Joe's stories of sexual exploits and examples from his readings on a range of different subjects seem more random and playful than exact and explanatory. Their communication, which is in its essence a non-communication, is *Nymphomaniac*'s presentation of itself as a contemporary film in accordance with the solitude of the postmodern subject.

Joe's ultimate loneliness as a nymphomaniac who must be outside the fabric of 'normal' society, Seligman's sterile loneliness, as well as *Nymphomaniac*'s isolation as an art-house cinematic production that enjoys its own being and its own minimal communication or even non-communication with the viewer, are natural extensions of Nietzsche's Western "free spirits" of "democratic taste and its 'modern ideas'", which, to him, are "not exactly the most communicative of spirits" but, on the contrary, are "born, sworn, jealous friends of *solitude* [...] most profound, most midnightly, most middaily solitude" (Nietzsche 245).

Joe's ultimate loneliness is stressed by nothing but her very openness to countless sexual relationships with countless men and her view of her own sexual organ as one of those doors with sensors that open at the slightest spur. Her position can be a precise answer to Lacan's question on the relation between "sexual symbolism" and the "metaphorical play of the signifier" when he asks "Why does one resurrect the metaphor 'fuck' in connection with something that is 'fucked up'?" To Lacan, this linguistic play on "phallic penetration" describes the radical presence of the signifier where it is precisely absent and which is there in the most ancient agricultural and handcraft activities of human civilization such as "opening the belly of the earth" or the "making of a vase"—activities that evoke not the "sexual act" but the "female sexual organ" itself in terms of "an opening and an emptiness" (*Ethics of Psychoanalysis* 168–9).

This opening-emptiness, which marks both the place of desire and the sign of castration at once, also marks the problem of the Lacanian subject whose sexual activity is nothing but a repetitive desperate expression of failure over "missing" its "effective jouissance" (Lacan, *On Feminine Sexuality* 121) thanks to "'the use of language'" which Lacan explains not in the sense that we use language but in the sense that "language [...] uses us [...] employs us, and that is how it enjoys" (*Other Side* 66). Joe, as a nymphomaniac who does not fit in 'normal' society, is not only "fucked up" because she fucks; she fucks in the first place because she always already perceives herself as fucked up.

In other words, Joe's position is precisely the position of the subject of language whose very inscription into it marks both communication/symbolic exchange with others and everlasting loss and melancholic loneliness—the paradoxical modeling of the self as indistinguishable from, yet threatened by and aggressive toward, the other, which *alienates it from itself* as it oscillates between an imagined individuality and a deceptive association with the other. The melancholic loneliness stems from the perception of a pre-subjective stage of fragmentation, of being nothing but "an inchoate collection of desires" (Lacan, *Psychoses* 39) in oneness with its surroundings, that is, a narcissistic world of non-being where the self *is* the other.

There is no doubt that the film provides an assortment of astute insights, but its main concern, from the present writer's perspective, is to deploy those insights for the viewer through alternate moments of gaiety and identification as well as interruption of the viewing experience and non-identification in a constantly changing mood that seems to be redolent of the experience of sex itself. Von Trier's *Nymphomaniac* is another illustration of Lacan's statement that "signifiers are not made for sexual relations" (*Other Side* 33). It is a film that overwhelms the viewer with literally hundreds of signifiers, images, linguistic riddles, political messages and ideas in order to show him/her that what constitutes the pleasure of viewing is precisely the inability of these signifiers to explain either the moments of gaiety or the moments of disturbance in the viewing, which, in the case of *Nymphomaniac*, seems to follow the experience of the sexual relationship that, we should not forget, does not exist[3] (*On Feminine Sexuality* 144).

Joe's loneliness reaches its very epitome as well as its uncanny identification with the viewer's loneliness in front of von Trier's most inaccessible film at the moment she utters "fill all my holes" while she lies beaten, bloody and near dead on the floor of the dark alley—the subject's indestructible libido speaking from the exact point of the subject's incompleteness and the emptiness that lies behind its fictional identity. Being a nymphomaniac, Joe's "fill all my holes!" seems to refer directly to her body's orifices, yet the dire situation in which this desperate wish is expressed does not seem more compatible with a polymorphous perverse need than a narrative one. The dialogues that follow between herself and Seligman come as a perfect answer to her wish. Lowry Pressly observes Seligman's "shallow, quasi-philosophic digressions", "intellectual superficiality", and his "maddening" character, which is seen as "*logos* to Joe's *eros*". "In the character of Seligman", Pressly argues, "it is as if von Trier has arranged a starscape of potential meanings and has left it up to the viewer to arrange the constellations of significance for himself" (Pressly).

This gesture, which is likened to young Joe's "looking up into the night sky and making sense of her life by drawing lines between the stars", is seen by Pressly as "an absurd and onanistic gesture" in which, however, "the failure of Von Trier's script to rise even to the philosophical heights of Sade's novels finds its redemption". Pressly concludes that "*Nymphomaniac* succeeds as a work of art insofar as it fails to live up to the terms it sets for itself as a film" (Pressly). Although this view quite justifiably sees *Nymphomaniac* as a work of art that succeeds in its very futility as neither a philosophical nor cinematic work, it doesn't see that it is precisely this narrative futility that Joe needs to deal with her nymphomania—inconsequential narrative as an answer to the human need to narrate and listen to narrative.

To put this in perspective, a comparison with the writing of the Marquis de Sade seems most appropriate in view of the focus on destructive libidinal energy. Sade's writing, as Pierre Klossowski asserts:

> Is not purely descriptive (objective) but interpretive. In interpreting the aberrant act as a coinciding of sensuous nature with reason, Sade humiliates reason with sensuous nature and humiliates the 'rational' sensuous nature with a perverse reason. (17)

Nymphomaniac clearly does not do that. Yet, it does much more than that. It puts reason *and* sensuous nature in the service of a dialogue that does not mean as much to the viewer as it does to Joe, who employs every object around her in order to turn her physical need to narrative need—indeed, another onanistic gesture. It is not surprising that she sees her countless lovers as one lover, after all; because all of her sexual relationships are nothing but different scenarios of onanistic fantasies.

Whereas the Sadean stories deal primarily with the body of the other as the site of the (im)possible act of transgression, Joe's many lovers do not seem to be anything but substitutable/disposable tools for her body's enjoyment of itself through countless fantasies. If Rousseau's onanism, according to Derrida, is that "maddening [supplement]" that is "neither presence nor absence" and which "enables one to affect oneself by providing oneself with presences, by summoning absent beauties" (*Acts of*

Literature 95–6), Joe's countless relationships enable her primarily to dive more and more into her own nymphomania, her own closed world in which the actual presences of so many lovers only accentuate their absences as effective others. Derrida's famous "*There is no outside-the-text*"[4] may be (mis)matched to Joe's position, which seems to announce that *there is no outside-the-self*.

To Joe, as well as to the viewer, Seligman seems to be a man who is able to recall everything he has read in books but who does not have any personal history. In a way, he resembles Umberto Eco's hero, Yambo, in *The Mysterious Flame of Queen Loana*, who suffers a bizarre form of memory loss that makes him remember every book he has ever read but nothing about his own life. In a sense, Joe is in front of a text, not in front of a man with a sexuality. When she asks him "what kind of a man are you?" and realizes soon after that he has no sexual experience whatsoever to guide her in determining what kind of man he is, the viewer realizes that he is not guarding any secret. Seligman is the very incarnation of Kafka's text *Vor dem Gesetz* (*Before the Law*) in a Derridean sense (*Acts of Literature* 181–220). The law is not guarding anything except itself. There is no story behind the text as an impenetrable surface. Sexuality to Joe is the primary method by which a human being can be read, understood, communicated with, analyzed, penetrated or even coerced. But being in the company of Seligman is like being before a story that is inaccessible or unreadable because there is "no itinerary, no method, no path to accede to the law, to what would happen there, to the *topos* of its occurrence" (196).

Joe seems somehow to live with that and she doesn't try to interpret anything. She takes Seligman as a best friend precisely in the sense that a best friend would be a good book or a text, a presumably benign companion, but not an other, not a reflection of the self. Seligman, on the other hand, even though he tries to relate Joe's sexual exploits to texts he has read, is nevertheless trying to reach for a human being behind the text; to interpret or to look for a meaning, to perform the "elementary 'phallic' gesture of symbolization"[5] (Žižek, *Žižek Reader* 23), to find something behind the door of the law. That is his fatal mistake. When he tries to fuck her he does so neither out of sexual desire as a desiring subject (and von Trier's camera insists on showing a penis that is not at all as excited as its holder at this point) nor out of a desire to make her regain her confidence in herself as a declared and dedicated nymphomaniac from the point of view of a humanist sympathizer.

At that moment, Seligman in Joe's view is neither simply a desiring subject nor a philosopher; he is literally *a corpus of literature trying to become a human being*. To put it in Lacanian language, he emerges as an "*Unheimliche*"; as the "most restful *desirable*, in its most soothing form" unpredictably "show[ing] itself as a *desirer*", or, as a "divine statue that is just divine" suddenly "com[ing] to life" (Lacan, *Anxiety* 271). This is a most horrifying moment for Joe who, by telling her story, has relieved herself by transforming her nymphomania into narrative. She kills Seligman not simply because she discovers that, after all, he is just another man who wants to fuck her, but because she sees in him at that particular moment her own self trying to be resurrected, trying to switch back from narrative to sexuality. It is this that scares her the most. By telling her story, Joe becomes like the Marquis de Sade in the sense that Beauvoir makes out of the Marquis as mainly a corpus of literature or as one long erotic narrative. And, when everything is said, once Joe becomes able to regard herself as narrative she, like Sade, becomes "afraid of the reality of the world" (Beauvoir 7).

The kind of panic that leads to murder in this sense is not simply because of the discovery of a lie or because reality turns out to be an illusion (that is, Seligman is not an asexual or an impotent intellectual; he is just another male who wants to fuck her); it is caused by the fear that what is perceived as illusory may turn out to be real. A good example of a murderous panic caused by the discovery of a lie (reality turning illusory) would be the murder scene in Paul Thomas Anderson's *There Will Be Blood* in which the hero, enraged by the discovery that the man claiming to be his long-lost half-brother is nothing but an impostor who stole the dead brother's name and personal history, shoots the stranger at point-blank range. A more radical murderous panic, however, would be an expression of great fear from the prospect of the reification of what is perceived as fictitious; indeed, from the idea that the world may be real after all, and not fictitious.

Orhan Pamuk's novel *My Name Is Red*—a circuitous mystery set in sixteenth-century Istanbul about the murder of one member of a cadre of miniaturists commissioned by the Sultan to create a book and illuminate it in the figurative European style banned by Islamic tradition—seems to touch on this idea when it concludes that, out of three suspect miniaturists, the murderer is neither the skillful materialist who creates art mainly to make money nor the egoistic perfectionist who creates art mainly to reflect on his own image. The murderer is the artist who identifies with his artwork to the point of disappearance in it, and thus fictionalizes the world. His identification with the fictitiousness of art is only matched by his violent religious beliefs. Even after being beheaded at the end of the story, his eyes seem to look on from a severed head, not at the final image of the real world but at the lines of a painting:

> What I saw from ground level filled my thoughts: The road inclining slightly upward, the wall, the arch, the roof of the workshop, the sky ... this is how the picture receded [...] If you stare long enough your mind enters the time of the painting. (Pamuk 405)

During his life, it was the disturbances of daily realities that interrupted his almost perpetual existence in the phantasmal world of art. As a nymphomaniac-turned-narrator, enjoyment to Joe now becomes primarily enjoyment telling her stories, like Sade who "attached greater importance to the stories he wove around the act of pleasure than to the contingent happenings" (Beauvoir 9). Narrated by Gainsbourg's ashamed and guilty yet somehow confident and cold voice, Joe's stories, like Sade's, are monotonous due to their rootedness in the sole subject of the act of pleasure, yet enlightening due to her politically incorrect and philosophical views.

On Sade's narrative form, Beauvoir writes that it "tends to disconcert us. He speaks in a monotonous, embarrassed tone, and we begin to be bored, when all at once the dull grayness is lit up with the glaring brilliance of some bitter, sardonic truth" (36). Similarly, from time to time, the viewer of *Nymphomaniac* comes face to face with such bitter sardonic truths in what Joe has to say in between descriptive episodes of her uncontrolled and endless sexual adventures. Thus, for example, "the pedophile, who manages to get through life with the shame of his desire while never acting on it, deserves a bloody medal". On the banning of the word "negro" as racially offensive, she tells Seligman that "each time a word becomes prohibited, you remove a stone from the democratic foundation" and that "society demonstrates its impotence in the face of a concrete problem by removing words from the language".

Joe's stories, like Sade's, are sometimes incoherent because coherence goes against their very purpose, which is to create and present images of her many sexual encounters in raw form such as they would be in a world of sexual fantasies, like Sade's. When Seligman objects to the part of the story in which young Joe strolls in a forest, finds fragments of torn photographs of Jerôme and his wife, then meets Jerome himself who "like a God pulls [her] up to him through the clouds", she asks him, "Which way do you think you'd get the most out of my story? By believing in it or by not believing in it?" The story of *Nymphomaniac* is primarily told in images and the dialogue between the images provides frames for them or holds them up to the viewer, but does not and cannot explain them.

Going over Beauvoir's analysis of Sade's writing, one is struck by the fact that it could as well explain what Seligman refers to as "unrealistic coincidences" in Joe's story or, more precisely, in von Trier's film. Sade, according to Beauvoir, "contented himself with projecting his fantasies. His accounts have the unreality, the false precision, and the monotony of schizophrenic reveries. He relates them for his own pleasure, and he is unconcerned about imposing them upon the reader" (37). There is no doubt that Lars von Trier's cinema has always been perceived as an imposition and his films have always been thought of as texts talking primarily to themselves. The unrealistic coincidences in Joe's accounts emerge from the fact that she is not telling a story at all; she is using images she can see in Seligman's house in order to try to project images of her nymphomania for him—and for the viewer.

Beauvoir:

> It is the image that Sade was imitating, even while claiming to give it literary opacity. Thus, he disregarded the spatial and temporal coordinates within which all real events are situated. The places he evokes are not of this world, the events which occur in them are *tableaux vivants* rather than adventures, and time has no hold on Sade's universe. (37)

In *Nymphomaniac*, the story and the action seem to have minimal roles; the most important parts of the film are made of static images, slow-motion scenes, or scenes of Joe's sexual encounters in which there is nothing but the repetitive act of lovemaking. By narrating her story—and she is narrating it in chapters with headings—Joe becomes Sade who "chose the imaginary" (9) and, through writing, "made of his sexuality an ethic" (7). Joe's nymphomania, like Sade's sexuality, "attains a real originality" by this "deliberate act" (7) of narration or writing respectively.

Through Joe's conversations with Seligman, we come to realize that what fascinates her now, much more than acting on her nymphomania, is understanding her nymphomania. Narration, to Joe, now constitutes a safe haven where she can live with her nymphomania in a literary sense without having to abuse her thoroughly hackneyed and worn-out body again. To a lesser extent, her nymphomania can be likened to a bad but irresistible habit that can be stopped only by transforming it into some readable text the way Richard Klein's book *Cigarettes Are Sublime*—a work which celebrates and romanticizes smoking cigarettes—comes out of an "urgent desire to stop smoking" (Klein ix). Through narration, Joe assumes a new subjective position from which she can look upon her nymphomaniac adventures as fiction. As narrator of her own personal history she seems to be a completely different woman. The stark contrast between the visual effects of the flashback scenes showing Joe's sensual feats and her composure as a narrator of those feats in Seligman's house suggests she is already looking upon herself as a nymphomaniac from a great remove; as if her insatiable sexual desire has been transformed into a desire to narrate her insatiable sexual desire.

That is why the act of killing Seligman calls for proper analysis. David Ehrlich explains it as one of the

> Definitive actions [which] guarantee that von Trier's clash between nature and the mind doesn't end in a stalemate. Nature wins, as it always does [in von Trier's films], and Joe is returned to the confines of her body, as she always will be. (*The Dissolve*)

However, the context of killing Seligman, from this writer's perspective, clearly defies this idea. Even though Ehrlich stresses that "von Trier is never to be trusted", he seems to trust him on the idea of the guaranteed victory of nature over the mind. Even though Joe states that "for a human being, killing is the most natural thing in the world. We're created for it", killing Seligman does not seem to belong to that thought either. If the killing had come as a conclusion of some sexual experience or the climax of a transgressive sexuality, it would have been easier to think about it as a case of nature winning over the mind.

Killing Seligman, on the other hand, takes place in order to prevent a sexual experience; it comes as a protestation against the shift from the narrative mode that defines the relationship between him and Joe to reality, or from the realm of the mind to the realm of the body (nature). The problem is that Joe's eroticism seems to have changed its direction, through the figure of Seligman and their conversations, from directly attending to the needs of the body to narrating the body and its needs. "It was not murder that fulfilled Sade's erotic nature: it was literature" (Beauvoir 33). Thus argues Beauvoir. Killing Seligman precisely at the moment of his transformation from an asexual corpus of literature to an 'other' with a sexuality may not be a marker of Joe's return to the "confines of her body" (Ehrlich) but of her freedom from those confines.

To her, Seligman's attempt to have sexual intercourse with her after establishing her newly acquired narrative identity through long hours of telling/listening to stories amounts to turning fiction into reality, or, to put it in Žižekan language, it means:

> *Realiz[ing] in 'external' social reality the 'stuff of her dreams'*; this 'forced actualization' in social reality itself of the [*now*] fantasmatic kernel of [her] being is the worst, most humiliating kind of violence, a violence which undermines the very basis of [her *new*] identity (of [her] 'self-image') by exposing [her] to an unbearable shame. (*Did Somebody Say* 189)

It is this sensitivity towards the problematic of the subject of language—which is manifestly present from the moment Joe utters "fill all my holes" through all of her conversations with Seligman and up to killing him—that makes *Nymphomaniac* something other than it appears to be. Lacan asserts that:

> Sublimation […] does not on all occasions necessarily follow the path of the sublime. […] the sexual acknowledged as such may come to light in sublimation. The crudest of sexual games can be the object of a poem without for that reason losing its sublimating goal. (*Ethics of Psychoanalysis* 161).

In accordance with this Lacanian idea, even though *Nymphomaniac* does deploy the crudest of sexual games, it makes those games through Joe's steely rebellious character the "object of a poem" and, precisely because of that, the film does not lose its sublimating goal, that is, to make the figure of the nymphomaniac sublime in spite of being an outcast in any decent society and, at the same time, to make the film itself intellectually sublime in spite of being too pornographic for mainstream cinema.

The sum of all this means that *Nymphomaniac* does not simply play on the idea of the law of desire as much as it deploys desire itself as law in an almost clinical style that is reminiscent of Sade's chillingly rational voice, by which he justifies the atrocities of perversion. The film's extremes acquire a certain value precisely because those extremes do not seem to properly define its disposition; on the contrary, it goes through complicated questions with regard to sexuality and human desire in order to justify its excessiveness. It is only logical that von Trier makes several thematic as well as stylistic connections between *Antichrist* and *Nymphomaniac* (both featuring Gainsbourg).

With the creation of *Nymphomaniac*, he adds a systematic narrative dimension that eventually alienates the heroine from her voracious sexuality. The excessiveness in both films is nothing but a desperate expression of the fact that the ideal transgressive film can never be realized, just as "the ideal erotic act was never to be realized" (Beauvoir 32) in Sade, or the ultimate crime by his evil characters. In Sade's *The 120 Days of Sodom*, Curval expresses his ultimate disappointment in the kind of satisfaction he gets from his sexual crimes by saying, "how many times, by God, have I not longed to be able to assail the sun, snatch it out of the universe, make a general darkness, or use that star to burn the world!" (364).

In *The Other Side of Psychoanalysis*, Lacan teaches that "materialists", like Sade, who "was the most intelligent of the materialists", "are the only authentic believers" because they believe in "divine *jouissance*" (66). In 'Kant with Sade', he asserts that "Christianity"—and of course we have every reason to add other spiritual doctrines similar to Christianity—"has assuredly taught men to pay little attention to God's jouissance, and this is how Kant makes palatable his voluntarism of Law-for-Law's sake" (*Écrit: The First Complete Edition* 651). There seems to be little doubt that Lars von Trier is another authentic believer in a God whose "only chance for […] existence […] is that He—with a capital H—enjoys, that He is *jouissance*". Sade's literature, to Lacan, is nothing but a display of Sade's "impotence to be anything other than the instrument of divine jouissance" (*Other Side* 66). If von Trier were asked by another angry journalist to justify the making of *Nymphomaniac* the way he was asked to justify the making of *Antichrist*, he would probably reply in the same way: "It is the hand of God, I am afraid. And I am the best director in the world." Yet, it would be much more to the point to say: it is the hand of God, I am afraid, because God enjoys, and I, Lars von Trier, am nothing but the instrument of His enjoyment.

Notes

1. Freud said once to Marie Bonaparte: "The great question that has never been answered, and which I have not yet been able to answer, despite my thirty years of research into the feminine soul, is 'What does a woman want?'," quoted in E. Jones, *Sigmund Freud: Life and Work*, Vol. 2 (London: Hogarth Press, 1953), p. 421. In a footnote, Jones gives the original German "Was will das Weib?"

2. From Derrida's audio comments regarding his notion of prayer at the 2002 Toronto conference. Prayer to Derrida must be "absolutely secret" and must embody a skeptical "suspension of belief and certainty". Derrida also confesses that his "first rebellion against [his] own religious environment had to do with public prayer", Toronto conference (2002), 'Other Testaments', accessed 7 May 2015, https://www.youtube.com/watch?v=FxgpZNtFxFU.
3. Lacan asserts that the sexual relationship does not exist because "one's jouissance of the Other taken as a body is always inadequate"; in the case of man, it is "perverse ... insofar as the Other is reduced to object *a*", and, in the case of woman, it is "crazy and enigmatic". *On Feminine Sexuality, The Limits of Love and Knowledge: Encore, 1972–1973*, trans. with notes by Bruce Fink (New York and London: W.W. Norton and Company, 1998), p. 144.
4. This is Derek Attridge's translation of Derrida's *Il n'y a pas de hors-texte*. Attridge explains in a footnote that "it does not mean "the things that we usually consider to be outside texts do not exist" but "there is nothing that completely escapes the general properties of textuality, *différance*, etc."— that is, as Derrida goes on to explain, no "natural presence" that can be known "in itself". But it is also true that there is no inside-the-text, since this would again imply an inside/outside boundary". *Acts of Literature*, ed. Derek Attridge (New York and London: Routledge, 1992), p. 102.
5. Žižek talks about this in the context of what the subject does when faced by a traumatic event or a sudden "loss of reality" as a way to "hang on to a sense of reality" by the conceiving of the self as "*radically responsible* for the intrusion of the Real". *The Žižek Reader*, eds Elizabeth Wright and Edmond Wright (Oxford and Malden, MA: Blackwell Publishing, 1999), p. 23. Indeed, Joe's intrusion on Seligman's secluded life with her nymphomaniac stories can be thought of in terms of this highly disruptive event, which needs to be somehow incorporated within his system of signification to be made sense of.

Bibliography

Assoun, Paul-Laurent. 'The Subject and the Other in Levinas and Lacan'. *Levinas and Lacan: The Missed Encounter*. Edited by Sarah Harasym. New York: State University of New York Press, 1998.

Beauvoir, Simone de. 'Must We Burn Sade?' *The Marquis de Sade: The 120 Days of Sodom and Other Writings*. Compiled and translated by Austryn Wainhouse and Richard Seaver. New York: Grove Press, 1953.

Bruns, Gerald L. *Maurice Blanchot: The Refusal of Philosophy*. Baltimore and London: Johns Hopkins University Press, 1997.

Derrida, Jacques. *Acts of Literature*. Edited by Derek Attridge. New York and London: Routledge, 1992.

Derrida, Jacques. Toronto conference (2002). 'Other Testaments'. Accessed 7 May 2015. https://www.youtube.com/watch?v=FxgpZNtFxFU

Eco, Umberto. *The Mysterious Flame of Queen Loana*. Translated by Geoffrey Brock. London: Vintage Books, 2006.

Ehrlich, David. 'Nymphomaniac and the Infinite Loneliness of Lars von Trier'. *The Dissolve*. Accessed 24 May 2015. https://thedissolve.com/features/exposition/483-nymphomaniac-and-the-infinite-loneliness-of-lars-v/

Heidegger, Martin. *Being and Time*. Translated by John Macquarrie and Edward Robinson. Oxford and Cambridge: Blackwell, 1962.

Jones, Ernest. *Sigmund Freud: Life and Work*. Vol. 2. London: Hogarth Press, 1953.

Kafka, Franz. *Three Complete Novels*. New York: Vintage, 1999.

Klein, Richard. *Cigarettes Are Sublime*. Great Britain: Picador, 1995.

Klossowski, Pierre. *Sade My Neighbour*. Translated by Alphonso Lingis. London: Quartet Books, 1992.

Lacan, Jacques. *Écrits: A Selection*. Translated by Alan Sheridan. London and New York: Routledge, 1989.

Lacan, Jacques. *The Four Fundamental Concepts of Psycho-Analysis*. Edited by Jacques-Alain Miller and translated by Alan Sheridan. Penguin Books, 1994.

Lacan, Jacques. *The Psychoses 1955–1956*. Edited by Jacques-Alain Miller and translated by Russell Grigg. New York and London: W.W. Norton and Company, 1997.

Lacan, Jacques. *On Feminine Sexuality, The Limits of Love and Knowledge: Encore, 1972–1973*. Translated and with notes by Bruce Fink. New York and London: W.W. Norton and Company, 1998.

Lacan, Jacques. *The Ethics of Psychoanalysis 1959–1960*. Edited by Jacques-Alain Miller and translated by Dennis Porter. London: Routledge, 1999.

Lacan, Jacques. *Écrit: The First Complete Edition in English*. Translated by Bruce Fink. New York and London: W.W. Norton and Company, 2006.

Lacan, Jacques. *The Other Side of Psychoanalysis*. Translated and with notes by Russell Grigg. New York and London: W.W. Norton and Company, 2007.

Lacan, Jacques. *Anxiety*. Edited by Jacques-Alain Miller and translated by A. Rae Price. Cambridge: Polity Press, 2014.

Lévinas, Emmanuel. *Collected Philosophical Papers*. Translated by Alphonso Lingis. Dordrecht, the Netherlands: Nijhoff, 1987.

Mann, Thomas. *Doctor Faustus; the Life of the German Composer, Adrian Leverkühn, as Told by a Friend*. Translated by H.T. Lowe-Porter. New York: A.A. Knopf, 1948.

Marcuse, Herbert. *One-Dimensional Man*. London and New York: Routledge Classics, 2002.

Miller, Michael. 'Foreword'. *The Cruelty of Depression: On Melancholy*. Translated by David Jacobson. Reading, MA: Addison-Wesley, 1997.

Nietzsche, Friedrich. *Basic Writings of Nietzsche*. Translated and edited by Walter Kaufmann. New York: The Modern Library, 2000.
Pamuk, Orhan. *My Name Is Red*. Translated by Erdağ M. Göknar. New York: Vintage International, 2002.
Poe, Edgar Allan. *Great Tales and Poems*. New York: Vintage Classics, 2009.
Pressly, Lowry. 'Nymphomaniac: Vol. 1: Fishers of Men, Meaning'. *Los Angeles Review of Books*. Accessed 11 May 2015. https://lareviewofbooks.org/essay/nymphomaniac-vol-1-fishers-men-meaning
Sade, Marquis de. *Marquis de Sade: The 120 Days of Sodom and Other Writings*. Compiled and translated by Austryn Wainhouse and Richard Seaver. New York: Grove Press, 1953.
Sade, Marquis de. *Marquis de Sade: Justine, Philosophy in the Bedroom, and Other Writings*. Compiled and translated by Richard Seaver and Austryn Wainhouse. New York: Grove Press, 1990.
Žižek, Slavoj. *The Sublime Object of Ideology*. London and New York: Verso, 1989.
Žižek, Slavoj. *The Žižek Reader*. Edited by Elizabeth Wright and Edmond Wright. Oxford and Malden, MA: Blackwell Publishing, 1999.
Žižek, Slavoj. *Enjoy Your Symptom! Jacques Lacan in Hollywood and Out*. New York and London: Routledge, 2001.
Žižek, Slavoj. *Did Somebody Say Totalitarianism? Five Interventions in the (Mis)use of a Notion*. London and New York: Verso, 2002.
Žižek, Slavoj. *For They Know Not What They Do: Enjoyment as a Political Factor*. London and New York: Verso, 2002.

Filmography

Antichrist. Directed and written by Lars von Trier. Irvington, NY: Criterion Collection, 2010.
Death and the Maiden. Directed by Roman Polanski. Written by Ariel Dorfman and Rafael Yglesias. Los Angeles, CA: New Line Home Entertainment, 2003.
Deutschland im jahre null (Germany, Year Zero). Directed by Roberto Rossellini. Written by Roberto Rossellini, Max Kolpé, and Sergio Amidei. Irvington, NY: Criterion Collection, 2009.
In the Mood for Love. Directed and written by Wong Kar-wai. Hong Kong: Distributed by USA Films, 2000.
Nymphomaniac. Directed and written by Lars von Trier. Hong Kong: Panorama Corporation Limited, 2014.
There Will Be Blood. Directed and written by Paul Thomas Anderson. Hong Kong: Distributed by Intercontinental Video Ltd, 2008.

INDEX

A
abocular hypothesis, 78
Abraham, 168, 171
   monotonous repetition of beating, 170
   psychotic moment of beating, 171
   repetitive beating of, 172
   scene of beating, 168, 170
   transgressive act of beating, 169
acting-out, 17, 18, 20, 64, 128
America, 25, 85–9, 91, 92
   Brecht's experience in, 90
   character, 98
   cinematic, 25, 86, 87, 93, 100, 106–7
   cinematic white, 121
   desexualized, 25, 87
   history of slavery in, 26
   image of, 97
   innocent and religious nature of small-town, 97
   society of small town, 100
   as woman, 105
America meant to Brecht, 88, 90
American cinema, 121
American cowboy, 100
American ideology, 100, 130
American innocence, 105, 106
American invention, cinema, as, 94
American musical, 74, 80
American phoniness, 80
American psychiatry, 181
American racism, 26, 113
Antigone, 100
anxiety, 19, 28, 167, 185
authentic idiocy, 62

B
being a father, 40
belief, 38, 45
the big Other, 36
Björk, 71–2, 75
   an anti-Odysseus figure, 75
   voice, 75
black Americans, 121
black body, 25, 26, 113, 124–9, 130
   flogging, 118
black man, flogging a, 126
black manhood, 115, 116, 124
black skin, 115
black slavery, 118, 126

black/white division, 26, 113
blindness, 71, 73, 78–80
blind viewer, 77, 78
blood knowledge, 73–5
Brecht's symbolism, 89

C
carnival, 57, 58
carnivalesque, 57, 58
carnivalesque spassing, 57
castration, 10, 14, 36, 69, 193
castration anxiety, 69, 78
censorship, 184
Chè vuoi, 19, 40, 126, 128, 185
  anxiety, 186
Christian belief, 41
Christianity, 22
cinematic gift, 25, 26
cinematic identification, 3
civilization, 118
civilized speaking subject, 81
Claire's muted scream, 165
collective suicide, 60
color 'black', 121
communism, 119
crowning/decrowning, 58, 59
cultural code, 12, 39, 124, 125
culture and religion, enemy of, 16
cynicism, 87, 88

D
Dafoe, Willem, 136, 137, 140, 144
decrowning, 59, 65
democracy, 118–20, 127, 129
Derridean supplement, 160
desexing and murder, affinity between, 100, 101
desire, 2, 28
  of the big Other, 39, 40
  as law, 28, 180, 201
  law of, 28
  to narrate, 200
  object cause of, 26, 114, 126, 129
  object-cause of, 4, 19, 165
  of the Other, 19, 20
  question of, 179
  real of, 4, 14, 29, 69, 166
  real of her own, 125
  real of one's own, 125
  real of that, 126
  sadistic, 186
  scopophilic, 179
  structure of, 18
  traumatic loss of, 4
desiring genderless subject, 129
desiring subject, 27, 155, 161, 167
disappointed love, 106
divine *jouissance*, 202
divine Law, 41
divine sacrifice, 41
divine split, 148
divine violence, 148
Dogma 95, 24, 53, 54, 62, 86
Dogville, satirical message of, 97

E
Edison, Thomas Alva, 92, 94
effective jouissance, 143
end of the world, 156, 161
end scene, 161, 167
enlightenment, 75
erotic affair between the inventing European subject and the invented feminized image of America, 87
eschatology, 98, 99
European nihilism, 163
European subject, 106, 107
Europe, desexualized mutant of, 86
eyes, function of, 79

F

failure to communicate, 2
fake crowning, 58
fantasy, 26, 40, 114–16, 126, 129, 186
  onanistic, 145, 195
Father Abraham, 171
father murder, 13
female
  jouissance, 16, 17, 47, 94, 107, 145, 147
  marginalization, 144
  nature, 144
  orgasm, 147
  sexuality, 145, 192
  subjectivity, 36, 149
female bodies, torturing, 2
female sexuality, 2, 3
female sexual organ, 193
female subjectivity, 15
feminine sexuality, 15, 28, 36, 138, 149, 191
feminine universe, 78
femininity, 10
  in Freud's thought, 10
feminist critique, 46
feminist discourse, 21
feminist reading, 28, 47, 167
feminist view, 7
femme fatale, 99
fertility, 103
fetishism, 78
fetishistic gaze, 74, 79
fetishistic scopophilia, 69
fetishistic viewer, 71
fictional identity, 194
figure of K, 185
film theory, 2
flagellation, 189
flogging scene, 124, 128, 129
foreign alien element, voice as, 142
freedom, 118–20, 122, 127
freedom of choice, 120
friendship, 95, 97

G

Gainsbourg, Charlotte, 26, 136, 137, 141–3, 148, 201
Gainsbourg's performance, 159
gaze, 3–5, 24, 26, 70, 79, 113, 125, 147, 149, 165
gender antagonism, 143
gender division, 2
genderless subject, 7
genocide, 27
gift, 26, 113, 114, 116, 118, 119, 121, 122, 125, 130
  of freedom, 116, 117, 122, 129
God, 5, 12, 16, 23, 24, 36–8, 40–7, 147
  beyond the Law, 41
  creation of, 147
  enjoyment, 48
  fall of, 24, 38, 48
  as Father, 42
  foreclosure of, 147
  impersonating, 41
  jouissance, 202
  in language, 17, 42, 43, 48
  Leìvinasian, 147
  love of, 40
  personal correspondence with, 40
  personal relation with, 37, 40
  private connection to, 37
  in real, 47
  in the Real, 42, 43, 47
  sacrifice, 41
group psychology, 183
group psychotherapy, 182, 184
group sex scene, 56, 60, 62
group therapy, 181
guilt confession, 188
guilty orgasm, 188

H

Handel's aria "Lascia ch'io pianga," 140
hole of the Real, 14
Hollywood musicals, 74
home universal dream, 87
House Committee on Un-American Activities, 90
human condition, restlessness of, 160
human sacrifice, 41
hysterical subject, 27, 155
hysteric category, 27, 155

I

ideology
  American, 130
  collapse of, 25–6, 239
idle talk, 192
imaginary identification, 170
infanticide, 143, 144, 150
innocence, 97, 98, 105
ISIL, 6
Islamic tradition, 37

J

jouissance, 13, 18, 20, 28, 36, 42, 47, 143, 149, 184, 187
  beyond pleasure principle, 19, 20, 28
  crazy and enigmatic, 142
  divine, 202
  female, 16, 17, 47, 94, 107, 145, 147
  masochistic, 188
  mysterious, 43
  mystic, 145
  perverse, 142
  phallic, 145
  sadistic, 188
  subtlety of female, 141

L

Lady Macbeth, 101, 103
  barrenness, 103
language subject, 201
Law, 41
Leìvinasian God, 147
libido, 72, 73, 194
  survival of the, 77
Lincoln, Abraham, statue of, 130
loneliness, 190, 193, 194
love, 3
  disappointed, 106
  ideological message of, 138
  in Lacanian thought, 106
  true, 142
  ultimate, 148

M

mainstream cinema, 2, 29
  interruption of, 191
male and black manhood, 126
  as unattainable objet petit a, 126
male gaze, satisfying, 80
man-like machine, 101
Marquis de Sade, writing of, 195
Martius, Caius, 101, 104
masochism, 186
masochistic enjoyment, 185
masochistic *jouissance*, 188
mass culture, 3
masturbation scene, 145
meaningless repetition, 141
melancholia, 27, 53, 54, 155, 161, 173, 174
  identification with, 161
  mourning to, 53
Melancholia, climactic scene, 167
melancholic loneliness, 194
melancholic passion, 166
melancholic position, 163
melancholy, 3, 54, 190
misogynist, 7

misogyny, 2, 7, 26, 80, 114, 124, 135, 136
monotonous repetition, 170
moral obligation, 118
moral question, 44
motherhood, 147
mourning, 24, 53–5
murderous desexualization, 101
murderous panic, 197
music
  defining, 1
  (im)possibility to speak about, 1
  Wagner's, 135, 162, 163
musical artificiality, 75
Muslim, 63
muted orgasmic scream, 141
mysterious jouissance, 16

N
name of the father, 13, 36, 39, 42, 43
narration, 199
  body and its needs, 200
narrative form, 198
narrative futility, 195
narrative identity, 200
natural father, 40
neurosis, 11, 38
neurosis condition, culture, 12
neurotic phenomenon, 38, 124
  culture as a characteristically, 124
neurotic subject, 12, 24, 38
next to last song, 76
nihilism, 163
non-cinematic acting, 72
non-communication, 193

O
objet petit a, 4, 19, 26, 107, 113–15, 124, 129, 165, 166
Odysseus, 74, 75, 79, 96

omnipotence, 162
omniscience, 162
omniscient knowledge, 158
onanistic fantasies, 145, 195
orgasm, 187, 189

P
passage à l'acte, 17, 18, 21, 63, 64, 144
passage to the act, 17, 18, 20, 63, 144
perverse *jouissance*, 142
perversion, 145
phallic *jouissance*, 145
phallic penetration, 193
phallus, 12–14, 20, 36, 40, 69
physical barriers, lack of, 95
pornographic imagination, 94
pornography, 28, 29, 61, 135, 141, 179
  mainstreaming, 191
power, 118, 124, 127
  gift of, 128
  secret of, 117
power and self-confidence totally and unequivocally collapse, 127
presentation, problematization of, 192
pre-subjective nature, 80
pre-subjective world, 79
pretense, 163
primitive song, 73
psychosis, 36, 38–40
psychotic moment, 146
psychotic phenomenon, 23, 38–40
psychotic subject, 39, 40

R
racism, 114, 120, 124
  Hollywood's ideological, 126
raping Grace, 94
regressive subject, 81

religion, 5, 17, 47
  history of, 42
  human dimension in, 38
religious discourse, 42, 44, 46
  feminist critique of, 46
religious eschatology, 98
remainder, 160, 161
  supplementarity of, 161
repetition pleasure, 20
representation, erotics of, 73
repressed return, 39

S

sacrifice, 19, 41, 42
  idea of, 99
  ultimate, 98
sadistic desire, 186
sadistic *jouissance*, 188
Schreber case, 38
scopophilic desire, 179
scopophilic fantasy, 72, 78
The Scream (Edvard Munch's painting), 164
self-alienation, 107
Seligman, killing, 200
Selma
  an anti-Odysseus figure, 75
  as pure song, 75, 76
sexuality
  female, 191
  feminine, 138, 149, 191
  lack of, 124
sexual organ, 193
  female, 193
sexual scenes, employment of, 136
sirens, 74–9
  singing, 74
  song of, 81
sisters, 145, 147
social suicide, 65
solitude, 191

song, 25, 70, 72, 74, 75
  next to last, 76
  survival of, 77
  survival of her as pure, 77
  survival of the mythical power of, 75
song and civilization, incompatibility between, 74
sonorous element, 164
sounds and voices, 140
spassing, 24, 55, 57, 60
speaking body, failure of, 146
speaking subject, 14
subject, death of, 149
subjectivity, 2, 3, 36, 64–5, 129
subject supposed to know, 158
symbolic exchange, 12, 39, 41, 116, 117, 122–4, 193
symbolic suicide, 64, 100

T

tearful gaze, 79
this failure is precisely what constitutes the element of enjoyment, 7
"Thomas Edison," 92, 94
transgression, 128, 168
  impossibility of, 168, 170
transgressive act, 169
traumatic enjoyment, 7
trembling body, 164
trembling figure, 164
true love, 142
true political act, 59

U

ultimate love, 148
ultimate martyr, 100
ultimate murderer, 100
ultimate sacrifice, 98
ungainly viewing experience, 72

V

viewing experience, 3, 4, 57, 58, 191
　interruption of, 194
viewing pleasure, 194
violence, 2, 135, 137, 138, 141, 148
voice, 138
　employment as an alienated object, 140
　foreignness of, 139
voice and sound, 139
　employment of, 136
von Trier and Björk, relationship between, 73
voyeurism, 69, 78
voyeuristic fantasy, 72, 78
voyeuristic gaze, 74, 79
voyeuristic viewer, 71

W

Wagner's anti-Semitic tendencies, 162
Wagner's fascism, 136
Wagner's music, 135, 162, 163
Wagner's Tristan Chord, 162
white-black division, 121
witch, 143
witchery, 145
witchery texts, 144
woman
　as an ideological cinematic tool, 25, 87
　desexualized, 94
　impossibility of becoming, 7
　indefinability of, 11
　inexplicability of the notion of, 35
　mechanical, 93, 94
　to write about, 1

The manufacturer's authorised representative in the EU is Springer Nature Customer Service Centre GmbH, Europaplatz 3, 69115 Heidelberg, Germany. If you have any concerns regarding our products, please contact ProductSafety@springernature.com

Printed and bound by CPI Group (UK) Ltd, Croydon, CR0 4YY

23/03/2026

02076736-0005